BROADCAST NEWS WRITING AND REPORTING

BROADCAST NEWS WRITING AND REPORTING

TED WHITE

Southern University

ST. MARTIN'S PRESS ■ NEW YORK

Editor: Jane Lambert
Managing editor: Patricia Mansfield-Phelan
Project editor: Talvi Laev
Production supervisor: Katherine Battiste
Art director: Sheree Goodman
Text design: Carolyn Joseph
Photo research: Inge King
Cover design: Jeanette Jacobs Design
Cover photo: Stock Boston/© Frank Siteman 1992

For information, write:
St. Martin's Press, Inc.
175 Fifth Avenue
New York, NY 10010

ISBN: 0–312–06150–1

Acknowledgments

Aaron, Betsy, "Marines in Lebanon," September 14, 1983. Transcript from "ABC News" reprinted by permission. Copyright 1983.

Atherton, Jack, "The Price of Fame" transcript, December 5, 1989, and "Ford Follow" transcript, July 16, 1991. Excerpts courtesy of National Broadcasting Company, Inc. All Rights Reserved.

Carter, Hodding, quotation about journalists today, from a speech on government and journalism by Hodding Carter, Assistant Secretary of State for Public Affairs/Department Spokesman.

Devine, Christine, "Deadly Fires" newscast, KTTV-TV, Los Angeles. Script excerpts courtesy of Fox Television Stations, Inc. © 1992 Fox Television Stations, Inc.

Dotson, Bob, "Cave Rescue." Excerpts courtesy of National Broadcasting Company, Inc. All Rights Reserved.

Ellerbee, Linda, "NBC News Overnight." Excerpts courtesy of National Broadcasting Company, Inc. All Rights Reserved.

Frederick, Pauline, report from United Nations, December 5, 1963 story. Excerpts courtesy of National Broadcasting Company, Inc. All Rights Reserved.

Gates, Paul, lead story on weather. Used with permission of WAFB-TV, Baton Rouge.

Harvey, Paul, "Rebirth of a Nation." Used with permission of Paul Harvey News.

Kirk, Bruce, marked script. Used by permission of Bruce Kirk, KPNX-TV Broadcasting, Phoenix, Arizona.

Kridel, Kris, David Chereck murder story. Used with permission of Kris Kridel, WBBM-AM, Newsradio 78, Chicago.

Kuralt, Charles, "On the Road in Montana," 1975, and "On the Road in Vermont," 1976. Used with permission of CBS News.

Murrow, Edward R., "Orchestrated Hell," "Permit Me to Tell You," and "The Fault, Dear Brutus," from *Murrow: His Life and Times* by Ann M. Sperber, Bantam Books, 1986. Originally published by Freundlich Books.

Olmsted, Jill, excerpts from "How to Find a Job in Radio/TV." Used with permission of Jill Olmsted, The American University.

Osgood, Charles, "Obituary for Dr. Seuss" and "Newsbreak." Used with permission of CBS News.

Acknowledgments and copyrights are continued at the back of the book on page 343, which constitutes an extension of the copyright page.

The late CBS News Correspondent
Doug Edwards

**MY GREATEST
ACCOMPLISHMENT,
FOUR WONDERFUL
DAUGHTERS:
KATHLEEN, IRENE,
JENNIFER AND ALEXANDRA**

**AND TO THE LATE CBS
NEWS CORRESPONDENT
DOUG EDWARDS, A
FRIEND AND COLLEAGUE
WHO WAS LOVED BY
ALL WHO HAD THE GOOD
FORTUNE TO WORK
WITH HIM.**

FOREWORD

roadcast news seems so simple that most viewers and listeners figure there's nothing to it. For several years now I have done four "Osgood File" broadcasts on the CBS Radio Network each morning. Each broadcast has two and a half minutes of editorial content. 4 x 2.5 = 10. Therefore, my friends figure, I only work 10 minutes a day—nice work if you can get it. As with most things that seem simple, however, there's a whole lot more to radio and television news reporting than meets the eye or the ear. It's been said that, as with sausage and cheese, it's better if the public doesn't ever find out exactly how our product is made or how early one has to get up every morning to make it. (In my case, 2:30 a.m. is the answer to the last part, by the way. Still want to be a news writer or reporter?)

At the heart of radio and television news broadcasting are the reporting and the writing. You can have the greatest studios in the world, the most state-of-the-art equipment, the hottest signal, the catchiest news theme music and the niftiest news set anybody ever designed, but if your reporting and writing aren't good, nothing is going to happen. You have to find out what's going on, talk with principals and witnesses, gather your information, assemble your facts into a coherent story and then tell it. The writing part is easy. As CBS News Correspondent Terry Smith's daddy used to say, all a writer has to do is open a vein and bleed all over the page. Nothing to it. Terry's daddy was the legendary sports writer Red Smith. What he said may be true, but it isn't very helpful advice about how to become a writer or reporter, whether for print or broadcast. Easier on your health, and easier on the carpet, is Ted White's approach.

Ted and I worked together for a time at CBS News in New York. Our colleagues were wonderful people like Walter Cronkite, Douglas Edwards, Eric Sevareid, Lowell Thomas, Hughes Rudd, Dallas Townsend and Richard C. Hotellet. We had great editors like Hal Terkel and Marian Glick who had learned from the masters, Edward R. Murrow himself and Murrow's own radio writer and editor, Ed Bliss. Our bosses were Joe Dembo and Emerson Stone, and their bosses were people like Richard Salant and Fred W. Friendly. That was the news broadcasting school Ted White and I went to. There was never a better one.

So, when Mr. White tells students about radio and television news, he knows whereof he speaks. And when he writes in this book about the nuts and bolts of how to gather news and organize it so that it makes sense, he knows whereof he writes. You may decide, after reading this book, that broadcast news writing and reporting are not for you. This would be a sensible decision nobody could argue with. But if you do decide to pursue this dodge anyway, you won't find anybody better to show you the ropes than Ted White.

Charles Osgood

PREFACE

roadcast News Writing and Reporting examines the skills, techniques and challenges of writing and reporting for broadcast. Along with complete coverage of the fundamentals, the text presents up-to-date examples and issues through actual scripts and interviews with the people who bring us the news.

As you examine the book, you may notice the extensive coverage of reporting. Eight of the book's 22 chapters focus on everything from basic skills and specialty reporting to research techniques and ethics. I believe this is the most complete treatment of reporting techniques and scripts by outstanding correspondents available in a broadcast news text. Journalists such as Betsy Aaron, Bob Dotson, Charles Kuralt, Charles Osgood, Susan Stamberg and Richard Threlkeld not only provided scripts for the book but discuss how they write and report. The work of such distinguished reporters as the late Edward R. Murrow and the late Pauline Frederick is also examined and analyzed closely.

Supplementing this is the emphasis throughout on real-life situations. The problems that reporters, writers, assignment editors and producers face every day are discussed in detail. You'll find entire chapters devoted to interviewing, covering breaking stories, delivering the news and finding a job. Whenever possible, I've relied on the voices of the experts—through interviews and transcripts of actual broadcasts—to teach future professionals how it's done.

As your students read this book, you may want to assign the writing, review and discussion exercises at the end of each chapter. They ask students to apply what they've read, not just summarize it. In conjunction with outside assignments, these exercises can provide enough material for an entire course.

You'll find answers to the exercises in the accompanying *Instructor's Manual*, along with sample syllabi and my suggestions for organizing the course, whether it be a reporting, writing, or all-in-one course. Also available with *Broadcast News Writing and Reporting* is a videotape with news clips your students can use as an exercise in writing to video.

This book would have been impossible to write without the assistance of a great number of people. Much of this help came from colleagues in the broadcast news industry with whom I worked over the years. Significant contributions also came from journalism professors, research assistants, editors and a variety of administrative assistants and public relations personnel throughout the country. I will try to thank by name all who have helped produce this book, but there have been so many of you over the past three years that I am likely to miss a few. Please forgive me if one of them is you.

At the top of the "thank you" list is Ben Silver. Our relationship goes back more than 20 years to when we both worked for CBS News. Ben, now professor emeritus of the Walter Cronkite School of Journalism at Arizona State University, was a gold mine of information. We have him to thank for locating some of the scripts and gathering much of the quoted material in the book.

Charlie Osgood too has been a friend and colleague over the years, and the foreword he wrote for the book is greatly appreciated. So are the scripts that he has permitted us to reproduce.

Charles Kuralt very graciously allowed us to include two of his "On the Road" scripts and a photograph from those splendid years when he traveled the back roads collecting stories about America. Speaking of help, we got lots of it from Charles' wonderful assistant Karen Beckers. Many thanks also to Lori Knight and Audrey Forman, who helped us to locate some of Charlie Osgood's best writings.

The list of CBS News correspondents who assisted us is long. Betsy Aaron and Richard Threlkeld allowed us to share their scripts and insights with you. We thank them also for providing photos from their private collections.

Our appreciation to Roger Welsch for sending us one of his "Postcard From Nebraska" stories, which air regularly on Charles Kuralt's "Sunday Morning." Thanks also to Correspondent Bob Faw and to "Sunday Morning" Correspondent David Culhane for all his help over the years.

"60 Minutes" Correspondent Ed Bradley gave us new insight into, among other things, the hopes and problems of African-Americans in broadcast journalism.

We thank CBS Correspondent Robert McKeown for sharing with us, as so many others did, what it was like to report during the Gulf War. And we appreciate CBS News Correspondent Bruce Morton's comments on the broadcast coverage of the sensational William Kennedy Smith rape trial.

The ABC News team also provided us with many pages of copy. Special thanks to all who took time to speak with us, including "Nightline" Correspondent Jeff Greenfield and news correspondents Morton Dean and Barry Serafin. News commentator Paul Harvey contributed a sample of his unique writing style; thanks also to his secretary, June Westgard.

Friend and former colleague Rob Sunde, news director of the ABC Information Network, provided useful information for young people trying to get started in broadcast news.

ABC News Vice President Walter Porges and Arnot Walker, press representative for ABC's "World News Tonight," were a great help.

News Correspondent Bob Dotson was more than generous, giving us not only a sample of his splendid writing but very detailed notes on how he thinks and works when he's putting a story together. NBC's Roger O'Neil is not only an excellent journalist, he's also refreshingly frank in describing the shortcomings of many of those working in broadcast news.

We appreciate the assistance we received from Don Browne, executive vice president of NBC News, from Katherine McQuay, manager of news information at NBC, and from NBC News Political Editor Kathryn Keeney.

The news staff at CNN was very cooperative. Bernard Shaw, in particular, gave us his views on a variety of subjects, including the Gulf War and the problems associated with reporting live and covering politics.

CNN Investigative Reporter Jim Polk provided a lot of good advice about a beat he has covered for several decades.

CNN Anchor Reid Collins, another former CBS colleague, gave us samples of his excellent writing, as did CNN Medical Correspondent Dan Rutz. Thanks also to friend and former CNN colleague Don Shoultz, an editor-producer for "Headline News."

Many thanks also to the people at NPR, where, as Susan Stamberg reminds us, women journalists have made tremendous progress.

We thank Susan and Cokie Roberts for their scripts and input on a variety of subjects and issues in broadcast news. We also appreciate the time that Nina Totenberg spent with us discussing her involvement in the leak of sexual harassment charges made by Anita Hill against Judge Clarence Thomas.

Some network producers were very helpful, among them Paul Friedman, executive producer of ABC's "World News Tonight"; Steve Friedman, executive producer of NBC's "Nightly News"; Linda Mason, executive producer of "Sunday Morning"; Joel Bernstein, a producer for CBS's "Evening News"; and Phil Scheffler, a senior producer for "60 Minutes."

We received a great deal of assistance from colleagues at radio and TV stations throughout the country. Much of that help was provided by stations in Baton Rouge, La. Special thanks to friend and colleague John Spain, station manager of WBRZ-TV, who has provided extraordinary information about a variety of aspects of broadcast news for two of my books.

Management and staff at WAFB-TV, the other major station in Baton Rouge, were equally cooperative. My thanks to Station Manager Ron Winders and News Director Nick Simonette and to anchor-reporters Nancy Parker and Paul Gates, who provided excellent examples of their work.

Thanks also to Chris Szechenyi, who is now with "60 Minutes," for providing us with a copy of an FOI request and details on how he wrote and produced an investigative report while he was still at WRC-TV in Washington.

Our appreciation to Will Wright, vice president and news director of KRIV-TV in Houston, for recalling how he rose from desk assistant at CBS to become one of only three African-American news directors at major TV stations. Wright and African-American anchor Sheila Stainback of WPIX-TV, in New York City, provide valuable information and advice for minorities who hope to succeed in broadcast news.

Others at local stations who provided information and scripts: Jack Atherton, WTVJ-Miami; Jerry Bell, news director of KOA-TV, Denver; News

Director Chris Berry and reporter Kris Kridel of WBBM Radio, Chicago; Tom Bier, news director of WISC-TV, Madison; Jerry Brown, weathercaster for KUTV, Salt Lake City; Christine Devine, anchor for KTTV-TV, Los Angeles; and Ed Godfrey, news director of WAVE-TV, Louisville.

Many thanks to the crowd at KPNX-TV, Phoenix: Remote News Coordinator Wally Athey, Art Director Kathy Beard, Senior News Producer Rod Haberer, Assignment Manager Al Macias, Reporter Cary Pfeffer and anchors Kent Dana, Bruce Kirk and Lin Sue Shepherd.

Our appreciation also to those at KTSP-TV in Phoenix: News Director Dave Howell, Executive Producer Mary Cox, Investigative Reporter Steve Kraft and Anchor-Reporter Claren Scott. Thanks also to Kathy Matz of KTVK-TV, Phoenix.

We received a lot of help from Marty Haag, vice president, news for A. H. Belo Corporation, which owns a number of stations, including KHOU-TV in Houston and WFAA-TV in Dallas. Penny Scott and Reporter Don Wall of WFAA-TV were a great help, as was Kerry Oslund, executive producer of news at KCAL-TV, Los Angeles, and Bill Bauman, news director at KCRA-TV, Sacramento.

Special thanks and a hug for friend and colleague Nan Siemer, an editor for radio station WTOP in Washington, who provided students with information on surviving in our business. Our appreciation also to WTOP Anchor John Lynker for providing a photo of himself in action—a nice reminder of the days some 20 years ago when I edited John's scripts at WINS, the first all-news station in New York.

Thanks also to the many journalism professors who shared information with us, including several at the University of Missouri: Karen Frankola, Department Chair Rod Gelatt, John Ullmann and Vernon Stone, who is also research director for the Radio and Television News Directors Association (RTNDA).

We thank Ed Bliss, professor emeritus at American University and another transplanted CBS News writer and editor. He's author of *Now the News*, a great new book on the history of broadcast news.

Other professors who made contributions to the book: David Dick, director of journalism at the University of Kentucky and a former CBS News correspondent; Robert Mulholland, chair of broadcast news at the Medill School of Journalism at Northwestern University and former president of the NBC-TV network; Susan Morris at the University of Pittsburgh; Lou Prato, who heads Northwestern's program in Washington, D.C.; Travis Linn of the University of Nevada at Reno, a former CBS News bureau chief in Dallas; and Bill Small of Fordham University, a former senior vice president of CBS News.

We owe Professor Jill Olmsted of American University a double thank you for reviewing the manuscript and allowing us to reprint articles she wrote on preparing resumes and resume tapes. Our appreciation to other professors who were commissioned by St. Martin's Press to review the manuscript in its early stages: Ben Silver, Arizona State University; Elmer Lower, former ABC News president; Jill Olmsted, American University; Marsha Della-Giustina, Emerson College; James L. Hoyt, University of Wisconsin at Madison; Kate Andrews, Syracuse University; Mark Harmon, Texas Tech University; Andrew Stern, University of California at Berkeley.

Special thanks also to Roz Polly for helping with the research and to my good friend and former student, Lennie Tierney, who has learned so much about TV news photography that he could teach his old mentor a few tricks.

Lots of people shot photos for us, and many others dug pictures and scripts out of files and archives, including Kathy Ozatko of Madison, Wisc., Kenneth Keller of Southern Illinois University and Marty Silverstein of CBS. The shooters included James Terry and Christopher Rogers of Baton Rouge and Mike Coscia of WFAA-TV, Dallas.

Special thanks to Carol Lichtenberg, curator at the Historical Photograph Collection at Washington State University, for finding photos of Edward R. Murrow for us. Thanks to Catherine Heinz, director of the Broadcast Pioneers Library, for telling us where to look for things we needed.

Help also came from Richard Lobo, president and general manager of WTVJ-TV in Miami, and from Carmen Perez, PR director for that station. We also thank Lori Konopka and Su-Lin Cheng of CNN for getting us pictures, as did Abenaa Abboa-Offei and Leslie Halpern at ABC Radio. Our appreciation also to Mata Goodwyn and Margery Sly, archivists at Smith College, for locating a script written by the late Pauline Frederick.

We are indebted to voice coaches Carol Dearing, Mary Berger and Jeff Puffer for providing excellent information on voice control and other aspects of anchoring and reporting for radio and TV.

During three years of writing and research, we attended many conferences and meetings of broadcast groups (particularly those held by the Radio and Television News Directors Association) and pored through many journals and magazines such as *The Communicator* and *Broadcasting* so that we could include the comments and observations of many whom we were unable to interview.

Here's a list of those we have quoted, in one way or another, throughout the book: investigative reporters David Anderson, Jack Anderson and Peter Benjaminson; NBC News Commentator John Chancellor; Bob Engleman of Scripps-Howard; former CBS News vice president Peter Herford; *Wall Street Journal* reporter Robert Goldberg; Craig Le May, editor of the *Freedom Forum Journal;* Robert Logan, director of the Science Journalism Center at the University of Missouri; CNN Environmental Reporter Deborah Potter; Jeffrey Marks, president of RTNDA; Walter R. Mears, vice-president and Washington bureau chief of the Associated Press; Professor William Metz, University of Nevada; attorney and former reporter Bruce Sanford; Penny Parrish, news director of KMSP in Minneapolis; Doug Ramsey of the Foundation for America Communications; and network news veterans Liz Trotta and Ed Fouhy.

We received additional help from Tom Goodman, director of media relations for CBS, and PR associate Eldra Gillman; Lynn Ross of AARP in Washington; Charlie Folds, PR director for WSVN-TV, Miami; Dr. Terry Kennedy, Southern University; and the Gallup and Roper research and polling organizations.

Thanks also to colleagues Frank Coakley and Dr. William Turpin for their friendship and support over the years.

Finally, thanks to all at St. Martin's Press who had to put up with the author's temperament over the years, especially Cathy Pusateri, Jane Lambert, Talvi Laev, Kim Johnson, Sam Potts and Denise Quirk.

Ted White

CONTENTS

JOURNALISTS AND SCRIPTS

INTRODUCTION

uch of this book was written during the conflict in the Persian Gulf and its aftermath. The timing offered a variety of opportunities to observe the broadcast media as they moved into a new role: the live reporting of a war on television. For the first time, the American people, along with most of the world, thanks to CNN, watched a war much as they would a Superbowl. The instant coverage of rockets falling on Israel and Saudi Arabia brought the war into living rooms as never before. This coverage of the war showed us how dramatically electronic journalism had matured technically. Yet it also showed us many other things that were not as positive and were, in the minds of many, controversial. For, unlike the Superbowl, the "replays" that Americans were seeing on their screens were censored and controlled by the military while frustrated journalists were often restricted to the "bench" or forced to take part in orchestrated pool coverage. There will be more on the war in Chapter 13, "Reporting Live."

The book also draws on the news coverage of the Gulf War to examine some of the positive and negative aspects of electronic journalism.

A CHANGING INDUSTRY

The media coverage of the war in the Persian Gulf illustrates some of the changes in the broadcast industry that will affect the roles many of you will play in the industry. Among the most important developments was the increased independence of local TV stations in covering a major news story. There was still heavy reliance on the networks for most of the war news, but there also was a great deal of coverage by reporters working for local stations and station groups. The Gulf War gave local stations an opportunity to demonstrate that their coverage of major events throughout the world was improving. Many TV news directors were saying, "Hey, we can have a presence in the gulf, too."

Long before the war, many TV stations had expanded their newscasts from 30 minutes to an hour or more in the evening, and some added an additional hour at noon. Some stations added an hour of news in the late evening. So, it was not unusual, especially in the larger markets, to see local reporters competing with network journalists during the Gulf War, a trend that continued in the coverage of subsequent world events. The significance of this trend for journalism students is that the more local TV stations rely on their staffs to cover events outside their listening area, the more jobs there will be for people breaking into the field.

Remember, however, that the competition for jobs in broadcast news is keen. The field is crowded because the profession is a dynamic one. It's exciting, colorful and often glamorous, attracting many people who want to be part of the action. But do not be overly alarmed. There always is room for the achievers. If you are determined to be among those broadcast journalism students who "make it," you need plenty of determination, motivation and hustle.

You do not have to be a born genius to become a good broadcast journalist. It never hurts, of course, but it's certainly not a requirement. As in all professional fields, you must be intelligent. However, there are other characteristics and skills that you must have or develop. These include an insatiable curiosity about the world around you; a desire to change those things and circumstances that you perceive to be unfair, improper or unlawful; and persistence and aggressiveness in discovering the truth.

IS JOURNALISM FOR YOU?

The late Frank Graham, a sports columnist, once observed that journalism will kill you, but it will keep you alive in the meantime. Something of an exaggeration, perhaps, but the lifestyle does not encourage a healthy or emotionally stable way of life. As one broadcast reporter puts it, "You have to be a little crazy to want to spend your life working lousy hours, eating bad food, probably drinking too much and fighting with your wife or girlfriend because you had to miss dinner for the 99th time or had to break a date."

ABC News Correspondent Barry Serafin says the broadcast news business is "just awful" on family and marriage life. "You must have a very understanding, tolerant wife or husband. They must be very supportive." He adds, "It is not the glamorous life that most people think. Last night I had a hot dog at an airport. After 25 years in the business, you wouldn't think it would be that way, but it is—that's the nature of the business."

Serafin recalls that earlier in the week he stayed up all night working on a complicated story. "We spent most of the next day on the story just to get it on the air," Serafin adds, repeating, "That's just the way the business is."

Betsy Aaron, a correspondent for CBS News who is married to CBS News Correspondent Richard Threlkeld, notes, "We see each other as much as we can. It's important for us to be together. But," she admits, "it isn't easy. It would be even harder if we were young and had kids."

NBC Commentator John Chancellor agrees that journalism is difficult work. "It's often frustrating, frequently exhausting, not the way to get rich." He says, "Every slip is out there in print or public view, to draw scorn, wrath—or lawsuits."

But in the book "The News Business," which Chancellor co-authored with Pulitzer Prize–winner Walter R. Mears of The Associated Press, the authors also write that journalism is "exciting, fascinating, constantly challenging and changing work."

WHAT ROLE TO PLAY?

Do you hope to be in front of the cameras or behind them? The majority of journalism students wish to be on camera as TV anchors. The odds are not quite as bad as for college quarterbacks making it to the NFL, but the competition is still formidable. Fortunately, there are a lot more TV stations—and an even greater number of radio stations—than there are football teams.

If you are determined to be an anchor, keep in mind that it takes more than a college degree or time spent as an intern. Most anchors earn their spot in front of the cameras by putting in their time as reporters. In time—and with appropriate skills—a reporter may be given a shot at anchoring on weekends and/or holidays when the "stars" have a day off. If you are intent on being an anchor, then, work hard at developing your reporting skills. If your goal is to be a broadcast reporter, sharpen your writing skills—the essence of good reporting.

Many of you will say, "I don't want to write or report, I want to be a producer." But when asked what kind of producer, most responders show an interest in "The Tonight Show" or some other area of entertainment. There are some talented people producing those shows, but their work is far removed from producing TV news, a more serious aspect of broadcasting.

TV news producers also pay their dues. They frequently start out as writers and associate producers, sometimes as researchers and even as desk assistants. Like the other people in broadcast news, producers get their jobs because they demonstrate many different skills. News judgment, the ability to sort out what should and should not go into a newscast, and what should be highlighted and what downplayed, is one of the most crucial. If the producer's news judgment is not sound, the program will not be successful.

One of a producer's concerns is ratings. A news manager whose newscasts are constantly running third in the ratings in a three-station market will probably be looking for a new producer. If that doesn't help, the news manager too will be looking for a new job. Reaching the top of the ratings chart is only part of the challenge in broadcast news. Staying there is even harder. A good producer knows how to attract and hold a large audience by keeping news programs interesting.

Whatever role you hope to play, this book will help you achieve your goals. It concentrates on two areas, writing and reporting, which are the cornerstones of broadcast journalism. If you are successful in finding a place in the broadcast news industry, you will probably find yourself using these skills every day. But before you start work on developing these skills, let's examine some other fundamentals that will help prepare you for your career in broadcast journalism.

YOUR COLLEGE EDUCATION

There is a continuing debate among news executives over the value of a journalism degree. Many professional journalists argue that a liberal arts education is more important than a program in journalism. "Give me young people with a well-rounded liberal arts education," say many news executives, "and I'll teach them how to be journalists."

It is a strong argument, which is why a great many college broadcast journalism programs require students to take most of their credits in the liberal arts. While you may want to focus solely on your journalism courses, keep in mind that all the history, economics, political science and language courses you are required to take will inform you as a journalist and will enrich your life as well.

An increasing number of job advertisements placed by news directors seek journalists who have some strong interest or background in such areas as health, business or law. Almost any concentration in a secondary area, including political science or sociology, may improve your chances of finding a position in broadcast news.

Another advantage for those entering the broadcast news market is a second language. Spanish is particularly useful for journalists working in markets in the Southeast, Southwest and West and also in major northern cities, such as New York and Chicago, that have large Spanish-speaking populations. For example, during rioting in Washington, D.C., reporters who spoke Spanish often "scooped" other reporters in their reports about the problems in the city and how they might be solved.

French, German, Japanese and Russian are also extremely helpful languages to know, especially if you hope to work overseas.

INTERNSHIPS

Never pass up a chance to work as an intern for a radio or TV station while you are in school. Such work can be a tremendous advantage because it gives you an opportunity to observe firsthand what you are learning in your classes. Interns are often asked to write and work at the assignment desk or to help the producer. Yes, there will probably be a lot of coffee runs, and you will take many calls from complaining listeners, but anything you do that gets you inside a radio or TV station is well worth it even if you do not get paid. However, interns sometimes do get the minimum wage or more.

Probably one of the greatest advantages of an internship is that you meet the people who do the hiring. Scores of students, after graduation, remain with the stations where they worked as interns. Many become reporters, producers and assignment editors. Even if there is no job waiting for you at the station after your internship, you have something substantial to put on your résumé. If you performed well, you have some good references too.

An internship also allows you to see what the world of broadcast news is really like. You may discover that it is not what you want to pursue as a career. Some students discover during an internship that it's not for them. If you are not "pushy" by nature and are not comfortable with pressures and deadlines, it is better to discover that as quickly as possible.

YOUR FIRST JOB

Like entry-level positions in many fields, your first job will not pay much. One disadvantage of working in broadcast news is that a lot of other people want to do it. News directors know that, and pay accordingly. They also know that if you "have what it takes" you will not be staying with the station for long. There is not much union representation except in larger markets, and you are unlikely to begin in one of those. But for most people who end up in broadcast news, money is secondary. There is always the hope of ending up in New York, Chicago or Los Angeles, where salaries are substantial, but you cannot depend on that happening. So, most people work in broadcasting for the very reasons that they got involved in the first place: it's fun, exciting and, yes, sometimes glamorous. There also is the satisfaction of knowing that you are doing your part in keeping people informed, sometimes making things better in your community, and correcting injustices.

RESPONSIBILITY AND ACCURACY

The two most important words in your vocabulary, starting right now, are *responsibility* and *accuracy*, the cornerstones of ethical journalism. To be a successful journalist, you need to learn to be responsible and accurate in everything you write or report. There is a well-worn phrase known to every journalist: "Getting it fast is no good unless it's right."

Responsibility is not just limited to checking information to ensure accuracy. It also means being fair. Journalists must learn to write and report without prejudice, despite their own personal views on a subject or an issue. To do otherwise is to betray the trust that is placed in them by the public. There will be much more on ethics throughout the book.

This introduction is designed to give you a brief look at some of the important requirements and rewards of a career in broadcast journalism. The remaining chapters focus on the process of developing the writing and reporting skills and techniques necessary for success in broadcast journalism.

At the end of each chapter, there are exercises to help you and your instructor determine how well you are absorbing all this new information. If you find that you are having trouble, go back and review the material. Much of the information you need to complete the assignments successfully is detailed in the chapter itself, but at times you will also have to use other resources. Locating outside information is the first step in a research process that will become a part of your everyday life if you become a broadcast journalist.

CHAPTER 1

BROADCAST NEWS
WRITING MECHANICS

efore you can race at Indianapolis, you have to learn how to drive a car. Before you write broadcast news, you must learn good grammar and know how to use a typewriter or computer. You also must understand what news *is* and how writing broadcast news copy differs from other types of writing. As noted in the Introduction, you must quickly learn about accuracy and responsibility. You also need to learn the vocabulary of broadcast journalism, terms such as *wrap, voice-over, standup,* and *cutaway.*

Before you have finished working with this book, you will have learned about all these things and many more. This chapter starts with the mechanics of broadcast news writing, the small but essential details of preparing a script correctly. Learning these mechanics is like learning how to use the controls on a dashboard.

SOME BASICS

Computers are rapidly replacing typewriters in news rooms and classrooms, but there are still plenty of typewriters in use. Regardless of which machine you use, the following instructions for typing broadcast copy on 8 1/2-by-11-inch paper are standard for radio news. (Television news writers work with what is called the *split page,* which will be discussed later in this chapter.)

Set the margins for 65 spaces, leaving approximately 10 spaces, or one inch, on each side. Depending on the make of typewriter, type the copy double- or triple-spaced to allow enough room between the lines to make corrections. If your typewriter has large, bulletin-sized type fonts, or you use a computer, double-space.

On a computer, you set these margins and spaces electronically, but the basic format remains the same. The major difference is that corrections will not be made between the lines on a computer screen. Corrections and changes in copy will be made electronically to the lines of copy themselves. The result is a much neater, easier-to-read script.

CORRECTING COPY

Corrections on a typewritten script must be made with great care. The words being changed must be completely crossed out, and the words being substituted must be written clearly just above the crossed-out words. If the required corrections are too elaborate and the script becomes difficult to read, retype it.

Standard newspaper copy-editing symbols are not permissible in broadcast copy. Here are two examples of corrected copy. The first is edited for print, the second for broadcast:

The mayor says he's binging the two sides in the newspaper stike to the

bargaining talbe today and is hupeful that an agreement can be reachd be-

fore the end of the week. The strike is now in its 3rd weeek. The major

issue are job security and the newspaper's demnand that the union accept

a 20% reduction in wages.

bringing *strike*
The mayor says he's ~~binging~~ the two sides in the newspaper ~~stike~~ to the

table *hopeful* *reached*
bargaining ~~talbe~~ today and is ~~hupeful~~ that an agreement can be ~~reachd~~

before *third week.*
~~before~~ the end of the week. The strike is now in its ~~3rd weeek~~. The major

issues *demand*
~~issue~~ are job security and the newspaper's ~~demnand~~ that the union accept

percent
a 20~~%~~ reduction in wages.

The important thing to remember is that poorly corrected copy increases the possibility that an anchor will make a mistake. As might be expected, anchors are particularly sensitive about stumbling over a word or sentence, and, if the mishap is the writer's fault, you can be certain that the newscaster will let someone know about it as soon as the newscast is over or, more likely, during a commercial break.

SLUGS

Every page of the news script must be identified. These identifications are called slugs, and they are placed in the upper left-hand corner of the page. The slug includes a one- or two-word description of the story, such as *Fire, Newspa-*

per Strike or *Missing Boy*. The slug also includes the date, the time of the newscast and the writer's initials. Here's an example:

Fire
2/10/93
9 a.m.
TW

Slugs are important because they allow the writer, producers, anchors, director and a variety of other people involved in putting a newscast together to locate quickly a particular story in the script. This can be vital when, for example, the position of the story in the script must be changed or the story must be dropped just as the newscast begins or when it is already on the air.

THE SPLIT PAGE

Preparing a TV script is somewhat more complicated than preparing a radio script. A TV script is divided into two vertical sections and is known as the *split page*. All technical instructions and identification of video and graphics fall in the left portion of the split page, and the script to be read by the anchor or reporter appears in the right column along with sound bite outcues and times. There will be a number of examples of split pages, and how they are used, throughout this book.

As you examine those scripts, you will notice that each station has its own way of using the split page. Experienced broadcast journalists adjust easily to the slight variations as they move from station to station.

AVOIDING ABBREVIATIONS

All words in broadcast news copy, with a few exceptions, must be spelled out. Abbreviations are not permitted because they would force anchors to interpret their meaning, inviting confusion and mistakes.

Wrong	Right
Lt. General	Lieutenant General
Ass't. Sec. of State	Assistant Secretary of State
Union Pres. Felix Jones	Union President Felix Jones
John St. and Norfolk Ave.	John Street and Norfolk Avenue

It is permissible to use abbreviations when the names of organizations are better known by their initials than by their full names—for example, FBI, NBC and CIA. However, to make it easier for anchors to read, place hyphens between the letters.

F-B-I

N-B-C

C-I-A

AVOIDING SPLIT WORDS AND SENTENCES

If there is not enough room on a line of copy to complete a word, the entire word must be carried over to the next line. Words should not be hyphenated because splitting words at the end of a line could confuse the anchor.

The same is true with sentences that cannot fit on one page. Part of a sentence should not be carried over from one page to another. Forcing anchors to jump from the bottom of one page to the top of the next when they are in the middle of a sentence invites trouble. It cannot be stressed too often that writers must avoid anything that increases the chance that the anchors will stumble over copy.

If a sentence cannot be completed on a page, it should begin on the top of the next page. Type the word *MORE* at the bottom of the page so the anchors know that there is more to the story on the next page. Otherwise, they may pause unnecessarily, believing a new story starts on the following page. Some newsrooms prefer to use an arrow at the end of the page to indicate more copy is coming.

PUNCTUATION

While the opening of this chapter stressed the importance of using correct grammar in broadcast copy, be aware that there are certain exceptions to standard grammatical rules. For example, use commas to indicate a pause, not simply for grammatical reasons. Some writers use a dash instead of a comma to indicate a pause, but dashes should be used sparingly, usually to indicate longer pauses. Unless you are writing for yourself (when you can do whatever is comfortable for you), you should not use an ellipsis (three dots) to indicate a pause or as a signal that you have eliminated part of a quotation because those dots could confuse anchors. Never use a semicolon.

Capitalize certain words, like *Not* and other words you think the anchors should emphasize. This is especially helpful when the anchors might not have an opportunity to go over the copy before they read it on the air. Keep such emphasis to a minimum, however, for the anchor is usually the best judge of which words to stress.

NAMES AND TITLES

Titles are always used before a person's name in broadcast copy, never after it. For example, *Secretary of Defense John Smith* should be used rather than, as newspapers write, *John Smith, Secretary of Defense.* Using the title first alerts the listener to the name that will follow, and it also reflects conversational style.

It is acceptable to break up the name and the title. For example:

The secretary of the Navy said today that joint maneuvers would begin in the Atlantic next week. John Smith told reporters that Canadian and British vessels would join part of the Atlantic fleet in the maneuvers.

If you use names in your copy, make sure you double-check their spelling and pronunciation. If you are reporting an accident or a fire in which there are inju-

The CNN newsroom in Atlanta

ries or deaths, ask the police officer or fire chief to confirm any names you're unsure about. Wire services are a good source for checking names and pronunciations; more on that in Chapter 8, "Delivering the News".

Names are not always essential to a story. Scripts written at a small-town radio or TV station should certainly include the names of those who were killed or injured in a fire at the local paper plant. But the names of three people from another state who were injured on the freeway would be of little interest to the local audience. It would be sufficient to say:

> Three Florida residents suffered minor injuries after their car spun out of control on the freeway and hit a guardrail.

If those three people live in a small town in the station's listening area, however, then the names and addresses should be mentioned. The story might read:

> Three Centerville people are recovering from minor injuries suffered this afternoon when their car went out of control on the freeway and hit the guardrail. Police identified the injured as Pam and John Rose of the 300 block of Blackwell Avenue and Peter Noyes, who lives at 177 Sunshine Road.

Some news directors prefer to omit the house numbers, limiting the address to the street. In many cases, the determining factor is the size of the community.

A radio station in a community of 5,000 will give more details about the injured than a station in a city of 100,000. A newscast in a larger city might merely identify the neighborhoods in which the injured people lived.

But in that community of 5,000, the second paragraph of the story might give more details:

> The injured were on their way home from a P-T-A meeting. The Roses both teach at Johnson High School. They were giving Noyes a ride home when the accident took place.

The added details are of interest because in a small community the chances are that many of those listening to the newscast know the three people. If they do not, they may still be interested for other reasons: most of the audience will be familar with Johnson High School, they may be members of the PTA, and some may have attended the PTA meeting.

MIDDLE INITIALS

Unless middle initials are part of the name a person is known by or they are needed in a story to identify people with similar names, do not use them. For example, some politicians and celebrities, like the following, always use their middle initials, so you would be correct to use them in the story:

> Edward R. Murrow
> George C. Scott
> The late President John F. Kennedy

The same goes for middle names. They should never be used unless the individual does. It would sound strange to hear the name of the late Dr. Martin Luther King Jr. mentioned without the *Luther*.

FOREIGN NAMES

It was sometimes amusing, but more often embarrassing, to hear radio and TV anchors trying to pronounce all the foreign names during the Gulf War. Everyone quickly learned the name and pronunciation of the president of Iraq, Saddam Hussein. The king of Jordan was easy: King Hussein. But anchors used a variety of pronunciations for the president of Syria, Hafeez Assad, and the emir of Kuwait, whose full name is Sheik Jabir al-Ahmad al-Sabah. Most of the time the emir was referred to simply as Sheik al-Sabah, and the Saudi Arabian monarch was usually called just King Fahd. PLO leader Yasir Arafat was almost always initially referred to by both names.

There will be more on pronunciation in Chapter 8, "Delivering the News," but for now remember that foreign names are used in broadcast copy only if they are essential. The names of foreign heads of state, ambassadors and foreign ministers who are frequently in the news must be mentioned, but secondary foreign officials can usually be identified by title alone.

When a foreign name is used, it must be used according to custom. In some foreign countries, such as China, the first name is the surname and important one, not the last. For example, the late Chinese leader Mao Tse-tung is referred to as Chairman Mao.

AGES

A person's age should be used in a news story only if it is significant for some reason. Most of the time it is irrelevant. There certainly would be no need to give the ages of Pam and John Rose or Peter Noyes, who were involved in the earlier accident example. However, if the Roses' 5-year-old daughter had been involved in the accident, her age would be worth mentioning because she is so young. And if Noyes' 87-year-old mother was in the back seat, her age should also be given.

Sometimes it is also acceptable to give ages in crime stories. If two teen-age boys were involved in a hit-and-run accident, their ages should be reported. If an 80-year-old man tried to hold up a bank, his age is the most interesting part of the story because it's unusual to hear of a senior citizen committing a violent crime.

If a 75-year-old woman's vehicle crossed a divider and collided head-on with another car, give her age. It could have been a factor in the accident. Perhaps not, but until police determine the cause of the accident, the woman's age should be included. It also should be noted if, for example, police said one of the tires on the woman's car had blown out and possibly caused the accident.

Other reasons for giving ages include exceptional accomplishments or unlikely occurrences. For example:

- A 16-year-old graduates at the top of her law school class.

- A 60-year-old Hollywood actor marries a 22-year-old woman.

- A 44-year-old woman gives birth to quadruplets.

MARITAL STATUS

It is not necessary to specify whether someone is married, divorced or single unless the information is directly related to the story in some way. There would be no reason to say whether someone who was arrested for driving while intoxicated is single or married. But when a candidate is running for mayor most people want to know whether he or she is single or married. It may influence how some people vote.

During the Gulf War, many servicewomen were on duty in the desert. A soldier usually was identified as a married woman when the reporter discovered that her husband was also in the service, or, perhaps, was home looking after the children. For the most part, however, reporters were more concerned with servicewomen's role in the Gulf War, not their marital status, and that was appropriate.

An anchor reviews copy.

RACE

As with marital status, race should be noted only if it is relevant to the story. For example, you would mention race or ethnicity if a city elected its first Hispanic member of the city council or if an African American graduated at the top of the class in a predominantly white college. But a person's race should be mentioned in a crime story *only* if it is necessary for identification purposes while police are still looking for a suspect. If a person has already been arrested for a crime, there is no reason to indicate the person's racial or ethnic background.

NUMBERS

The fundamental rule to remember about the use of numbers in broadcast copy is that they should be rounded off and spelled out when there is any chance for confusion. For example, a budget figure of $60,342,960,000 should be rounded off to "more than 60 billion dollars." Such a figure is spelled out because it would be virtually impossible for a newscaster to deal with all those numbers in the middle of the copy.

The convention is to spell out single-digit numbers, and eleven, and to use figures for 10 and for 12 through 999. For larger figures, use words or word-figure combinations. Here are some examples:

- There are only eleven days left until Christmas.

- There were 45 students in the class.

- There were three people at the table.

- There were 600 prisoners of war.

- There were 75-thousand people in the stadium and another 15-thousand were turned away.

Single-digit numbers with *million, billion,* and so on are expressed in words, such as:

⇥ It will take another three million dollars to complete work on the project.

Some figures reaching the news desk are expressed in decimals:

⇥ The stock market was up 6.88 points.

⇥ Unemployment was down .01 percent for the month.

⇥ The Navy asked for an additional 5.5 billion dollars.

Some newscasters will say the stock market was up "six point 88," but most prefer to eliminate the decimal and round off the figure to "almost seven points." As for the other examples: recast them for broadcast copy to read, "Unemployment was down one tenth of one percent for the month," and "The Navy asked for an additional five and one-half billion dollars."

TIMING STORIES

It is essential to know how to time copy. If you are writing for yourself, use a stopwatch as you read each page of copy aloud, and then write the time on the page. Be sure to read the copy aloud because the timing would be different if you read it silently.

If you are writing the copy for someone else, it is more difficult to estimate time because everyone reads copy at a different pace. On average, newscasters read at a speed of about 15 or 16 standard lines of copy per minute.

For television, because of the split page and the use of bold type for the teleprompter, most newscasters take about one second to read each line of copy. When computers are used to write TV scripts, the timing may be different. (Some computers will time each story.) As you become familar with the equipment you use to write scripts, you'll learn how best to time the material. You must know this information so that you will be able to estimate how many lines of copy you need to write for a given story. You may often be told by a producer, "Give me about 20 seconds."

REVIEW QUESTIONS

1. Why can't you use standard newspaper copy-editing techniques when you are correcting mistakes in broadcast copy?

2. What is a *slug*, and where does it go on your copy?

3. Most abbreviations are not permitted in broadcast copy. Give examples of some exceptions.

4. What should you do if you cannot complete a sentence on one page?

5. Do titles go before or after a name in broadcast copy?

6. Explain when you should and should not give the street address of someone involved in a car accident.

7. Should you ever give a person's middle name or initial in broadcast copy? Explain.

8. When is it proper to give a person's age in broadcast copy?

9. When should you mention a person's racial or ethnic background?

10. How would you express the following sentence in broadcast copy?

   The Centerville School Board approved a budget of 1.5 million dollars.

11. How would you express the figure in the following sentence?

   There were 49,883 people at the game.

EXERCISES

1. Photocopy the following broadcast copy or retype it exactly as it appears and then, with a pen or pencil, correct the errors.

   The President caled on Iraqis to overtrow the regime of President Haddam Hussein. He suggested this solution would be the best way to bring Iraq buck into the community of peace-luving nations.

   Pete Williams, Assistant Secretary of Defunce, praised the press fo its coverage of the Guld War and defended the militry's use of the pool system in reporting the war. Williams said the press accurtely reported the war. He denied complaints that the press was unnable to report the war accurately because of interference by the military.

2. Rewrite the following to reflect good broadcast style:

   Ted Kennedy, the Democratic senator from Massachusetts, said he would vote against the Supreme Court nomination.

   General Colin Powell, the Chairman of the Joint Chiefs of Staff, will visit NATO bases in Europe next week.

3. Read through your local newspaper until you find three stories that use numbers that would have to be changed for broadcast. Type the material so that it reflects proper broadcast style.

4. Using the same newspaper, find three examples of names and titles that would have to be rewritten for broadcast. Type the material in broadcast style.

5. Rewrite a one-page story from a newspaper and, after you have corrected the copy, time it and note the time on the page.

BROADCAST NEWS WRITING STYLE

n the last chapter, you became acquainted with some of the rather tedious but necessary basics of broadcast news writing. The next step is learning broadcast news writing *style*. Broadcast style is very different from other styles of writing, principally because broadcast copy is written for the ear, not the eye, unlike most other writing.

Much of the news "writing" heard on radio and television is actually "rewriting." Although broadcast news reporters write original copy when they are covering a story, a considerable portion of the news heard on radio and television is gathered from the news wires and rewritten in broadcast style or taken off the broadcast wire and read on the air without a rewrite. This chapter focuses on rewriting the wire.

REWRITING WIRE COPY

One semester, a student stopped me at the end of a class and said, "Professor White, I need some help. I have an internship and an opportunity to write some broadcast copy. Can you give me some tips?"

I was puzzled and amused. He was carrying a copy of my textbook under his arm. "It's all in the book," I told him. "Everything I've learned about writing is there. I have no secret, no 'quick fix.' It's all important."

He looked at me, nodding his head in agreement. "I know," he said, "I've read it all, but isn't there something special, something particularly important that I should remember when the editor gives me a piece of wire copy and says, 'rewrite this'?"

I was still amused by his question and his apparent panic at the idea of having to write a story from a piece of wire copy in an actual broadcast newsroom, rather than in the classroom.

Then suddenly I remembered being in a similar situation before this young man was even born. There was, indeed, one essential point to learn about rewriting wire copy.

"Look," I said, "there actually is one thing that you can do when you are given that wire copy, that you must learn above all else. Get rid of it as fast as possible. Read it, digest it and then discard it. After that," I said, "write what

Newsroom at WAFB-TV, Baton Rouge
PHOTO BY CHRISTOPHER J. ROGERS

you remember and don't look at the wire copy again until it's time to check your facts."

You may find it difficult to surrender the wire copy and rely only on memory, but that is the only way to be certain that you rewrite what is basically newspaper-style wire copy into conversational broadcast copy. The wire services do offer a broadcast wire written in a conversational style, but we are not concerned with that wire. This book will, in effect, prepare you to do what the broadcast news service writer does with the service's newspaper wire copy.

Getting accustomed to reading and absorbing material and then expressing it in your own words takes practice. But once you have conquered the temptation to refer to the original wire or newspaper copy as you write, you will discover that your broadcast copy will be easy and natural for you, or anyone else, to read on the air.

CONVERSATIONAL STYLE

Writing in *conversational style* means writing for the ear. Newspapers, obviously, are written for the eye, which means that if readers do not understand something, they can return to the paragraph or sentence and read it a second time. In broadcast news, the audience has no such luxury; they hear the copy just once. So, broadcast copy must be written clearly and simply. Thoughts must be expressed quickly with brief, crisp, declarative sentences. They must be aimed at ordinary people, which means the words must be understood immediately, without second thought. If the audience does not understand the copy, nothing else matters.

CONTRACTIONS

Broadcast news writers must write the way most people speak. When we have a discussion with another person, we automatically do a number of things of which we usually are not aware. For example, we almost always use contractions. We are more likely to say "I'm going to work now, Frank," than "I am going to work now, Frank." And we might add, "Let's get together for lunch again soon," instead of "Let us get together again soon." In other words, if we contract our words in conversation, we should do the same in broadcast copy. Here are some other examples:

> Good Morning, I'm Jack Jones with the late news.
>
> Here's a rundown of the top stories we're covering.
>
> We've just received word that teachers are walking out of classrooms at Willow Street High School. . . .
>
> If you're driving to work, expect serious delays on the freeway because of an accident at the James Street exit. . . .
>
> There's no word from the mayor yet on rumors he'll resign. . . .
>
> Those are the headlines. Now here are the details. . . .

In the above copy, most pronoun-verb combinations have been contracted. However, sometimes—for emphasis—it is better not to contract words. For example:

> The mayor says he will seek re-election.

Because the word *will* is key to this particular sentence, it would be better to avoid the contraction *he'll*. The newscaster would want to emphasize the word *will*.

READING YOUR COPY ALOUD

Reading copy aloud helps you determine when words should be contracted, which words should be emphasized, how clear the sentences are, and how well the copy flows from sentence to sentence. Writers should not be embarrassed about reading copy aloud in the newsroom. The ear, not the eye, is the best judge of well-written broadcast copy. It is almost impossible to catch some poorly written phrases or sentences without testing them on the ear. In particular, you may not realize how complicated a sentence is until you read it aloud.

AVOIDING INFORMATION OVERLOAD

Often, copy that is difficult to understand contains too much information in any one sentence, a situation known as *information overload*. Some of the nation's finest newspapers are guilty of overloading sentences, but, as mentioned earlier, readers can always reread complicated passages. Here's an example of some copy from a major city newspaper and how it could be simplified for broadcast:

> President Saddam Hussein of Iraq, besieged by tenacious domestic rebellions that continued to threaten his control of key cities, Saturday promised broad political reforms that he said would transform his totalitarian regime into a multiparty democracy.

Quite a mouthful. It is not well written even for a newspaper, but in its present form, it would be outrageous to read it on the air. The first phrase to go should be "besieged by tenacious domestic rebellions," which is obviously not "conversational" copy. The next passage to be revised would be "transform his totalitarian regime into a multiparty democracy."

The example sentence would be greatly improved if it were broken into two sentences. What is the most important detail? It is Hussein's promise to make reforms. So, the story could start out like this:

> Iraqi President Saddam Hussein promises sweeping political reforms that he claims would lead to a multiparty democracy.

Then the second sentence could deal with the other major thought, about the rebels:

> Saddam made the promise Saturday as rebels continued to threaten his control of key cities.

Notice that the word *tenacious* was dropped. *Tenacious* is not a bad word, but it works better in print than on the air. It is an "elitist" word, and not everyone in the audience will know its meaning. Remember that unless the words are understood, nothing else matters. In a report heard on network radio, two elitist words were used within 20 seconds of each other: *ubiquitous* and *eclectic*. Such words have no place in broadcast copy. The reporter who used them had a good story to tell, but many in his audience missed the meaning of the story because they did not understand the words.

Here's another newspaper lead that needs revising for broadcast:

> The Energy Department proposes to spend $2.4 billion next year and up to $3.7 billion in each of the following four years to bring the nation's paralyzed nuclear weapon production plants into compliance with environmental and safety laws, according to Energy Secretary James D. Watkins.

If you read that sentence to some friends, and then ask them to tell you what it says, you would probably find that unless they have unusual abilities of concentration and recall, they would be unable to repeat all the details. That lengthy, involved sentence could be turned into good broadcast copy:

The Energy Department wants to spend almost two and one-half billion dollars next year to improve the nation's nuclear production plants. The funds would be used to bring the paralyzed plants into compliance with environmental and safety laws. Energy Secretary James Watkins says the government is willing to spend almost 15 billion dollars over the next four years to continue the cleanup and safety checks at the nuclear weapon production plants.

If you read the new sentences to your friends, they would probably remember more about the story than they did when you read the newspaper version. Let's examine how the newspaper copy was rewritten.

First, it was broken into three parts to reduce the number of details in one sentence. It is easier for listeners to understand the information if they hear it in small doses. The newspaper version mentions two large figures, $2.4 billion and $3.7 billion. In the broadcast version, the first figure was explained in the first sentence, and the second figure was mentioned in the third sentence.

The first figure, $2.4 billion, was rounded off to "almost two and one-half billion dollars." It is best to round off figures and to eliminate use of the decimal in broadcast copy because the result is easier for most people to understand. The second figure, "up to $3.7 billion in each of the following four years," was totaled and rounded off. The result, "the government is willing to spend almost 15 billion dollars over the next four years," is easier for listeners to grasp because they don't need to do the math in their heads. Notice, too, that *dollars* is spelled out in broadcast copy.

No attempt was made in the first sentence to discuss exactly how the Energy Department plans to spend the money. It was enough to tell the audience that the department wants to spend this money to improve the plants. Now that the audience has digested that information, it is told how the money is going to be used, "to bring the paralyzed plants into compliance with environmental and safety laws." And then, in the third sentence, the audience learns that the energy secretary wants even more money in the coming years to complete the job. Just in case the audience was not paying complete attention, how the money is to be used was mentioned again in the closing words—"to continue the cleanup and safety checks" at the plants.

Last, the middle initial *D* was dropped from Secretary Watkins' name because the secretary does not use the initial consistently.

AVOIDING RELATIVE CLAUSES

Other sentences that produce information overload are those that contain relative clauses. *Relative clauses* are introduced by the relative pronouns *who, which, that, what, whoever, whichever,* and *whatever* and add information to simple sentences. Newspapers often use relative clauses to stress one point about a person or thing over another in a particular sentence. Because relative pronouns refer to nouns that precede them, TV and radio audiences may have trouble identifying the noun and pronoun as the same person or thing. Take this example found in a newspaper:

> The comments from the State Department spokesman came in response to a report in the English-language Tehran Times, which quoted a source as saying Iran would definitely intercede to gain the release of the hostages if Washington gave assurances it would release frozen Iranian assets.

Whereas newspaper readers would immediately know that *which* refers to *Tehran Times* because the words are next to each other, a broadcast audience might have to stop and think about what *which* refers to. When this copy was rewritten for broadcast, the relative pronoun *which* was removed and the sentence was cut in two. The noun *newspaper* was used again instead of the pronoun:

> The State Department spokesman made the comments after a report appeared in the English-language newspaper The Tehran Times. The newspaper quoted a source as saying Iran would definitely help win release of the hostages if Washington promised to release frozen Iranian assets.

Other changes included recasting the passive construction in the first sentence as active and replacing the phrase *intercede to gain* with the single word *help*. Likewise, *gave assurances* was simplified to *promised*. The second version is better for a broadcast audience because it does not use pronouns or wordy phrases that could cause misunderstanding.

Which, when used as part of a clause that adds descriptive detail about a noun, also presents unnecessary problems for broadcast writers. Take this print copy:

> Two people were killed today when a small plane, which was on a flight from Key West to Miami, crashed into the ocean off the coast of Key Largo.

All these details will be simpler for your audience to digest if you give the number of dead and where the crash took place in the first sentence and explain the departure and destination of the plane in the second sentence. Here's a broadcast version:

> Two people died today when a small plane crashed into the ocean off the coast of Key Largo. The plane was on a flight from Key West to Miami.

Relative clauses introduced by *that* contain information important to the meaning of a sentence, not just additional details. For example:

> The truck that jackknifed on the freeway today was carrying flammable liquid.

The *that* clause identifies which particular truck was carrying flammable liquid.

In some sentences, *that* can be omitted because the sentence sounds more natural and is clear without it. For example:

The governor says that he'll leave the capital by plane this evening.

Dropping *that* makes the sentence more conversational:

The governor says he'll leave the capital by plane this evening.

ELIMINATING LONG WORDS

Short words are usually easier to understand than long ones and, crucially for broadcast news, where time is precious, they take less time to deliver. For example:

Police *abandoned* the search.

is more difficult to say than

Police *gave up* the search.

Here are examples of long words and some shorter ones that could replace them in broadcast copy:

AVOID	USE
extraordinary	unusual
acknowledge	admit
initiate	start, begin
transform	change

Certain words should be avoided because they are difficult to pronounce on the air. Here are some examples:

AVOID	USE
burst into	broke into
coaxing	tempting
recrimination	countercharge
autonomy	independence
deteriorate	grow worse
allegations	charges
intermediaries	go-betweens; negotiators

If you are unsure about other words you find yourself using, remember that reading them aloud is the best way to decide whether they are appropriate broadcast words. If a word is difficult to say or sounds strange or confusing to the ear, don't use it.

CONJUNCTIONS

Coupling pins such as *but* and *and* are often helpful in connecting sentences or parts of sentences. Using conjunctions to link ideas to one another often can help broadcast copy sound more conversational. However, do not overuse conjunctions. Remember also that some conjunctions that work in print, such as the *however* in the previous sentence, do not always work as well in broadcast copy. Use *but* instead of *however* in broadcast copy.

PREPOSITIONS

Prepositions can also be helpful in making copy more conversational, particularly when used to eliminate the possessive, which tends to make listeners work harder to follow the meaning. Here are some examples; the first uses the possessive:

> The Senate Armed Services Committee's spokesman announced a series of new hearings on budget cuts.

Here is a preposition used in the same sentence:

> A spokesman *for* the Senate Armed Services Committee announced a series of new hearings on budget cuts.

See how much easier it is to read the version with the preposition. It is more natural. The preposition is more likely to be used than the possessive in conversation.

PRONOUNS

We use a lot of pronouns during conversation, and they serve a useful purpose in broadcast copy. They eliminate the need to repeat a person's name. Some difficulty arises, however, when pronouns are used too far from the person's

News Director Susan Brown of WJBO-Radio works on a newscast.
PHOTO BY CHRISTOPHER J. ROGERS

name or more than one name is mentioned in the sentence or paragraph. Examine this troublesome use of a pronoun:

The Boy Scout of the Year award was given to Frank Jones by Mayor Harris. Immediately after the presentation he slipped and fell on the stage.

Who slipped and fell on the stage, the mayor or the Boy Scout? The pronoun *he* does not work here because two males are mentioned in the sentence. The person who fell should be identified by name.

MODIFYING PHRASES

Some writers, in their eagerness to tell the story, often get the details right but put the words in the wrong order, thus changing the meaning of the sentence. Look at the following example:

Soviet officials said political prisoners arrested by the KGB during former communist regimes would be released at a news conference today.

Because of the placement of the modifying phrase *at a news conference,* this sentence implies that the prisoners would be released at the time of the news conference. What the writer meant to say is:

Soviet officials said at a news conference today that political prisoners arrested by the KGB during former communist regimes would be released.

When you use modifying phrases, be sure to place them as close as possible to the word(s) they describe or identify.
Here's another example:

The two cars collided in heavy rain on Interstate 95 during the rush hour.

It's true that the "heavy rain" did fall on the highway, but it also fell elsewhere. Recast to be less ambiguous, the sentence would read this way:

The two cars collided on Interstate 95 in heavy rain during the rush hour.

AVOIDING CLICHÉS

During the Gulf War, I watched television news in a number of major cities. The reporting was often good, but the writing was just as often horrible. When you watch and listen to news for hours at a time, you realize how badly broadcast copy can be written, not only on local stations but on the networks as well.
Newspaper writers, including those working for such distinguished publications as the New York Times, Washington Post and Los Angeles Times, turn out a lot of long, cumbersome copy that sometimes takes several readings to

digest. But, to these newspaper writers' credit, their writing is rarely as cliché-filled as the copy produced by broadcast writers and reporters.

Broadcast news managers often argue that their writers do not have as much time as newspaper writers to produce copy, which is often true. They also point out that some of the cliché-filled copy I complain about is not very different from the way people talk. "We're writing conversational copy, aren't we?" asked one news director, "so what's wrong with a few clichés? We use them all the time in conversation."

Some people might find that argument persuasive, but writing in a conversational style does not mean adopting all the bad habits of conversation. Many people hold conversations without using clichés.

The American College Dictionary defines a cliché as "a trite, stereotyped expression." In his book "Newswriting," William Metz says a cliché is "a phrase that has been used so often that it has no zip, has outlived its usefulness. A cliché is a worn-out phrase." He adds: "These barren, impotent word combinations are used by careless and lazy writers."

In Gulf War broadcast copy, Americans were almost always "glued" to their TV sets. That cliché conjures up awful pictures of American heads attached to televisions. There also were lots of "wary eyes" during the Gulf War, but they belonged mostly to administration officials, diplomats and members of Congress.

We all use clichés from time to time, but you should avoid as much as possible using clichés in broadcast copy, even though some clichés are heard every night on news programs. For example, killers are often "coldblooded"; "slaughter" is always "bloody"; and events "come on the heels of" other events. Broadcasts during political campaigns in particular inundate listeners with clichés, such as "hats in the political ring," "campaign trails," "political hay" and "political footballs."

Here are some more clichés that should be (if you will excuse the cliché) "deep sixed":

- Airliners that become "ill-fated planes" after they crash

- Politicians and others who "take to the air waves"

- Lobby groups and others who "are up in arms"

- People who end up "in the driver's seat"

- Facts that are "difficult to swallow"

- Plans brought to a "screeching halt"

- Comments or actions that add "fuel to the storm" (a mixed metaphor)

- Troublesome situations that are a "can of worms" or a "Pandora's box"

And why are so many things "put on the back burner"? What is wrong with "delaying action" or referring to something as having "a low priority"? Say simply that people are "delaying" or "avoiding" something, rather than "dragging their feet." Police should be "searching for" or "looking for" or even "hunting for" a missing person, not "combing the woods" for him or her.

Broadcast writers who use "cooling their heels," "tight-lipped" and "Mother Nature" should be "tarred and feathered." Although some news makers insist on referring to something as being "miraculous," do not use the word to describe some spectacular escape from death or injury unless you are quoting the newsmaker. Use instead "unbelievable," "amazing," "incredible."

"Rampage" is another "worn-out" word that will never go away. Instead of using the cliché to tell a prison riot story, describe what's actually going on inside the prison. For example:

> Prisoners at Center City jail this afternoon took five guards hostage, burned cellblocks and demanded that Governor Wilson come to the jail to hear their demands.

A Miami TV station, in its story about the arrest of a suspect in the Florida State University serial killings, reported the following:

> People are breathing easier tonight because a suspected serial killer is behind bars.

As it turned out, the suspect was then released for lack of evidence, so we can assume that the breathing in the community became heavier again.

A network sportscaster reporting about a series of injuries in the NBA wrote this sentence:

> Officials are scratching their heads for an explanation.

All of the above are examples of "lazy" writing. Whenever you are tempted to use a cliché, make the extra effort to think of a fresh way to express your point.

WRITING WHAT YOU MEAN

During the Gulf War, the English language also came under attack. It was not an Iraqi *boat* that was sunk in the gulf, it was a *ship*. A boat is something you paddle or sail. If you are referring to anything larger, use *ship*.

In writing broadcast copy, be precise. Use the right word. If you do not, your credibility, a key factor in building a career, comes into question.

Here are a few words and phrases commonly used incorrectly on the air:

- The *consensus of opinion* is that the war will be over within a few months. [*Of opinion* is redundant; *consensus* means "general agreement."]

- There was bad weather over the gulf *due to* a fast-moving storm front. [*Due to* means "owing to"; use *because of*.]

- The fighting is different *than* last week's. [*Different* here takes the preposition *from*. However, it is correct to say: The fighting is different *than* he expected.]

- The number of people injured was *over* a dozen. [*Over* implies a spatial relationship; use *more than*.]

- The house is *further* down the road. [*Further* means "in addition to"; use *farther* to refer to distance.]

- *Since* you are going downtown, please get me a newspaper. [*Since* refers to a relationship of time; use *because* to indicate a causal connection.]

These are just a few examples of improper word usage. A good background in English grammar is important. Most college journalism programs insist that you take one to two years of English, but it is not always easy to find classes that work on grammar. Ask your adviser to recommend a teacher who does.

GOOD GRAMMAR AND SOME EXCEPTIONS

The same rules of grammar apply to both print and broadcast copy, most of the time. Writers do take a few liberties in broadcast copy because of its conversational nature. You'll recall that commas can be omitted from broadcast copy unless they indicate a pause and that subordinate clauses should be avoided in broadcast writing. Another exception: verbs can be dropped from some sentences, as is frequently done in conversation.

For example, if you are talking to your letter carrier and say, "Looks like snow today, Helen," no one is going to object because you did not say, "It appears as if we are going to get snow today, Helen." Therefore, it would be natural for a newscaster to say, "Three injuries tonight on the turnpike, that story when we return." Few people will take offense because the newscaster did not say "*There were* three injuries tonight on the turnpike." Verbs will be discussed further in Chapter 3, "More Style Rules."

SUMMARY

This chapter suggests that you use conversational style in writing broadcast copy. The material in the chapter is meant to help you learn to write as you speak. Most of us use brief sentences, with few subordinate clauses, and choose easy-to-understand words in everyday conversation. Communicating information to a radio or TV audience is best done in everyday language, simply and with sincerity.

Keep in mind that reading your copy aloud is the surest way to test how well you are using conversational style. Your ears, not your eyes, will tell you if your copy is good.

1. Where would you use contractions in the following sentences?

The governor says he will leave on vacation tomorrow.

There will be a dozen people at the reception.

The workers say they will walk off the job at noon.

Here is the latest word from the Weather Bureau.

Now let us take a look at what happened in baseball tonight.

2. Would you use a contraction in the following sentence? Explain.

The president says he will sign the bill.

3. What's wrong with the following sentence, and how could it be improved for broadcast?

Two years after the crash of a helicopter into the Washington channel, the D.C. Fire Department has not provided scuba equipment and training for its fireboat personnel, despite an order from Congress to do so accompanied by an appropriation to pay for it.

4. Here is another complex sentence. How could you improve it for broadcast?

Higher rates for electricity could be one result of the miners' strike against the Pittston Coal Company, which has forced some utilities to curtail sales of power to neighboring companies and to buy more expensive types of fuel, according to an industry spokesman.

5. Here is a list of words that are not particularly good for broadcast. Think of an appropriate substitute for each.

emblazoned	facilitate
ascent	perquisites
capitulation	stupefied
exodus	disperse

6. Keeping in mind the suggestions for using prepositions and conjunctions, how could the following sentence be improved for broadcast?

The circus's chief lion trainer did not take part in the show because he was sick. However, the apprentice trainer took over and his performance was loudly applauded.

7. There's a pronoun problem in the following sentence. Identify it, and explain how the sentence should read.

The governor accused his opponent, Frank Smith, of mudslinging. After the exchange, he predicted he would win the election.

8. What words and phrases might you use to replace the clichés in the following sentences?

The prisoners rampaged for more than an hour.

The White House announcement came on the heels of Iraq's invasion of Kuwait.

The Republican candidate said he had no doubt that the tax issue would become a political football.

The gun lobby was up in arms because of congressional approval of the Brady bill.

EXERCISES

1. Correct any misused words and phrases in the following sentences:

The consensus of opinion was that Saddam Hussein would be out of power within months.

Due to the bad weather, we decided not to go boating.

There were over a thousand people in the ballroom.

The car rides like an expensive one should.

2. Rewrite the following wire-service sentence for broadcast.

Thunderstorms that raged through the South, and bad weather elsewhere, have been blamed for at least 23 deaths and the presumed drowning of a North Carolina man swept away by a swollen creek the night before he was to be married.

3. Take a story from the wires or a newspaper. Read it carefully, and then put it aside. Now rewrite the story in broadcast style without looking at the copy again. When you have finished, look at your copy, and make a note of anything important that you forgot or any information that you wrote incorrectly.

4. Watch a program of any kind on television, and then write a story about it, describing it as you would to a friend.

5. Read over your story from exercise 3 or 4, and make any changes you think will improve the copy. Then read the copy *aloud,* and note any changes you would make that you did not notice when you read the copy to yourself.

6. Find a newspaper story that has at least one subordinate clause in the lead, and rewrite it in broadcast style.

7. Look through your newspaper for words that you feel are too long or might be difficult for a broadcast audience to understand. Look them up in a dictionary or thesaurus to find synonyms that would be more appropriate for broadcast copy.

CHAPTER 3

MORE STYLE RULES

ike the last chapter, this one focuses on broadcast style rules. Much of this chapter is devoted to the use of verbs, adjectives and other parts of speech. It also examines the various ways broadcast writers express time, quote people, and attribute information.

VERBS

PRESENT TENSE

Broadcast news must always present an image of immediacy. Without deceiving an audience by treating an old story as if it were fresh, the broadcast news writer's job is to tell the news as though it is in progress or has just recently happened. If a story is still developing or has just cleared the wires, a news writer should make it sound as new and exciting as possible because most of the audience will be hearing the story for the first time. Use of present-tense verbs, particularly present-progressive verbs, which suggest ongoing action, adds to that immediacy. For example, in covering a meeting at the White House that is still in progress, a writer would best say:

> The president is meeting with his cabinet this morning to discuss the budget.

Only if the meeting had ended by the time of the newscast would the writer use the past tense:

> The President met today with his cabinet to discuss the budget.

When writers use the past tense they tell the audience that the event has already taken place, while some aspect of it may actually still be in progress. Look at the following examples to see how the use of present-tense verbs focuses on the continuing action:

> *Poor:* Members of Congress ended their session today and headed for home.

> *Good:* Members of Congress are on their way home today after ending their session.

Poor: A hurricane warning was issued tonight for Florida and Georgia.

Good: A hurricane warning is in effect tonight for Florida and Georgia.

PRESENT PERFECT TENSE

Another verb tense that gives a sense of immediacy is the present perfect, which suggests that an action started in the past and is continuing into the present. For example:

The president has left Camp David for Andrews Air Force Base.

The present perfect tense is useful when the status of the story is not certain. In this case, it may be known that the president left Camp David, but it may not be clear when he is going to arrive at Andrews Air Force Base.

MIXING TENSES

Because a news story may mention events that happened at different times or report a statement that still holds true but was made earlier, it is acceptable to mix tenses in broadcast copy. For example, a story may begin with the present tense and then change to the past tense in later sentences so that the story makes sense. Here's an example of changing tenses:

Mayor Jones says he hopes to keep property taxes at their present level. He made the comment during a speech earlier today before a meeting of the Chamber of Commerce. The mayor told the group he expects an improving economy and a reduction in city expenses will eliminate the need for higher property taxes.

The first sentence uses the present-tense verb *says,* but the rest of the paragraph uses past-tense verbs because it would sound strange to continue the present tense once it is established that the mayor made the comments earlier in the day.

But suppose the mayor has not yet delivered the speech. The story might be handled this way:

Mayor Jones says he hopes to keep property taxes at their present level. Jones will say this tonight in a speech to the Chamber of Commerce. The mayor says he believes that an improving economy and a reduction in city expenses will eliminate the need for higher property taxes.

In this case the present tense is used to describe opinions the mayor holds now, and the future tense is used to describe when he will express those opinions. The fourth and fifth sentences might continue with the future tense:

The mayor will also tell his audience that he expects to attract new business to the city. He'll say he has a promise from Governor Williams for extra state funds to take care of the city's needy.

ACTIVE VERBS

Good broadcast copy also makes use of active verbs, not passive ones. Active verbs speed up copy and give it more punch because they focus on the action rather than the receiver of the action.

Poor: Three areas occupied by Bosnian forces were attacked by Serb tanks.

Good: Serb tanks attacked three areas occupied by Bosnian forces.

Poor: The Dow Jones was pushed up 30 points today after buyers took over on Wall Street.

Good: Buyers took over today on Wall Street, sending the Dow Jones up 30 points.

SAYS IS A GOOD VERB

Don't be afraid to use *says.* Many writers think they have to find different ways to avoid using a form of *say* because they think it is a boring verb. So, they will use forms of *exclaim, declare, assert, announce* and other words that they believe mean the same thing as *say.* The problem is that these other words are not synonyms for *say;* each has a different connotation.

STRONG VERBS

Although these verbs should not be used in place of *say,* sometimes they do accurately describe the situation. For example:

- ➨ The United Nations Security Council declared today . . .
- ➨ The White House announced that Peter Grant would become the new Secretary of the Interior.
- ➨ "We'll walk this picket line 'till hell freezes over!" exclaimed union leader Frank Chilton.

As for *assert,* it is difficult to think of an occasion when it would be appropriate to use that word in broadcast copy.

In writing broadcast copy, look for strong verbs that vividly describe the action:

- ➨ *smother,* rather than *put down,* an uprising
- ➨ *snuff out,* rather than *defeat,* a rebellion

➡ *echo,* rather than *repeat,* an opinion

➡ *clash,* rather than *disagree,* over strategy

➡ *lash out at,* rather than *attack,* opponents

➡ *muster,* rather than *collect,* enough votes

When choosing verbs, think about the image you want to create. For example, a tornado *roars,* but it also can *sweep* through a neighborhood. A hurricane can *destroy* a beachfront, but *demolish* gives a stronger picture. A high-school student might be *expelled,* but a deposed leader would be *exiled.* Battalions can *move* through the desert, but if they are doing it quickly, as they were in the Gulf War, they might be said to *race* through.

LIMITING USE OF ADVERBS AND ADJECTIVES

Like good verbs, adjectives and adverbs sometimes add color to broadcast copy, but for the most part they should be avoided. Many adjectives add unnecessary detail, and rather than enliven the copy, they weigh it down. Here's an example of a sentence with too many adjectives and adverbs:

The *diesel-powered* train was quickly moving around the *very sharp* curve when suddenly there was a *loud, screeching* noise and the cars near the *very* front of the train *rapidly* started to leave the track.

The sentence would be more effective without most of these adjectives and adverbs because they add little meaning. It is not important to know that the train is *diesel-powered,* because most are. *Quickly moving* could be replaced by the strong verb *racing,* and the adverb *very* could be omitted because intensifiers are "filler" words that rarely add meaning. *Rapidly* could be eliminated because it is a given that the cars would leave the tracks quickly if the train was *racing* around the curve. Finally, *started to leave* could be replaced by the more vivid *jumped.*

The cleaned-up sentence would read:

The train was racing around the sharp curve when suddenly there was a screeching noise as the cars near the front of the train jumped the track.

Screeching was left in the sentence because it is a strong, colorful adjective that describes the noise. *Loud,* however, was eliminated because a screeching noise is, by definition, loud.

ATTRIBUTION

One of the basic requirements of good news writing and reporting, whether for newspapers or broadcasts, is proper attribution. The chapters on reporting will deal with the various types and methods of attributing information. Right now, let's examine the proper style of attribution used in broadcast scripts, which differs from the style used in newspapers and newspaper wire copy.

For the most part, newspapers use attribution at the end of a sentence, what is called *dangling attribution.* For example:

> Hundreds of people have been killed in Yugoslav army attacks on Croatia, according to The Associated Press.

Attribution in broadcast copy, if used in the lead sentence, is always at the top of the sentence. For example:

> The Associated Press reports hundreds of people have been killed in Croatia following Yugoslav army attacks.

The attribution can also be *delayed;* that is, it can be mentioned in the second sentence. For example:

> Hundreds of people reportedly have been killed in Yugoslav army attacks on Croatia. The report comes from The Associated Press.

USING QUOTES   Most of the time, quotes are paraphrased in broadcast copy. Newspapers have the luxury of providing long, detailed quotes of politicians, government officials and other newsmakers. But broadcasting time restrictions require a distillation of such information. There will be times, because of the importance of statements, when direct quotes can be used. But even then, the writer must keep them to a minimum.

Here is sample of a quote that appeared in a newspaper:

> "This is an example of the worst brutality I have ever come across," was the way the judge described the beating of a man arrested by police.

The broadcast version would read:

> The judge said the beating of a man arrested by police was—in his words— "the worst brutality I have ever come across."

The quote also could have been paraphrased:

> The judge described the beating of the arrested man as the worst brutality he had ever come across.

If a quote is too important to paraphrase, such as President Bush's denunciation of Iraqi President Saddam Hussein's aggression against Kuwait, the actual words must be used. Most writers and broadcasters avoid using the terms *quote*

"60 Minutes" Correspondent Ed Bradley reports live from the 1992 Republican Convention in Houston.
COURTESY OF CBS NEWS

and *unquote* at the beginning and end of a direct quote, but you will occasionally hear them on the air. There are better ways of handling a direct quote. Here's one way:

> President Bush today denounced Iraqi President Saddam Hussein, saying—and this is a direct quote—"I am determined as I have ever been that this aggression will not stand."

Some newscasters will use a direct quote after saying "and these are the president's exact words." Other anchors will simply pause a second before a direct quote and change the inflection of their voices, but not all newscasters do this effectively. If you are writing the script, be explicit and use an introductory phrase to indicate you will be quoting someone directly.

The president's actual remarks about Saddam Hussein were much longer. Here's a paraphrase of some of them along with direct quotes for some key phrases.

> The president expressed his anger over mistreatment of American hostages. The president noted that the American flag is still flying over the embassy in Kuwait and our people inside are—as the president put it—"being starved by a brutal dictator."
>
> Mr. Bush added: "I have had it with that kind of treatment of Americans."

Because the final quote follows the previous one so quickly, it is not necessary to point out again that it is a direct quote.

EXPRESSING TIME

Because broadcast news usually reports or describes events that are currently happening, it is not always necessary to use the word *today* in broadcast copy. If events are not current, point that out quickly.

If a story says that 18 people have been injured in a train crash in Center City, listeners are going to assume that the accident occurred today unless the broadcaster explains that it happened last night or at some other time. Repeating the word *today* throughout a newscast, then, would become tiresome.

Those writing or reporting for an evening or late-night newscast should be specific. If the story is about something that is going on while the newscast is on the air or took place a short time earlier, the copy should stress the word *tonight* or use a phrase such as *at this very moment, a short time ago, within the past hour* or *earlier this evening* to alert the audience that this is fresh news.

A story should never lead with the word *yesterday*. If a story happened the day before, something new must be found to freshen the story and eliminate *yesterday* from the lead. There will be details on the subject of updating leads in Chapter 4, "Writing Broadcast Copy."

LOOKING AHEAD

Some newscasts alert the audience to events that are expected to happen in the future. The information should be as specific as possible. An example:

> The president is expected to leave the White House in the next 15 minutes or so for Andrews Air Force Base, where he'll board Air Force One for the trip to London.

Another example:

> At any moment now, members of the United Nations Security Council will be considering new proposals on the crisis in the Middle East. We were told a few minutes ago that members were already beginning to arrive at the Security Council chamber.

This sort of specific time reference adds immediacy and drama. It's much better than saying:

> The Security Council meets today to consider new proposals on the Middle East.

One final note: Whenever you use a specific time reference, such as *tonight* or *a few minutes ago,* place the reference as close as possible to the verb whose action it describes.

TRANSITIONS

Transitions are phrases and words that signal relationships between sentences. Some broadcast writers use transitions to carry listeners from one story to another, but in a newscast, transitions should be used with care and in moderation. If a transition is natural, it can be effective, but most transitions tend to sound contrived.

Here's an example of good use of a transition:

> Centerville Mayor Frank Jones is flying to New York City at this hour to take part in talks with other mayors on how to deal with Washington's cut in funds for American cities.
>
> Also traveling today is Centerville Police Chief Robert Potter. He's on his way to Chicago to meet with officials in that city to discuss the fight on drugs.

The transition *also traveling today* works here because it links stories about similar events of equal importance. But here's a bad example:

> Centerville Mayor Frank Jones is flying to New York City at this hour to take part in talks with other mayors on how to deal with Washington's cut in funds for American cities.
>
> Also traveling tonight, Hurricane Dorothy. It's headed our way at about 10 miles an hour and could slam into the mainland in the morning.

In this example, the transition is forced. Unlike the natural connection of two city officials who are traveling on government business, there is nothing logical about connecting the movement of the mayor and that of a hurricane.

That example was not made up. The names have been changed, but the transition tying together the movement of an official and a hurricane was actually broadcast.

Here is another example of an effective transition:

> The Justice Department wants to know if there are patterns of police brutality anywhere in the country. Attorney General Richard Thornburgh has ordered a review of all police brutality complaints filed with the department's civil rights division during the last six years. The order comes amid an outcry over the police beating of a motorist in Los Angeles—an attack videotaped by a witness and aired across the country.
>
> Los Angeles isn't the only place where authorities are investigating allegations of police brutality. In Georgia, witnesses say more than a dozen police officers pounced on a suspected prowler they caught after a chase from Atlanta to Stockbridge. The Atlanta and Clayton County police departments are conducting internal investigations. (*AP Radio*)

The transitional sentence *Los Angeles isn't the only place where authorities are investigating allegations of police brutality* is quite logical.

The prize for bad transitions must go to a Miami TV station:

The pope wasn't the only one celebrating a birthday today. Five years ago today, Mount St. Helens volcano erupted.

PEOPLE, NOT *PERSONS*

One final style note, on the use of the term *people* as opposed to *persons.* When more than one person is involved in a story, it is more conversational to refer to them as *people,* even though some style books continue to insist that a small group should be referred to as *persons.* For example, in conversation we are more likely to say that "five *people*" are going to join us for dinner than we are to say that "five *persons*" will be joining us.

SUMMARY

Verbs play a vital role in broadcast news writing. One of the most important messages of this chapter is: use present-tense verbs in broadcast copy as much as possible. People turn to radio and television because they want to know what is happening *now.* When you write broadcast copy, try to make the news sound fresh without being dishonest or misleading.

Using the *right* verb is also crucial. Remember that you don't always need to look for ways to replace *says.* It's a good verb. Look for strong verbs that vividly describe the action, but make sure they don't send the wrong message.

This chapter also discusses attributing information in broadcast copy. If you *need* to include an attribution, always place it at the beginning of your sentence.

REVIEW QUESTIONS

1. How could the verb tenses in these sentences be improved for broadcast?

President Bush said the invasion of Kuwait "will not stand." He spoke to reporters at the White House a short time ago.

Rescuers went through the wreckage looking for more bodies. They said they expect to work all day and night.

The hurricane slammed into Hollywood, Florida, a few minutes ago, and our reporter had this report from the beach area.

2. What's wrong with the verbs in these sentences?

There was applause when the birthday cake was brought out by the chef.

The robber was grabbed by the sheriff as he tried to run from the bank.

3. How could the verbs in these sentences be improved for broadcast?

The teacher declared that the student outing was postponed because of rain.

The mayor asserted that she would seek another term.

The president exclaimed that he would go to Camp David for the weekend.

4. What's wrong with the attributions in the following sentences?

The nation's economy is going to get worse before it gets better, according to a leading economist.

Hundreds of people were injured in rioting in Los Angeles following the Rodney King verdict, according to the police.

5. What's wrong with the transition used to link the following sentences?

Forest fires swept through a number of states on the West Coast today, destroying hundreds of thousands of acres of trees. Also under fire is our town's police chief, who is accused of failing to control some of his officers.

EXERCISES

1. Using stronger verbs, rewrite the following copy.

An earthquake has hit San Francisco. Police say several people may have been killed. There is no report on injuries. But rescue workers looked through several wrecked buildings for possible victims. Hundreds of frightened residents left their homes. It was the strongest quake to hit the city in several years.

Power lines were down in some areas. Police say they fell when cracks developed in the pavement.

Utility company officials are in the area to examine damage. They said some power lines were broken during the quake and present a danger.

2. The following remarks were made by former President Bush. Write a story showing how you would use them in broadcast copy.

"What keeps a kid in school, away from drugs, and off the street? It's not government spending. It's not the number of SBA loans or HUD grants. It's whether a child lives in a home where they are loved and cared for and kept on the right path."

3. Find two related stories on the wires or in the newspaper. Rewrite them in broadcast style, and use a transition to tie them together.

4. Using wire copy or newspaper stories, find three sentences that use the passive voice, and rewrite the sentences in broadcast style.

5. Find as many verbs as you can on the front page of your local newspaper that you feel could be stronger or more colorful. Replace them.

CHAPTER 4

WRITING BROADCAST COPY

he hardest part of writing broadcast copy is getting started. There are times when you will have difficulty moving your fingers. Your brain will seem dead. You may feel hypnotized by the white paper in your typewriter or the glow from your computer screen. Break the spell! Type the first thing that comes into your mind. Don't worry whether it is good, just write. Get started. It will get easier.

You may find that the first sentence you write works as an opening for your story, or you may need to write a few sentences before you come up with one that you like. This chapter focuses on writing an effective opening sentence, or *lead,* for a news story.

LEADS

The lead is the most important part of a news story because it sets the tone for all that follows. The lead must grab or "hook" the audience's attention in as few words as possible. The hook can be an exciting or dramatic sentence, a clever phrase, an intriguing fact or a provocative quote.

THE FIVE *W*'S AND *H* RULE

Unless the story is a feature, the lead must include an element of news. It must begin to address the traditional journalistic concept of discovering information. To guarantee that all of the important news elements are reported in a story, journalists have devised a rule that requires news writers to answer six basic questions—*who, what, where, when, why* and *how.* This rule is referred to as the "five *W*'s and *H* rule."

At one time, most newspaper editors expected every lead to answer all of these questions. But few newspaper editors still require this, and broadcasters never follow the rule. However, at least one or more of the questions must be answered in the lead of the story for it to be news. By the end of the story, most—if not all—of the questions should be answered.

An opening sentence that contains no news is referred to as a *non-news lead,* and such leads are unacceptable in a news story. Here's an example:

The chairman of the Joint Chiefs of Staff has met with reporters.

This lead could become news by answering some of the journalistic questions. *Why* did the chairman meet with reporters? *What* did he tell them? For example:

> The chairman of the Joint Chiefs of Staff, General Colin Powell, told reporters this morning that the United States would continue to keep troops in Iraq for a number of months.

This revised lead does not deal with all five *W*'s and the *H*, but it is a start. The *Who* is the chairman of the Joint Chiefs of Staff. The *what* is the issue of maintaining troops overseas. The *where* is Iraq. The *when* is for a number of months. Still unanswered are the *why* and the *how.* These questions will be answered in the balance of the story, if the answers are available.

This revised lead is an example of a *hard lead.* Such leads address the most important aspect of a story immediately. There are a variety of ways to lead your story, and all of them will be examined in the following sections. The decision about which kind of lead to use depends on a number of factors; the most important is the nature of the story. Is it a feature or breaking news? Is the story sad or upbeat? Is it about people or an event? Is the story about politics, a war, a medical development or the kidnapping of a child? Is the story brand new or a continuing one? The lead is like the foundation of a house. How the foundation is built determines how the rest of the house will look. The lead sentence determines how the rest of the story should be constructed.

An anchor and producers go over a script at WTVʃ-TV, Miami.
COURTESY OF WTVʃ-TV, MIAMI

HARD AND SOFT LEADS

In choosing a lead, decide first whether it will be hard or soft. As you saw in the previous example, a hard lead tells the audience the vital details of the story immediately. Hard leads are usually used for breaking news:

> Yugoslav army tanks strike across the Croatian border and attack the republic's last eastern strongholds.

> At least five people are reported dead in the crash of a DC-10 at Center City Airport.

> Burglars break into Cartier's and steal an estimated two million dollars in gems.

A *soft lead* takes a more subtle approach; it alerts the audience to the news that is to follow. This approach is sometimes called "warming up" the audience. The following soft leads could be used for the above stories:

- The fighting in Croatia has entered a new phase. Yugoslav army tanks struck across the border and began attacking the republic's last eastern strongholds.

- A fatal airliner accident at Center City Airport. At least five people are reported dead in the crash of a DC-10.

- A major robbery in New York City. Burglars broke into Cartier's and stole an estimated two million dollars in gems.

The soft leads may not sound as exciting or dramatic as the hard leads, but they do invite the audience to keep listening. Notice that two of the example soft leads are not full sentences but phrases that serve the same purpose as headlines in a print story. Soft leads can be helpful to listeners carrying out other tasks or fighting traffic on the way to the office, by giving them time to shift their attention to the news.

Many editors discourage soft leads because they tend to slow down a newscast, particularly if used too often. But used in moderation, soft leads add variety to broadcast copy. Experienced editors tend to be flexible in dealing with a writer's style, including the kinds of leads writers choose. Good editors recognize that there is not just one way to write a story. They might say, "Well, it's not the way I would have written it, but it's not bad."

THE "RIGHT" EMOTION

One challenge in writing a lead is deciding on the appropriate emotion, or *tone,* to express in the story. The tone depends largely on the kind of story you are going to tell. For example, if the story is about something amusing, you would establish a lighthearted tone in the lead. Let's look at an example:

A Center City schoolteacher got enough kisses today to last—well, maybe not a lifetime, but a few weeks, anyway. Patricia Roberson kissed 110 men at the annual fund-raiser for the local zoo. At ten bucks a kiss, Roberson raised eleven hundred dollars for the zoo, and when she turned the money over to zoo officials she joked that all the animals were not behind bars.

Even stories about accidents can sometimes be treated lightly:

"I'll never drink hot coffee in the car again." That's what John Semien said when he left the Center City hospital. This morning, Semien's car struck a fire hydrant, bounced off a tree and smashed into the window of a flower shop.

Semien said he had bought a container of coffee at a McDonald's drive-through and as he tried to add sugar and cream he lost control of the car when the hot coffee fell between his legs.

Stories about tragedies, as you would expect, require a more serious, straightforward approach:

- It's now believed that the death toll in the earthquake in Mexico has reached more than 50.

    or

- At least three people are reported dead in the collision this morning of a half-dozen cars on the freeway.

For these leads, the writers chose to give just the facts, a decision that creates a quiet tone that underscores the loss of life described in the stories.

While every story requires the writer to choose a certain tone, features and non-breaking news stories allow more flexibility than does breaking news. Some writers are very effective at evoking joy, pathos and other emotions from an audience through the tone they create. Look, for example, at these leads written by CNN anchor Reid Collins. His story about the invasion of Kuwait began: "A rich little country died at dawn today." On the rioting at the Viennese Opera Ball, Collins wrote: "A night at the opera in Vienna was a Marxist nightmare—part Karl, part Groucho." And his lead on a story about Mikhail Gorbachev's busy day was: "Like a juggler with too many plates in the air, Mikhail Gorbachev was stage right, stage left and stage center today. So far, no breakage."

Notice that Collins creates an air of sadness in his Kuwait lead, whereas he suggests the chaos and confusion of the riot in his lead about the Vienna opera. Similarly, his image of Gorbachev as a juggler effectively elicits a picture of Gorbachev frantically rushing around trying to hold his country together. These leads tell the audience not only what the stories are about, but how the writer wants the audience to feel about them.

THE QUOTE LEAD

Sometimes a *quote*, like the "hot coffee" example used earlier, can provide an excellent hook for a story:

> "Life is short and life is sweet. So take time to enjoy what you have." Marine Captain Russell Sanborn says that's one of the lessons he learned as a prisoner of war in Iraq. He and some other former P-O-W's told their stories today at news conferences in the Washington area. (*AP Broadcast Wire*)

Here is another example:

> "The first thing I'm going to do is quit my job and take a trip around the world." That's what lottery winner Bill Turpin said when he redeemed his ten million dollar winning lottery ticket.

Quote leads should be used sparingly, however. Unless the quote is comparatively short, the listener may miss its connection with the rest of the story.

THE SHOTGUN LEAD

The *shotgun,* or *umbrella, lead* can be effective for combining two or more related stories:

> Forest fires continue to roar out of control in California, Oregon and Washington State. The drought that has plagued the three states is now in its second month. Fires have scorched more than a million acres of timberland in California and another half million acres in Oregon and Washington.

The advantage of the shotgun lead is that it allows the writer to eliminate the boring alternative of reporting the fires in three separate, back-to-back stories.
Here is another example:

> Congress today is looking at administration proposals that would increase the number of crimes punishable by the death penalty and make it easier for police to collect evidence.

The writer would then devote a few sentences to each of the White House recommendations.

THE SUSPENSE LEAD

The object of the *suspense lead* is to delay telling the key information until the end of the story.

National Public Radio's Susan Stamberg used an effective suspense lead in her story about a famous photographer:

Stamberg: Edith Shane had run over to Times Square from her job at Doctors Hospital. She wanted to be part of the celebration. Off duty, she wasn't supposed to be in her uniform, but she was. The sailor, Bill Schwhitzgood — all these names popped up years later, by the way, and the two never did meet formally — the sailor grabbed the nurse in glee just as he had grabbed all those other women, but this was different. The nurse is caught gracefully in the sailor's arms. Her body twists a bit in his embrace. They look as if they could be dancing. It's the Eisenstadt moment.

Eisenstadt: If this nurse in white would have been in a dark uniform, wouldn't have been a nurse, wouldn't have been a picture or vice versa. If the — if the nurse was in white and he would be in white, wouldn't be a picture either. It was just a coincidence that he was in navy blue and she was in white and she was thin. If she would have been fat, it wouldn't have been a good picture either.

Stamberg: Alfred Eisenstadt was one of the original staff photographers for Life magazine, not a person to snap five rolls of film to get the single perfect shot. He has been seen standing absolutely motionless for an hour or more, waiting for a sailboat to move to exactly the right spot before he released the shutter. That August day in 1945, the day of the Eisenstadt moment, he took more pictures than usual and knew he had something.

Eisenstadt: I know this was the best picture I took on that day. I knew that.

Stamberg: What Alfred Eisenstadt didn't know then is that of all the thousands of images in his long career, this one of the sailor and the nurse would be the one he's known for.

Eisenstadt: When I someday go to heaven and I'm not living anymore, maybe probably everybody will say, "Oh, this is the photographer who took that picture," and everybody remembers that picture.

Stamberg: Photographer Alfred Eisenstadt just celebrated his 92nd birthday. He lives in New York, still goes into the Life magazine offices every day and still takes photographs, Eisenstadt moments. US troops continue coming back from the Persian Gulf, and it is possible one of the homecoming

```
photographs will capture the end of Operation Desert Storm,
but in this age of the moving image, it's unlikely that the
picture will mean to future generations what VJ Day Times
Square has come to mean in the past nearly half century. In
Washington, I'm Susan Stamberg.
```

Stamberg does not tell her audience until the final paragraph that Eisenstadt has just celebrated his 92nd birthday and that this is why she is talking about him and his work on this particular day. She decides to grab her audience with a story about a sailor and a nurse. The listeners have no idea why she is telling them the story, but it is bound to get the audience's attention. And the picture Stamberg paints is a colorful one:

> ... the sailor grabbed the nurse in glee just as he had grabbed all those other women, but this was different. The nurse is caught gracefully in the sailor's arms. Her body twists a bit in his embrace. They look as if they could be dancing. It's the Eisenstadt moment.

The last sentence of Stamberg's opening introduces Eisenstadt for the first time, but listeners still do not know who Eisenstadt is unless they guess he is the famous photographer. Then, Stamberg intrigues listeners some more by letting Eisenstadt speak for himself. At that point, the audience realizes that the story *is* about Eisenstadt the photographer and about a famous picture he took more than 45 years earlier.

Stamberg doesn't fill up her script with a lot of details about the career of the famous photographer. She decides to remind listeners of the man by telling about his most famous picture, one that captured a moment in history at the end of World War II.

THE DELAYED LEAD

Instead of saving the most important information until the end of the story, as in the case of the suspense lead, the *delayed lead* just withholds the most important details for a few sentences.

> The scene in the locker room of the Center City Rockets was quieter than usual last night although the team won by three goals. There also was a lot less swearing than usual and no nudity. Also new in the locker room last night was Heather Tierney.
>
> The sports reporter for the Center City Times is the first woman to be allowed in the team's locker room. Club officials broke the female ban after Tierney threatened to go to court to win the right to enter the locker room after games.

If the delayed lead had not been used, the story probably would have started out this way:

> For the first time, last night a woman reporter was allowed in the locker room of the Center City Rockets.

The delayed lead gives writers another option for adding variety to a script, but, like some other leads mentioned earlier, it should not be overused.

NEGATIVE LEADS

Negative leads, which include the word *not,* should be avoided. A positive lead can easily achieve the same result. There is always the chance someone in the audience might miss the word *not* and reach the wrong conclusion about what is happening. Here are some examples:

> *Avoid:* Striking newspaper workers say they will not return to work.

> *Use:* Striking newspaper workers say they will continue their walkout.

> *Avoid:* The mayor says he will not raise the city sales tax.

> *Use:* The mayor says he will keep the city sales tax at its present rate.

UPDATING AND REWORKING THE LEAD

One of the most effective methods of attracting and holding listeners is to convince them that the news is fresh. There will be days when news is plentiful, but on slow days writers need certain skills to make the news sound exciting and timely. One of those skills is the ability to *update* leads, which means finding something new to say in stories used in an earlier newscast. Another is the ability to *rework* the original lead to include new developments. For example, take a story about the arrest of a dozen men on narcotics charges. Police say the men were found in a cocaine "factory" where they were "cutting" more than one hundred million dollars' worth of cocaine.

Here's the first version of the lead:

> Police have arrested a dozen men during a raid on a cocaine factory in Center City. They say the men were cutting more than 100 million dollars' worth of cocaine.

An hour later, the lead might say:

> A dozen men are under arrest after police raided a building in Center City. Police say the men were cutting more than 100 million dollars in cocaine.

Still later, the lead might read:

Police are guarding an estimated 100 million dollars in cocaine that they scooped up in a raid on a Center City building. A dozen men are behind bars in connection with the raid. Police say the men were cutting the cocaine when the raid took place.

Another possible updated lead might say:

A dozen men are being held for arraignment on narcotics charges following a raid on a Center City building. Police say they found about 100 million dollars' worth of cocaine in the building. Police say the men were in the process of cutting the cocaine when the officers broke into the building.

As new developments occur in the story, there will be added opportunities to rework the lead. Within a few hours, detectives may reveal details about how they found out about the cocaine factory. They also may give more details about the raid. For example:

Center City police now say that their raid on a cocaine factory that resulted in the arrest of a dozen men came after two months of surveillance by detectives.

A skilled writer will be able to tell the story many times without its sounding stale.

CONSTRUCTING THE REST OF THE STORY

Once you have the lead of a story, its foundation, you are ready to construct the rest of the story by building on the lead. The audience has been prepared for what is to come. Now you must provide the details in a clear and logical manner.

In broadcast news, you can use more than just words to accomplish your goal. You can employ sound on radio and use both sound and pictures to help tell the story on television. Those techniques will be examined later. For now, let's just deal with words, returning to the story on General Colin Powell mentioned earlier in the chapter.

We'll start with a hard lead:

The chairman of the Joint Chiefs of Staff, General Colin Powell, says United States troops will stay in Iraq for a number of months.

The listeners now know part of the story. It's not much, but it is sufficient to grab interest. A general whom they have come to know over the months is telling them something important: that their sons, daughters, husbands, wives, and other relatives and friends—at least some of them—are not coming home right away. The audience will want to hear the general's explanation.

General Powell says American forces will stay in Iraq to enforce provisions of a pending U.N. cease-fire agreement. He says the troops would also prevent Iraq from using chemicals and air strikes to defeat rebels trying to overthrow President Saddam Hussein.

Now the audience knows why troops will remain in Iraq. What it does not know yet is how the troops are going to prevent Iraq from using chemical weapons and air attacks against the rebels. The next sentence addresses the question:

General Powell did not explain how U.S. forces would prevent Iraq from using chemicals and air attacks against the rebels.

Once the general made reference to the chemicals and air attacks, the statement had to be explained to the audience even if the general did not elaborate. Otherwise, the audience might have been asking the question and accusing the newscaster of withholding the information.

What next? Because the third sentence mentions the rebels, that aspect of the story could be expanded:

General Powell also said he was surprised by the strength of the revolt against the Saddam regime. He also denied that the U.S. forces are trying to play a role in influencing the outcome of the rebellion.

The general had much more to say to reporters, and newspapers carried the story in greater detail. But the broadcast news writer, who had eight other stories to cover in a three-minute newscast, told the Powell story in just 20 seconds. The essential details were given; nothing vital was left out. This is key to broadcast news writing: condense the important material; eliminate the unimportant without distorting the story or the facts.

SUMMARY

Writing broadcast copy is like building a house. This chapter focuses on the foundation, the lead. You now know many different ways to open your story. Some leads may be more appropriate than others, depending on the nature of the story, but remember that there is always more than one way to lead your story.

In the first four chapters, the emphasis has been on the basics of broadcast news writing. Now that you know how to construct a news story and include all the important details in your story in a logical manner, you are ready to learn about what many believe is the most important aspect of news writing: color, the subject of Chapter 5.

REVIEW QUESTIONS

1. Many writers have problems writing the first sentence of a story. How can they overcome this block?

2. What is the most important part of a news story? Why?

3. Although the five *W*'s and *H* rule is basically a print journalism concept, it does have application for broadcast journalism. What are the five *W*'s and *H*, and what is the major difference in the way they apply to print and broadcast journalism?

4. What is the difference between hard and soft leads?

5. How does emotion play a role in determining the lead sentence and how the rest of the story is written?

6. Do quote leads work for broadcast? Explain.

7. What is a shotgun lead?

8. What is a delayed lead?

9. How do you update a lead?

EXERCISES

1. Using the following information, write both hard and soft leads:

A tanker registered to the Zabo Oil Company of Panama has run aground. This happened off the coast of Charleston, South Carolina. One half million gallons of oil already have spilled into the Atlantic. It is believed that another half million gallons are still on the ship.

2. Write a quote lead based on the following information:

A man on welfare, Bill Nelson, found a purse on the street. When he opened it there was $5,000 inside. Nelson counted it a dozen times. After two hours, he went to the police station and turned over the money to the officer at the desk. When questioned about his honesty, Nelson said, "I may be poor but I am honest."

3. Using the information from exercise 2, write a delayed lead.

4. Write a shotgun lead using the following information:

Forest fires in Oregon have burned more than 10,000 acres of timberland and the flames are threatening thousands of additional acres. In California, firefighters are battling flames that already have destroyed 15,000 acres of woodland.

5. Use your imagination to figure out ways to update these leads:

The president is scheduled to leave this afternoon for a vacation in Florida, where he will work on a new budget.

The hurricane is off the coast of Jacksonville, Florida, and could hit the mainland within the next three hours.

Striking autoworkers are meeting at this hour to decide whether or not to accept the auto industry's latest contract offer.

The countdown has begun at Cape Canaveral for the launching of the space shuttle Atlantis.

6. Using any of the types of leads discussed in this chapter, write a story from the following information:

Lorry and Kevin were married today.

It was exactly 30 years ago to the day that they met.

When they were teen-agers the two had dated for about a year after meeting on a blind date in 1963. "I remember the date, of course, because it was my birthday," said Lorry Scott. Lorry and Kevin Rowce broke up following a fight. They both married and had children and had not seen each other for 29 years. Kevin contacted Lorry when he heard from a friend that her husband had died. Kevin had been divorced a number of years ago. They decided to marry after dating for the past year. They were married on New York's Staten Island ferry. "That's what we did on our first date," Kevin said.

CHAPTER 5

COLOR: THE KEY TO GOOD WRITING

he last few chapters stressed that broadcast news writing should be conversational—written the way we would speak with a friend at a restaurant or on a street corner. What makes such conversations memorable? An element known as *color*.

Who are the people who most hold our attention in social conversations? Interesting people, of course; people who can tell a yarn with a flair; people who make us laugh; people who sometimes shock us and on occasion make us cry. They may be people who fascinate us because of the way they use the language or the way they dress or because they just act differently. The people we like to meet are colorful people. They may not know it; that's just the way they are. Their style comes naturally. Color in broadcast copy should be just as natural.

COLOR SHOULD BE NATURAL

Color should not be forced or achieved with clichés or hype. Strong verbs, and adjectives used in moderation, add color, but they must be selected carefully. Poorly chosen verbs and adjectives can destroy copy. "Colorful" words do not always produce colorful copy.

The people involved in a story, and what they have to say, are likely to add color. Broadcast writing should honestly reflect the feelings and emotions of those people. Sound bites and pictures of the news makers themselves often provide the humor, pathos and other emotions that make the story a success. But using the voices and pictures of colorful people to provide the color for the story is almost a given. The real challenge is bringing color to the script through words, much as a good painter adds the proper strokes to a canvas to bring it to life.

Observing, paying close attention to details and using those details in copy provide color. Listen to and watch carefully people engaged in conversation. Does John use his hands like an orchestra leader to make his point? Does Mary whisper and look away in embarrassment when she tells her story, as though she's afraid someone will hear her? Is there a hole in the sole of Frank's shoe? Does Ann look directly into Pat's eyes as she speaks? Do Paul's hands shake? These are the things that good writers look and listen for if they hope to let the audience know and understand Paul and Ann and John and Mary.

Ernest Hemingway's name often comes up during a discussion of good news writing. Hemingway was one of America's best storytellers, and as one of his biographers noted, Hemingway's work as a journalist taught him "certain lessons in verbal economy" that he carried over to his novels. It was Hemingway's short, crisp, uncluttered, journalist-like sentences that marked his career as a novelist—skills he learned as a newspaperman for the Kansas City Star.

Here's a sample of Hemingway's writing from "The Old Man and the Sea":

> He was an old man who fished alone in a skiff in the Gulf Stream and he had gone eighty-four days now without taking a fish. In the first forty days a boy had been with him. But after forty days without a fish the boy's parents had told him that the old man was now definitely and finally *salāo*, which is the worst form of unlucky, and the boy had gone at their orders in another boat which caught three good fish the first week.

Consider what Hemingway tells us in only three sentences. We know that the fisherman is old and that he fishes in the Gulf Stream and that he certainly is very unlucky. We also know that he had a young companion in his boat until the boy's parents also reached the conclusion that the old man was unlucky. The old man is now fishing alone.

Hemingway tells us more about the character of the boy in the next sentence:

> It made the boy sad to see the old man come in each day with his skiff empty and he always went down to help him carry either the coiled lines or the gaff and harpoon and the sail that was furled around the mast.

And we quickly learn about the condition of the boat:

> The sail was patched with flour sacks and, furled, it looked like the flag of permanent defeat.

Hemingway's description of the old man is next:

> The old man was thin and gaunt with deep wrinkles in the back of his neck. The brown blotches of the benevolent skin cancer the sun brings from its reflection on the tropic sea were on his cheeks. The blotches ran well down the sides of his face and his hands had the deep-creased scars from handling heavy fish on the cords. But none of these scars were fresh. They were as old as erosions in a fishless desert.

In only two paragraphs we already have a clear picture of this fisherman and his young friend. We can see them together by the sea, the young boy sad with worry about the old man and the fisherman weary and broken by age and bad luck.

Consider Hemingway's detail, the kind of detail mentioned earlier that is so important in the development of colorful copy:

The old man was thin and gaunt with deep wrinkles in the back of his neck.

The brown blotches of the benevolent skin cancer . . .

The blotches ran well down the sides of his face.

. . . his hands had the deep-creased scars . . .

But none of these scars were fresh. They were as old as erosions in a fish-less desert.

We know more about this old man in just two paragraphs than most writers could tell us in two pages.

EMULATE THE BEST

A good way to learn how to use color in a story is to look to the masters of the craft. Read E. B. White, James Thurber and other good essayists and listen to the words of such distinguished broadcast journalists as David Brinkley, John Chancellor, Charles Kuralt, Bill Moyers, Charles Osgood, Cokie Roberts, Diane Sawyer and Susan Stamberg. Examine the writing of the late Pauline Frederick of NBC News and the late Edward R. Murrow of CBS News, the most distinguished of all broadcast journalists. One of the best ways to practice good techniques is to adopt the styles of successful writers.

CBS News Correspondent Charles Kuralt, a master of colorful writing, suggests that you also look in style manuals and usage guides—"browse through Fowler or Eric Partridge or Bergen Evans from time to time." He wonders how many people keep Otto Jesperson's seven-volume "Modern English Grammar" on a shelf in the bathroom.

CBS News Correspondent Charles Osgood, also known for his colorful writing, is "fascinated by the writings of people like John McPhee and Loren Eiseley, both wonderful craftsmen and artisans in their use of the language, who like to deal with subjects that have to do with science." He also says, "You can get a lot out of reading novels simply because we refer to every news story that we do as a story."

Osgood notes that all stories, whether they are novels or news, have to be constructed "according to some kind of logical plan with a beginning, a middle, and an end." He comments that if there has to be development and character and other elements in a novel, writers "should at least pay some homage to it in doing a news story."

Interestingly, both Osgood and Kuralt speak of rhythm and music when they talk about writing. Osgood says language starts with the ear: "A child learns the language by hearing people speak it. He hears words. He learns to say words long before he learns to read them. There's music in language." Osgood says that, like music, language has rhythm: "There's a shape, form and character to it. It's language, it's music, it's a noise."

Kuralt comments, "I know that I hear the rhythms of writers I have read and admired in my head. Sometimes," he adds, "I can even remember which writer's rhythm I am feeling. I think good writers hear the music of good writing they've read. The great writers compose new music for the rest of us to hear when we sit down at the typewriter."

Kuralt also says that good writing "takes patience." He thinks "it's worth sitting there until you remember the right word," recalling that Mark Twain once said that "the difference between the right word and the nearly right word is the difference between lightning and a lightning bug."

KURALT ON THE ROAD

Many of Charles Kuralt's colleagues would say that *his* name should be added to the list of great writers. Kuralt is by everyone's definition a "writer's writer." Many successful network correspondents acknowledge that they have learned from him.

Kuralt's "On the Road" TV series brought joy to millions. In 1975, he did a special series called "On the Road to '76" to mark the upcoming 200th anniversary of the nation's independence. Kuralt did a historical story from each of the 50 states, and one of his stops was Little Bighorn, Montana.

```
On The Road to '76
MONTANA
Kuralt-Bleckman-Colby-Quinlan
September 4, 1975

Kuralt on camera SOF          This is about a place where the

                              wind blows, the grass grows,

                              and a river flows below a hill.

                              There is nothing here but the

                              wind and the grass and the river.

                              But of all places in America,

                              this is the saddest place I know.

SOF pullback from             The Indians called the river
sparkle on river
                              the Greasy Grass. The white men

                              called it the Little Bighorn.

Saddle gap in                 From that gap in the mountains
mountains, pullback
to wide grassy plains         to the east, Brevet Major General

                              George A. Custer's proud 7th
```

Cavalry came riding early in the morning of June 25th, 1876, riding toward the Little Bighorn.

Looking down at river

Custer sent one battalion, under Major Marcus Reno, across the river to attack what he thought

grassy valley

might be a small village of hostile Sioux. His own battalion he galloped behind the ridges to ride down on the village from the rear.

pan down
from hill . . .

When at last Custer brought his 231 troops to the top of a hill and looked down toward the

. . . to broad plain below (right after slate in roll 2)

river, what he saw was an encampment of 15-thousand Indians stretching for two and a half miles — the largest assembly

zoom back from river

of Indians the plains had ever known — and a thousand mounted warriors coming straight for him.

view of hills . . .

Reno's men, meantime, had been turned, routed, chased across the river, joined by the rest of the regiment, surrounded, and now

. . . pull back to Meador's grave on hill

were dying, defending a nameless brown hill.

pan from grass . . .

In a low protected swale in the middle of their narrowing circle, the one surviving

. . . to post with
red cross on it

shallow rifle
trench . . .
. . . and peer
over side

Kuralt on camera

doctor improvised a field hospital
and did what he could for the
wounded. The grass covers the
place now, and grows in the
shallow rifle trenches above
which were dug that day by knives
and tin cups and fingernails.

Two friends in H Company,
Private Charles Windolph and
Private Julian Jones, fought up
here, side by side, all that day,
and that night stayed awake,
talking, both of them scared.

Charles Windolph said, "The next
morning, when the firing
commenced, I said to Julian,
'We better get our
coats off.' He didn't move. I
looked at him. He was shot
through the heart."

camera tilts down
to gravestone

view from hilltop

Charles Windolph won the Congressional Medal of Honor up here, survived, lived to be 98 — he didn't
die until 1950 — and never a day
passed in all those years that
he didn't think of Julian Jones.

wide shot showing
white stones in
distance

one you can read

And Custer's men, four miles
away? There are stones in the grass
that tell the story of Custer's
men. The stones all say the same

montage of grass and
and stones first one
or two, then —

Another bunch of
stones, larger group

Then a big group

Zoom through
grass . . .

 . . . to stone
that has Custer's
name on it

WS battlefield,
stones in distance

More grass
and stones

Kuralt on camera

thing: "U.S. Soldier, 7th Cavalry,
fell here, June 25th, 1876."

The warriors of Sitting Bull
under the great Chief Gall struck
Custer first and divided his
troops. Two Moon and the Northern
Cheyenne struck him next. And
when he tried to gain a hilltop
with the last remnants of his
command, Crazy Horse rode over
that hill with hundreds of
warriors, and right
through his battalion. The
Indians who were there later
agreed on two things — that Custer
and his men fought with exceeding
bravery, and that after half an
hour, not one of them was left
alive.

The Army came back that winter.
Of course, the Army came back —
and broke the Sioux and the
Cheyenne, and forced them back to
the starvation of the reser-
vations, and in time murdered
more old warriors and women and
children on the Pine Ridge
Reservation than Custer lost
in battle here.

That is why this is the saddest

place. For Custer and the 7th
Cavalry, courage only led to
defeat. For Crazy Horse and the
Sioux, victory only led to
Wounded Knee.

Saddest shot of
battlefield, maybe
backlit stone with
grass

Come here sometime, and you
will see. There is melancholy
in the wind, and sorrow in
the grass. And the river
weeps.

Maybe one last
zoom to river

Charles Kuralt, CBS News, on
the road to '76 in Montana.

*CBS News Correspondent Charles
Kuralt delivers one of his "On the
Road" reports.*
COURTESY OF CBS NEWS

Kuralt once commented that the Little Bighorn story was a challenge: "There was really nobody to interview there. There's nothing there but grass, water and gravestones, but I wanted to do a story anyway. We were not in a hurry to do this one; we had a whole day to walk around the battlefield and think. We didn't shoot anything."

Kuralt said he had been reading about the battle and had several books about the Little Bighorn battlefield. After the daylong tour of the battlefield, he said, "I went back to the bus and wrote the story, and afterwards we went out and shot it." The CBS news correspondent admitted, "We broke my rule and reversed the order, but I was writing to pictures I knew we were going to shoot." Kuralt said it was one of the few times that he worked "almost like a movie script writer."

Kuralt said that when the story went on the air, "it was beautiful ... all mood, all writing and some beautiful photography." He added, "You can fill the story with words and not do any interviews at all if you have a good story to tell and a skillful photographer at work."

Kuralt stresses how important it is to write to the picture. "Write something that will add to the experience of the viewer in seeing the picture," he says, "but when you can, have the courage to remain silent and let the picture tell the story. Give people time to feel something."

There is another Kuralt script in Chapter 14, "Putting the Television Story Together," where the CBS news correspondent discusses the importance of pictures.

"A POSTCARD FROM NEBRASKA"

Colorful writing and good pictures make good TV news. CBS News Special Correspondent Roger Welsch's success in marrying the two elements has made him a frequent contributor to Charles Kuralt's "Sunday Morning" program. Here is the script of one Welsch story, with Kuralt's introduction:

```
Kuralt O/C                        To prepare us for Thanksgiving,

                                  the great harvest festival we

                                  celebrate this Thursday, Roger

                                  Welsch has sent us another post-

                                  card from Nebraska. This one is

                                  reverent. Between the lines you

                                  can hear Roger giving thanks.

V/O                                      (Welsch)

Video of corn fields              It won't be long before these

                                  fields are empty. The corn picked,
```

	the squash tucked away in the cellar. Well, we managed to get some sweet corn into the freezer. It'll be a long time before we taste the sweetness of corn dripping with butter right off the cob. As for the
Video of melons and Placke's Market	melons, there's no saving them. They're here . . . and then they're gone. But it wasn't long ago back in Dannebrog, when Dan or Eric, maybe it was Harriet, said, "Hey, Roger, Placke's has sweet corn and melons for sale, let's go." It doesn't take me long to respond to an invitation like that. It's a special time of the year. An ephemeral moment that has to be grasped right now before it's gone and the fields are empty and cold.
Video of people at Placke's	(SOT Unidentified Person) "That ought to do it." V/O
Video of highway and produce places	Highway 281 near Saint Libory is peppered with produce stands. Some little more than rustic sheds, some fairly fancy markets where local farmers sell their squash, tomatoes, peppers, onions

	and sweet corn. This is my idea of a supermarket.
Video of people at market	There's no question that the merchandise here is fresh. It was picked this morning from fields
Video of produce picking	within walking distance of where we're standing right now.
SOT	(SOT Unidentified person) "Those have got a high sound to them. You've got to have a low sound."
V/O Market footage	V/O Personal service? Well, the family that's selling me my groceries this morning picked it and planted it, watered it and weeded it. In every sense of the word this watermelon is the Plackes' watermelon, until I pay for it. Then in every sense, it's mine.
Video of watermelons and watermelon eating	(SOT Unidentified person) "You guys going to eat that?"
V/O	V/O And taste? Nothing beats the taste of melon straight out of the field.
SOT	(SOT Unidentified person) "That's good, waited all summer for that."

V/O	V/O
Video of Welsch at market	Spaghetti squash?
SOT	(SOT Unidentified person)
	"Yes, they're very good."
V/O	V/O
Video of market	Well, I'm going to try some of those.
SOT	(SOT Unidentified person)
	"OK."
V/O	Sure, part of the attraction of buying produce like this is the price. It's not expensive and the Plackes usually consider 13 ears of corn a dozen and round off the total of your bill from $9.37 to $9 even.
	I don't know what I'm going to do with these red peppers, but they're too pretty to pass up.
SOT	(SOT Salesperson)
	"OK . . . a dollar, 78, 40."
V/O	V/O
Video of people picking produce	But, do you know what I think makes this food taste especially good? Handing over my money to the very folks who grew the sweet corn and who picked the water-melon and know the peppers by name. Sure the food is cheaper.

But frankly I'd pay more knowing that the money goes to the farmers. And, of course, it's better tasting, but I attribute part of that to the fact that the folks who sell it to me want it to taste better.

Welsch O/C at market

They have to look me in the eye when they sell it to me and when I come back the next week and next year.

I've been buying produce at the Placke stand now for 15 years. One of the Plackes' nephews was a classmate of mine at the University of Nebraska 10 or 20 years ago or so.

Thanks a lot, Marilyn. I appreciate it.

SOT

(SOT Unidentified person) "Yeah."

V/O

Video at market

                    V/O

These folks are not just businessmen, they're friends and neighbors.

There are a lot of reasons to complain about the weather out here on the plains. Sometimes it

```
                              seems as if complaining is our

                              favorite of all season sports.

                              But when the heat of summer is

                              gone and before the winter's

                              blizzards sweep across these

                              fields . . . at that short and

                              lovely moment when the sweet

                              coolness of autumn is evident,

                              it's then that the Saint Libory

                              produce stands remind us how

                              good things out here can be.

                              How rich and how full and how

                              tasty.
```

Welsch's story relies heavily on words as well as pictures. Welsch had only a few short sound bites to punctuate the narration, which meant the narration had to be longer, particularly because the stories on "Sunday Morning" usually run at least twice as long as the two-minute stories on most other news programs.

The story succeeds only because the script is so well written. Normally, without interviews it is difficult to sustain so much copy. But the combination of excellent pictures and colorful words allowed this story to run as long as it did. In the hands of a less talented writer, the story most certainly would have been shorter.

CRISP AND CLEAR

Welsch's writing style is crisp and clear. He picks short sentences and phrases and makes each word work for him. His sentences are conversational and often incomplete.

> It won't be long before these fields are empty. The corn picked, the squash tucked away in the cellar.

The squash could have been *stored* in the cellar, but *tucked away* is so much more colorful.

The first section of this chapter discussed the importance of using your senses in writing broadcast copy. Welsch uses his senses well:

It'll be a long time before we taste the sweetness of corn dripping with butter right off the cob.

Welsch also involves the audience. He brings the viewers into the story with lines such as:

I don't know what I'm going to do with these red peppers, but they're too pretty to pass up.

Most of us have said the same thing at one time or another as we shopped and spotted food that we just could not resist buying. We identify with Welsch's feelings, and that makes his writing effective.

He involves the audience again later in the script:

But, do you know what I think makes this food taste especially good? Handing over my money to the very folks who grew the sweet corn and who picked the watermelon and know the peppers by name.

Welsch speaks *with* us, not *to* us. It's conversation, not narration.

His script effectively mixes strong and tender thoughts:

But when the heat of summer is gone and before the winter's blizzards sweep across these fields . . . at that short and lovely moment when the sweet coolness of autumn is evident, it's then that the Saint Libory produce stands remind us of how good things out here can be.

And then he reinforces the thought with the final line of the script:

How rich and how full and how tasty.

If you spot some similarity between the writing styles of Roger Welsch and Charles Kuralt, you may see why so many Welsch stories wind up on "Sunday Morning."

The novelist William Burroughs once observed that if a writer "can't see it, hear it, feel it, and smell it he can't write it." You will not be able to use all of your senses every time you sit down at a typewriter or computer. But on most occasions, you should be able to draw on the two senses most useful to a journalist—seeing and hearing.

Here's an excellent example of how a writer used those senses, a script written by NBC News Correspondent Bob Dotson about a cave rescue in Carlsbad, N.M. The actual script is produced in its entirety because it shows an unusual technique employed by Dotson. In the left-hand column, among the video notes, Dotson tells in great detail what he is seeing and hearing.

```
SLUG         SHOW       WRITER   DATE                         TIMING  LC
Cave Rescue  = =NN/DD =  dotson   Thu May 16 10:48 1991 HOLD   2:11   260
```

"NN CAVE" 4/4/91
W/BOB DOTSON
CARLSBAD, NEW MEXICO

SPOT RUNS: 2:31

SUPERS: BOB DOTSON
        CARLSBAD, NEW MEXICO
        (_:_-_:_)

[LEAD INFORMATION]

   Imagine slithering through a block
of swiss cheese a mile and a half
long. Climbing up a thousand foot
maze dragging a broken leg. That's
what it was like for Emily Mobley.
She clawed her way beneath the earth
for 4 days, after an 80 pound boulder
slipped and crushed her in a cave. It
took 60 people to rescue her. Emily's
ordeal ended at 3:15 EDT this morning.

═══════════════════════════════════

   ANCIENT INVASIONS OF ICE HAVE CRE-
ATED AN ENORMOUS UNDERGROUND CATHE-
DRAL. ONE LONE CLIMBER — HIGH ABOVE —
CLINGS TO ITS SPIRE. THE LIGHT FROM
HIS HELMET LAMP DABS THE CAVERN WITH
COLOR.

                              NATSOT: (RESCUER)
                              "IS THE WHOLE TEAM
                              READY?"

   OTHER RESCUERS APPEAR IN THE BEAM OF
LIGHT. THERE IS A SQUEAKING OF PULL-
IES AND ROPES. RESCUER IS RAPPELLING
DOWN.

V/O

Shadows chase shad-
ows. Now and then a
whisper of sliding
rope.

ONE RESCUER SLITHERS IN AND OUT, MO-
MENTARILY LOSES CONTROL. TUMBLES, BUT
RIGHTS HIMSELF.

NATSOT: (RESCUER)
"OKAY, EASY, EASY!"

A THIN LINE OF RESCUERS, CARRYING
EMILY, HUFF THEIR WAY THROUGH A TIGHT
OPENING, THEN PICK CAUTIOUSLY ALONG
LOOSE GRAVEL.

V/O

The anxious, uneven
breathing of 60 peo-
ple lugging one of
their own.

MOBLEY IS LASHED TO A MAKESHIFT
STRETCHER. ONLY THE RESCUERS' WITS
AND A LENGTH OF ROPE KEEP HER FROM
PLUNGING INTO ETERNAL FREE FALL.

NATSOT: (RESCUER)
"I GOT IT!"

V/O

Emily Mobley was at
the bottom of the
deepest cave this
country has ever
seen. In a cavern
so big there are ex-
plorers at the oppo-
site end that don't
even know the 4-day
rescue took place.

A RESCUER SQUINTS ACROSS THE BLANK
STONE, TRYING TO SEE THE CRACKS HE
HAD MEMORIZED THE NIGHT BEFORE, THEN
COMMENCES AGAIN THE STEADY ROUTINE OF
THE CLIMB.

NATSOT: (RESCUER)
"MUCH BETTER! MUCH
BETTER!"

V/O

The darkness would
have been total
without her friends.

NATSOT: (RESCUER)
"LOOKING GOOD!!"
"MOVE A LITTLE
FASTER."
"KEEP HER COMING!"

RESCUERS MUST BE MORE THAN BRAVE.
THEY MUST BE METICULOUS AND ABOVE ALL
ORDERLY. EACH STEP MUST BE THE SAME.
EXACTLY THE SAME. AGAIN AND AGAIN.

V/O

They tugged her to
the top an inch at
a time. One-and-a-
half miles.

NATSOT: (RESCUER)
"KEEP ON MOVING."

EMILY IS BREATHING OUT THE PAIN.

(MOBLEY) "YEAH, I'M
FINE. JUST KEEP MOV-
ING ME."

THE RESCUERS LIE ON THEIR BACKS AND
PASS THE STRETCHER OVER THEIR HEADS.

                                                  V/O

                                     In places they cush-
                                     ioned her weight
                                     with their own bod-
                                     ies. And always
                                     kept a light for
                                     her to see above.

                                     NATSOT: (RESCUER)
                                     "REAL SLOW AND EASY
                                     GUYS."

    EMILY'S SMILE SHOWS THROUGH THE DUST
AND GRIME ON HER FACE

                                                  V/O

                                     Emily showed her ap-
                                     preciation with a
                                     grin . . . lit from
                                     inside.

                                     SOT: (MOBLEY) "UM,
                                     IF I HAVE TO BREAK
                                     MY LEG, I CAN'T
                                     THINK OF BETTER PEO-
                                     PLE I'D RATHER BE
                                     AROUND."

    SHE IS HOOKED TO ROPES THAT WILL
LIFT HER INTO DARKNESS. SHE SPINS UP
AND AWAY.

                                     NATSOT: (RESCUER)
                                     "ON THREE . . .
                                     ONE, TWO . . ."

                                     NATSOT: [THE CLANK-
                                     ING AND HUFFING
                                     BELOW CONTINUES
                                     UNDER DOTSON's
                                     STANDUP]

    CUT TO DOTSON ON CAMERA WITH RESCUE
TEAM NEAR MOUTH OF CAVE.

SUPER: BOB DOTSON
       CARLSBAD, NEW MEXICO
       (_:-_:_)

[Standup] The ordeal below did not build character, but it revealed it. What matters down there are energy, muscle and will. Qualities her friends had in abundance. Otherwise she would not have survived.

TEAM STRUGGLES FOR FOOTING AT THE BOTTOM OF A TALL STACK OF LOOSE ROCKS.

NATSOT: (RESCUER) "OKAY, WE CAN CARRY HER ON OUT."

EMILY'S WORDS ARE BRAVER THAN SHE LOOKS.

SOT: (MOBLEY) "AS LONG AS I DON'T STEP ON MY LEG, I'M FINE."

THEY FACE THIS LAST CHALLENGE WITH HOPE AND A CERTAIN HORROR. RISK IS AS MUCH A CLIMBER'S TOOL AS A ROPE.

V/O

They are all expert climbers. So is Emily. She was mapping this new cave when a loose rock started this test of friendship.

NATSOT: (RESCUER) "ALL RIGHT . . . ."

EACH CLIMBER STEADIES THE NEXT. HAND HOLDING HAND, THEY LIFT EMILY OUT OF THE DARKNESS.

V/O

Pals came from all
around the country.
A cry of need seems
to carry further in
darkness. Or per-
haps we listen
closer.

THEY SCRAMBLE UP, HUNGRY NOW TO
REACH THE TOP.

NATSOT: (RESCUER)
"HOLD ON!"

THE COMMONPLACE HORIZONTAL WORLD OF
MORTGAGES, GIRLFRIENDS AND FAMILY
SEEM FAR AWAY. THEY HAVE FORGED AN IN-
TENSE RELATIONSHIP WITH EACH OTHER
AND THE ROCK.

NATSOT: (EMILY)
"AM I EXCITED! YOU
BET I AM!"

AT LAST! THEY ARE OUT. UNDER A FULL
MOON. HUGS. HANDSHAKES. CONQUEST!

V/O

Finally, the
light above did not
need batteries.

NATSOT: (RESCUER)
"CHEERS FOR EVERY-
BODY!"

NATSOT: [CROWD
WHISTLES AND AP-
PLAUSE]

Emily's friends
felt as old as
thick mud.

Nearly 100 hours
in that pewter
world.

RESCUER ON CAMERA TURNS AND SPEAKS FOR ALL WHO LABORED SO LONG.

SOT: (RESCUER)
"WE'RE REAL PLEASED
TO GET HER OUT
ALIVE. AND GET HER
OUT IN ONE PIECE.
IT WAS REAL SPECIAL
TO ALL OF US."

EMILY'S FRIENDS GENTLY SLIDE HER INTO A WAITING AMBULANCE. SHE GIVES THEM A THUMBS UP THROUGH THE WINDOW AS IT DRIVES OFF INTO THE NIGHT.

Deep within them-
selves they had dis-
covered the people
they wanted to be.
Bob Dotson, NBC
News, Carlsbad, New
Mexico.

NBC Correspondent Bob Dotson
COURTESY OF NBC NEWS

If you go back to the Welsch script, you will note that there is limited information in the video column. The Dotson notes, in contrast, are so literary, and include such detail, that they could have easily provided a second script for the story.

Dotson's broadcast script is lean by comparison with the notes. You may find yourself wondering why Dotson did not employ more of the well-written notes in the actual script. One very important reason is time. The story that was broadcast ran 2 minutes and 11 seconds. Dotson did not really have the option of adding more narration because of the time constraints placed on him by his producers. And second, although Dotson is a splendid writer, he is primarily a "picture person." He selects his pictures first and then writes his script to the pictures. Some reporters believe that the script should be written first and then the pictures selected to support the words. That long-standing debate will be discussed later in detail, in the reporting section. For now, let's examine Dotson's writing style.

Dotson gives his script a lean, almost poetic quality. He captures emotion and color by selecting his words carefully:

Shadows chase shadows. Now and then a whisper of a sliding rope. . . .

The anxious, uneven breathing of 60 people lugging one of their own. . . .

The darkness would have been total without her friends. . . .

In places they cushioned her weight with their own bodies. . . .

Emily showed her appreciation with a grin . . . lit from inside. . . .

Pals came from all around the country. A cry of need seems to carry further in darkness. Or perhaps we listen closer.

Dotson's words—like Emily's rescuers—are strong, caring and proficient. Both got the job done.

Now examine the words that did *not* get into the script. They tell us that their author, although a "picture person," has mastered the skill and art of good writing:

Ancient invasions of ice have created an enormous underground cathedral. One lone climber—high above—clings to its spire. The light from his helmet lamp dabs the cavern with color. . . .

Only the rescuers' wits and a length of rope keep her from plunging into eternal free fall.

A rescuer squints across the blank stone, trying to see the cracks he had memorized the night before, then commences again the steady routine of the climb. . . .

They face this last challenge with hope and a certain horror. Risk is as much a climber's tool as a rope.

Remember that these words are not written for a broadcast audience but for Dotson's and the editor's reference. He and his co-workers are the only people who will read the video notes. We will examine Dotson's work in more detail in Chapter 14, "Putting the Television Story Together."

COLOR COMES IN MANY SHADES

You have read some examples of outstanding, colorful writing by top broadcast journalists. All of the scripts display an element of entertainment, humor and enlightenment. They may have brought a smile to your face and, perhaps, even a tear or two. But color comes in many shades; it is not just humorous or entertaining.

Color can be expressed in writing about dramatic or frightening situations:

The man held his gun to the side of the woman's head and you could see that both of them were scared. Her eyes were bulging. So were the veins on her neck as she looked down at the grey steel barrel moving down to the side of her neck. The gunman's hand shook nervously and menacingly.

Color can appear in the middle of a report on a congressional debate:

The senator's face was beginning to turn red. His fists were tight and you could see he was about to give in to the anger that was swelling within him. I don't think I have ever seen the senator from Oregon as angry as he was at that moment.

Color can be used to describe an FCC hearing:

Neither side was happy about the decision. The networks warned they could go broke and the Hollywood producers said the decision could mean the public would see fewer creative programs. Someone said it was a battle between the rich and the wealthy.

In discussing color in broadcast copy, NBC News Correspondent Roger O'Neil says, "If I am successful it's because I take a great deal of pride in telling a story rather than giving people facts and figures, most of which no one remembers anyhow. It seems to me," he continues, "the great failing of local reporters that I watch across the country is that they are not good storytellers."

For a story to be successful, O'Neil says, an audience "must be provoked" by the story or "moved by it, or be happy or sad about it." He adds that he is talking about a human interest story, not a news story from the White House.

**COLORFUL
OBITUARIES**

Just about any event or situation that is worth news coverage has potential for colorful writing—writing that influences and affects an audience in a dozen different ways. This is true even of obituaries. CBS News Correspondent Richard Threlkeld has written many obituaries over the years. Here is an example that displays his special talents.

V/O	Threlkeld
Montage of Dr. Seuss characters	Dr. Seuss wasn't a real doctor, but he was at least as instrumental in the upbringing of a couple of generations of kids as Dr. Spock.
Clips from various Seuss videos	And not just American kids. Everywhere, in 18 languages, they know about ziffs and zuffs and nerkles and nerds.
Seuss video clips and kids reading books	They called his books "children's books," but the children knew better. "Children like my books," said Dr. Seuss, "because I treat them as equals."
SOT of kids reading books and commenting on them. Video of Cat in Hat	(SOT . . . kids) V/O And the books are about grownup things, after all. About taking responsibility.
PIX of Cat in Hat book	"I know it is wet and the sun is not sunny, but we can have lots of good fun that is funny."
PIX of Horton Hatches the Egg	About loyalty. "I meant what I said and I said what I meant. An

	elephant's faithful, one hundred percent."
Seuss movie	About prejudice.
SOT	(SOT)
	"Ronald, remember when you are out walking, you walk past a sneetch of that type without talking."
V/O	V/O
Seuss video	So, Dr. Seuss wasn't all stuff and nonsense, even though creatures in his world were pretty weird and called each other funny names. When you grew up, you were always amazed at how many people in the real world reminded you of somebody you met in Dr. Seuss. Somebody asked him once, who was his favorite?
SOT T. S. Geisel	(SOT)
	"I think the Grinch, maybe."
SOT Grinch video	"I'll be coming back someday."
V/O Grinch movie	V/O
	The Grinch has been coming back to our living rooms every holiday season for 25 years now, trying and failing to steal Christmas.
SOT END of Grinch Xmas movie, sad kids	(SOT)
	Dr. Seuss never had any children

```
in window and cat              of his own. But he is survived
walks by
                               by millions of children, past

                               and present, all over the world.

                               Richard Threlkeld, CBS News,

                               New York.
```

Threlkeld says that he tries, in his obituaries, to capture the "essence" of the particular person. He says that because of time limits in broadcasting, "You aren't able to include all the nuances as you would in a newspaper obit. But," he adds, "the advantage in broadcasting is that the nuances, quite often, come in the pictures and sound."

For the Dr. Seuss (T. S. Geisel) obit, Threlkeld said, "I got every piece of information in print that I could find and culled through it looking for particular things that would lead me to the essence of the person and his work." Threlkeld said that he was fortunate to have the Dr. Seuss TV special that is broadcast every Christmas, and he bought all the Dr. Seuss books available.

Threlkeld said that he had the advantage of living through two generations of Dr. Seuss—as a child himself and as a parent reading the stories to his children. "As I looked at all the visual material," he said, "I thought of the things that affected me when I was a kid. I realize now, of course, that Dr. Seuss was

CBS News Correspondent Richard Threlkeld prepares to do a report.
COURTESY OF CBS NEWS

not only entertaining but also teaching children things. I asked myself what was he trying to teach and, in the case of Horton the Elephant—'an elephant's faithful one hundred percent'—he was teaching loyalty to children." The CBS news correspondent said that in the Dr. Seuss books he was able to find three or four examples to demonstrate "these principles of good, decent living that [Dr. Seuss] was trying to teach."

Threlkeld said that it was not easy finding sound bites because Geisel was something of a recluse. But he was able to find one bite that worked. As for the readings from Dr. Seuss' books, Threlkeld said he decided he was the right one to read them because he had "read them out loud" to his children.

"I tried to let the viewer look at the life's work of this man," he said, "that's what you do in an obituary."

Dr. Seuss was special—and an inspiration—to another CBS news correspondent, Charles Osgood, who likes to use rhyme in many of the stories he writes for the "Osgood File" on CBS Radio. The title of Osgood's first book is "Nothing Could Be Finer Than a Crisis That Is Finer in the Morning," and he dedicated the book to Dr. Seuss, who, he said, "gave me a new way to look at the *neuss*." Dr. Seuss sent Osgood a note in reply saying, "Nothing could be finer than to be an Osgood inspiriner."

In his script about Dr. Seuss' death, Osgood used his marvelous flair for rhyme to express some "personal thoughts about inspiration . . . and immortality."

```
And now the news . . . what can I say? My inspiriner passed
away?
That he just died and went to heaven . . . at the age of 87?
I do not like that . . . Sam I am.
For in his books . . . Green Eggs and Ham . . .
The Cat, the Grinch, and Lorax too . . .
There's something that keeps coming through.
It's there, if anybody looks
In 47 of his books.
The ones that kids enjoy so much . . .
His play with words, his special touch.
And yet in just that way he told
Of war and peace . . . and growing old . . .
From the sublime to the absurd . . .
He always picked the perfect word.
And if no perfect words were known . . .
He made up new ones of his own.
You read his stuff . . . I'm sure you did
And as you read it to your kid
You smiled because you really knew
That it was also meant . . . for you.
Your kids will read those books again
As grown-up women . . . grown-up men.
```

```
And their kids also will enjoy . . .
Reading to THEIR girl and boy.
Although it's true the MAN is gone . . .
His genius will go on and on.
A spark that was much more than clever
Dr. Seuss will live forever.
So tell the kids they shouldn't cry.
Inspiriners never die.
```

Osgood says that one of the nice things about radio is "you don't have the problem of fighting pictures, because there you're creating a picture from the very beginning." He adds, "I think radio is a superior visual medium because the picture is not literal."

The CBS news correspondent recalls that when the late Rod Serling made the move from radio to television he wrote a line for a drama that said, "'Once there was a castle on a hill' and he was asked 'What kind of a castle do you want? Do you want ramparts? Is this a medieval castle? What kind of castle is it?' Serling answered, 'I don't know. Let each person build his own castle.'"

Osgood says, "That's what you do in radio. The listener fills in. But you have to help him, you have to give him enough information so that he can build his castle. You give him materials to build with."

FREDERICK, ELLERBEE AND AARON

No discussion of good writing would be complete without examining the writing of one of the nation's best journalists, the late Pauline Frederick, who was United Nations correspondent for NBC News for many years. The following is the script of a broadcast from December 5, 1963, two weeks after the assassination of President Kennedy.

```
Frederick: This is Pauline Frederick, NBC News, New York,
with

EMPHASIS: United Nations. A time to heal. I'll return with
this observation on people and the times, in a moment.

Frederick: This is Pauline Frederick. EMPHASIS: United Na-
tions. The rifle shots that were heard around the world,
reverberated through the halls of the United Nations.

Then came a time to weep, a time to mourn and a time to be
silent. Slowly the tempo of living resumed — the carrying
out of assigned duties — the pleading for and against causes
— the passing and defeating of resolutions.

Even though it could be assumed that all was the same, it
was not. An accustomed underpinning was gone, a certainty
that permitted assault on the accepted, a questioning of the
```

unquestioned. There is a new subdued quality about business here.

One important Western Delegate says that Africans who were once talking freely about drastic measures have lost their fire. They seem frightened, not because they fear the tangible but because suddenly where there was the known there is the unknown. As when a father drops the hand of his child in the dark. This feeling has been particularly evident in the Security Council.

The Africans had demanded an urgent meeting of the Council to take new steps to force South Africa to free all of its people or be read out of the community of nations. The Council was called for Monday morning, November 25.

Instead, this became a time to be silent.

When the Council did convene a week ago, President Sir Patrick Dean gave voice to the sudden realization of members of a change that affected them all, afflicted them with a sense of uncertainty because there was change. Sir Patrick said: "Inevitably, and rightly, the United States assumes a large share of our total responsibility under the Charter of the United Nations for the continuing peace of the world. President Kennedy was second to none in his recognition of that fact and in the steadfast support he gave, in word and deed, to the purposes of the United States and to the authority of the Council."

After all the urgency for Council action, only two visiting African foreign ministers were ready to speak. After their words, the Council adjourned until Friday.

The debate since then has repeated most of the words that have been said many times on the subject — there have even been suggestions that South Africa should be deprived of its privileges in the General Assembly. But they were spoken with less zeal than has marked the African demands heretofore. And when Norway's Sievert Nielsen proposed a compromise to bridge the demands of the Africans for sanctions and the more moderate views of the western industrial powers, he succeeded in gaining African support.

The resolution would deny materials for arms-making to South Africa, and the Secretary-General is asked to set up a group of experts to work with South Africa in peacefully according human rights to all of its people.

    Not that the Africans have given up thoughts of extreme
    pressure against South Africa eventually, if necessary.

    But the moment appears to be a time to heal.

    This is Pauline Frederick, NBC News, United Nations.

Frederick began her career with ABC, where she became the first woman correspondent with the networks. She went on to spend 22 years with NBC. She
retired at 65. She continued to work for National Public Radio and was the first
woman to moderate a presidential debate. She died in 1990.

   Another respected woman journalist is Linda Ellerbee, who also spent many
years with NBC before moving to ABC. Here is one of her stories, written for
"NBC News Overnight":

    LINDA ESSAY:

    Doing something just because you really want to do it can
    make trouble. Especially if you're about the only one who
    does it. Consider the case of Roy Warren and Elizabeth
    Sargeant of Massachusetts.

    They got married on June 12. Mr. Warren has six brothers.
    Miss Sargeant has none. For that reason, Roy Warren took her

*The late NBC Correspondent Pauline Frederick files her report
from the United Nations.*
SOPHIA SMITH COLLECTION, SMITH COLLEGE

surname and became Roy Sargeant. The priest, said Mr. Sargeant, freaked out. The Department of Motor Vehicles told the ex-Marine it was illegal to change his name on his license. It wasn't. The Social Security office considered the name change for three days.

Mr. Sargeant is still carrying his marriage certificate to prove he is not Mr. Warren. Perhaps we ought to be more easy about something that is really a simple thing, but we're not.

On the other hand, we may take pride in being somewhat more advanced in our notion of equality than the Irish government. The European Economic Community, or Common Market, pointed out to the Irish government that it had not yet implemented the agreed sex-equality legislation. The Dublin government immediately advertised for an equal-pay enforcement officer to correct the situation. The advertisement offered different salary scales for men and women. And so it goes.

Another woman who managed to break through the "women need not apply" attitude at the networks in the 1940s and 1950s was Betsy Aaron. She had too much talent to be ignored Before moving to CBS, where she is a news correspondent, Aaron worked for ABC. Here's one of her 1983 reports from Lebanon:

```
Marines in Lebanon
9/14/83
Aaron/Irving
```

NATL SOT: POEM	What Lebanon Means To Me: I lay on the ground with my face in the dirt and wonder what I'm doing here. The bullets go by, the mortars explode, the rockets scream in my ear.
V/O	Corporal Thom Stephenson. Hometown Cherry Hill, New Jersey. In Beirut since May . . . and now much older than his 23 years.
NATL SOT: STEPHENSON	approx: how has this changed you? I think about what's going on in the world now.

V/O	The Americans occupy three positions protecting Beirut's Airport. Alpha . . . hugging the runway . . . the company with four men killed in action. Bravo . . . overlooking the airport. The company taking the most shelling. And Charley . . . way out at the end of the runway. The company closest to the Lebanese Army troops. The company hit with the heaviest artillery.
SOT: POEM	I wait for a minute and I run for my hole and dive for the comfort inside. Sand in my tee shirt, sand in my socks, and the temperature's at least 105.
V/O	He's not kidding. It's just plain hot here . . . all the time. Hot and dirty.
SOT: SGT FOSTER HILL	Most everybody is used to the luxuries of home and it's hard when it's taken away from you.
V/O	Just over a week ago it rained shrapnel all over Charley Company . . . for most of a day and a night. There's only one way to handle shrapnel.
SOT: SGT HILL	We got an old saying here in the first platoon. If you want to

	hide behind the wall you must dig behind the wall.
V/O	So that's what they do . . .
SOT: LT ARTHUR HARRIS	The deeper the better. And we're trying to make it a little more comfortable in our bunkers because it looks like we'll be there for a while.
V/O	And when they're not digging, they're filling sandbags . . . more bags than they'd ever dreamed they'd fill. Walls of sandbags lining bunkers dug deeper since the Marines began taking casualties.
NATL SOUND SEQUENCE WITH GUNFIRE = OBSER- VERS IN BUNKERS ON BINOCULARS AT MAP . . . ON PHONE	
V/O	It's a front row orchestra seat to a show where the plot unfolds daily
CONTINUE NATL SOT:	
V/O	The Marines call them men. They are very young men.
SOT: POEM	As I sit here melting sweating away, I'll remember her voice on the phone . . . She said keep your head low, don't be a hero, we all want you home in one piece.
NATL SOT: PROMOTION CEREMONY	
V/O	A month ago all 165 men in

	Charley Company would have turned out for this promotion ceremony. But it's dusk now, and the fighting in the mountains is picking up. It always does . . . in the evening.
CONTINUE CEREMONY	
V/O	There is a tradition in a Corps long on tradition. For officers above the rank of those promoted to pin the stripes on . . . so they'll stick.
CONTINUE SLAPPING SEQUENCE	
V/O NATL SOT:	And at sunset . . . Lowering of the colors.
V/O	So far just another day in Lebanon . . . a place where Marines are glad to get eggs and pancakes for dinner . . . when it's the first hot meal they've had in 9 days.
NATL SOT: W/ SGT HILL	Oh goody — give me the one with the big bug.
V/O	Meals and mail — pretty big items in a Marine's day. Time to try and forget the fighting. But then there is news of shelling at

	company headquarters. There are casualties . . . but no details.
SOT: SGT HILL	We haven't done anything to hurt anybody. We just trying to keep the peace and somebody just wants to hurt us and provoke us into violence against whoever is doing this to us. EDIT What's going through your mind? Just praying we get through the night.
V/O	Charley Company is now operating under Condition One. No lights . . . everyone under cover. The men in headquarters sit in the dark and talk.
SOT: TAPE 5 5:00	I wanted to see what it would be like in a hostile environment. This was the most hostile you can get.
SOT: TAPE 5 4:30	There was so much incoming and they dropped boom, boom, boom. All you could see of the three of us was the tops of our boots. I was petrified, I just dove for my life.
V/O	And finally with the Druze and the Lebanese Army still going at each other . . . Charley Company goes to sleep.
NATL SOT GUNFIRE IN DARK	
V/O	Reveille is 4:30 a.m. An ungodly

	hour to get up save for one
	one thing: It is clear . . .
	and cool.
NATL SCENES OF UP AND AT 'EM. END SEQUENCE WITH NATL SOT:	"First shot of the morning."
V/O	The monotony of the routine can
	get to you . . .
	a little breakfast . . .
	a little work . . .
	write a letter . . .
	chase your dog . . .
	blow off steam.
	There is no more jogging . . .
	no more basketball.
NATL SOT:	listening post . . . gunfire.
SOT: POEM	I can't help but wonder why these people fight. I guess diplomacy isn't their style. Bombs and grenades, death and destruction. We'll keep our heads low for awhile.
STANDUP	Despite the casualties . . .
	despite the sitting duck con-
	ditions, despite the debate in
	Washington . . . the Marines who
	are here say they should be here.
	And they're convinced that, no
	matter how bad things get here,
	they'd be worse without the
	Marines. Now the Marines are sup-

	posed to say that. But they say it as if they really believe it.
NATL SOT: PVT MICHAEL MCCARTY	". . . we have a job to do."
V/O	And yet both enlisted men and officers freely talk about the problems of this peacekeeping mission, especially the problem of staying on the defense when you're being attacked.
CAPT CHRIS COWDREY CHARLEY COMPANY COMMANDER	We are not out here banging away at the drum and trying to start something up, or trying to take lives unnecessarily. We are here really taking more licks than we really deserve, or are justified in receiving. EDIT Is this a real war? . . . out cue: it looks like a war to me.
SOT: MCCARTY	If they would let us get out and fight and move around or if they would take us out of here. The choice doesn't really matter. But it's just a fact sitting here in this particular area it's like we're trapped down.
SOT TO STEPHENSON	Should you and the Marines be in Lebanon? Approx? I don't know . . . that's a tough one I think about all the time.
V/O	Betsy Aaron for Nightline with Charley Company in Beirut.

Aaron said the package was designed to accomplish several goals: to show the American people what it was like in Lebanon for Marines and to reveal that the Marines didn't understand why they were there and what they were supposed to accomplish. "They had a little boy attitude," she said, "they thought that

CBS News Correspondent Betsy Aaron reporting from Lebanon while she was still with ABC

they were there to do some good." Aaron said that some of the Marines in her story were later seriously wounded in the bomb attack on the barracks that killed 220 Marines.

"We were the first reporting team to spend the night with the Marines," she said, "and we wanted to know how they felt because we were convinced it was an ill-fated mission. You could look at the mountains and the sea that surrounded them," Aaron said, "and you knew they were sitting ducks. That was important for Americans to see, to let them know what we had stepped into."

Aaron said that wasn't the first war she covered. She reported on the Six Day War in the Middle East and the war on Cyprus between the Greeks and Turks, which she said was the worst "slaughter" she had ever covered.

You have read scripts written by some of America's top broadcast journalists—communicators effectively using language in a colorful, eloquent and sometimes classic manner. The best of these men and women point to one individual who set the standard on a rooftop in London more than 50 years ago.

MURROW AND HIS "BOYS"

Shortly before World War II, the head of CBS, William S. Paley, decided that he wanted the nation's top broadcast news operation. Edward R. Murrow would get it for him.

Murrow was already on the payroll, working in London for CBS, when he was told by his New York office to start hiring the best reporters he could find to work in the key capitals of Europe. He did, and "Murrow's Boys," as they came to be known, *did* give Paley the best broadcast news team in the nation. It also established a dynasty that would allow CBS to dominate broadcast news for more than 40 years.

Among the "boys" were Bill Downs, Charles Collingwood, Richard C. Hottelet, Alexander Kendrick, Larry Le Sueur, David Schoenbrun, Eric Sevareid, William L. Shirer and Howard K. Smith. The team was to broadcasting what the Babe Ruth Yankees were to baseball. CBS would continue its successful recruiting, adding to its roster the talented Winston Burdett, Walter Cronkite, Douglas Edwards, Robert Pierpoint, Harry Reasoner, Daniel Schorr and Robert Trout.

"THIS IS LONDON"

In the 1940s, Murrow quickly established a reputation as the most notable broadcast journalist covering the war in Europe. His nightly reports from London rooftops—with sounds of bombs and anti-aircraft and sirens in the background—became a ritual for millions of Americans.

It was Murrow's skill with words that set him apart from other broadcast journalists. Here are some excerpts from some of Murrow's reports:

```
There are no words to describe the thing that is happening.
[But he found them.] A row of automobiles, with stretchers
racked on the roofs like skis, standing outside of bombed
buildings. A man pinned under wreckage where a broken gas
main sears his arms and face . . . the courage of the peo-
ple; the flash and roar of guns rolling down streets . . .
the stench of air-raid shelters in the poor districts.

The fires up the river had turned the moon blood red . . .
Huge pearshaped bursts of flame would rise up into the smoke
and disappear. The world was upside down.
```

This rooftop report was delivered as anti-aircraft fire lighted the sky:

```
Out of one window there waves something that looks like a
white bedsheet, a . . . curtain swinging free in this night
breeze. It looks as if it were being shaken by a ghost . .
. The searchlights straightaway, miles in front of me, are
still scratching that sky. There's a three-quarter moon
riding high. There was one burst of shellfire almost straight
in the Little Dipper.
```

One of the best examples of Murrow's writing is a report he made after flying on a combat mission to Berlin aboard a British bomber called "D for Dog." Here are excerpts from Murrow's script that display his extraordinary use of words to capture the mood and drama of everything that passed before him:

```
We went out and stood around a big, black four-motored
Lancaster, D for Dog. A small station wagon delivered a
```

*The late CBS News Correspondent
Edward R. Murrow risked his life to go
on a bombing raid over Germany during
World War II.*

*HISTORICAL PHOTOGRAPH COLLECTIONS,
WASHINGTON STATE UNIVERSITY LIBRARIES*

thermos bottle of coffee, chewing gum, an orange and a bit
of chocolate for each man. Up in that part of England the
air hums and throbs with the sound of aircraft motors all
day. But for half an hour before takeoff, the skies are
dead, silent and expectant. A lone hawk hovered over the
airfield, absolutely still as he faced into the wind. Jack,
the tail gunner, said, "It would be nice if we could fly
like that . . ."

The take-off was smooth as silk. The wheels came up, and
D-Dog started the long climb. As we came up through the
clouds, I looked right and left and counted fourteen black
Lancasters climbing for the place where men must burn oxygen
to live. The sun was going down, and its red glow made
rivers and lakes of fire on the tops of the clouds. Down to
the southward, the clouds piled up to form castles, battle-
ments and whole cities, all tinged with red.

We were approaching the enemy coast. The flak looked like a
cigarette lighter in a dark room — one that won't light.
Sparks but no flame. The sparks crackling just above the
level of the cloud tops.

The blue-green jet of the exhausts licked back along the

leading edge, and there were other aircraft all around us. The whole great armada was hurtling towards Berlin. . . .

We were still over the clouds. But suddenly those dirty gray clouds turned white. We were over the outer searchlight defenses. The clouds below us were white, and we were black. D-Dog seemed like a black bug on a white sheet. . . .

The same moment the sky ahead was lit up by bright yellow flares. Off to starboard, another kite [plane] went down in flames. The flares were sprouting all over the sky — reds and greens and yellows — and we were flying straight for the center of the fireworks. . . .

Suddenly a tremendous big blob of yellow light appeared dead ahead, another to the right and another to the left. We were flying straight for them.

And then with no warning at all, D-Dog was filled with an unhealthy white light. I was standing just behind Jock and could see all the seams on the wings. His quiet Scots voice beat into my ears. "Steady, lads, we've been coned." His slender body lifted half out of his seat as he jammed the control column forward and to the left. We were going down.

Jock was wearing woolen gloves with the fingers cut off. I could see his fingernails turn white as he gripped the wheel. And then I was on my knees, flat on the deck, for he had whipped the Dog back into a climbing turn. . . .

The small incendiaries were going down like a fistful of white rice thrown on a piece of black velvet. . . .

The cookies — the four thousand pound high explosives — were bursting below like great sunflowers gone mad. . . .

I looked down, and the white fires had turned red. They were beginning to merge and spread, just like butter does on a hot plate. . . .

We flew level then. I looked on the port beam at the target area. There was a sullen, obscene glare. The fires seemed to have found each other — and we were heading home. . . .

Two other journalists, on other Lancasters in that raid over Berlin, did not return home.

Murrow had the incredible ability—and it was the reason he was so effective—to use words to transport the listener onto a plane or a London rooftop or into an air-raid shelter.

Listen also for the rhythm of Murrow's words in the "D-for Dog" report:

> . . . the skies are dead, silent and expectant. A lone hawk hovered over the airfield, absolutely still as he faced into the wind. . . .

> The sun was going down, and its red glow made rivers and lakes of fire on the tops of the clouds.

> . . . clouds piled up to form castles, battlements and whole cities, all tinged with red. . . .

> The flak looked like a cigarette lighter in a dark room—one that won't light. Sparks but no flame. The sparks crackling just above the level of the cloud tops.

> The blue-green jet of the exhausts licked back along the leading edge. . . .

It was no wonder that Murrow won great respect from his audiences and peers. Traveling on a near-death ride through hell, Murrow captured and held pictures of everything that was going on, including details like Jock's "woolen gloves with the fingers cut off." Then, like a composer, he put a score to the word pictures he brought back to the studio: he added the dozens of different sounds and sights that were exploding around him, the "fistful of white rice thrown on a piece of black velvet" and the fires that were "beginning to merge and spread like butter does on a hot plate." The broadcast became known as "Orchestrated Hell."

"PERMIT ME TO TELL YOU"   One of Murrow's most moving reports from Europe came from his visit to the infamous Buchenwald concentration camp after the fighting was over.

> Permit me to tell you what you would have seen, and heard, had you been with me on Thursday. It will not be pleasant listening. If you are at lunch, or if you have no appetite to hear what Germans have done, now is a good time to switch off the radio, for I propose to tell you of Buchenwald. It is on a small hill about four miles outside Weimar, and it was one of the largest concentration camps in Germany, and it was built to last. . . .

> There surged around me an evil-smelling horde. Men and boys reached out to touch me; and they were in rags and the remnants of uniform. Death had already marked many of them, but they were smiling with their eyes. I looked out over that mass of men to the green fields beyond where well-fed Germans were ploughing.

> A German, Fritz Kersheimer, came up and said, "May I show

you around the camp? I've been here ten years." . . . I asked to see one of the barracks. . . . I was told that this building had once stabled eighty horses. There were twelve hundred men in it, five to a bunk. The stink was beyond all description.

When I reached the center of the barracks, a man came up and said, "Remember me? I'm Peter Zenkl, one-time mayor of Prague." I remember him, but did not recognize him. He asked about Beneš and Jan Masaryk. I asked how many men had died in that building during the last month. They called the doctor; we inspected his records. There were only names in the little blackbook, nothing more — nothing of who these men were, what they had done, or hoped. Behind the names of those who had died there was a cross. I counted them. They totalled 242. Two hundred and forty two out of twelve hundred in one month. . . .

As we walked out in the courtyard, a man fell dead. Two others — they must have been over sixty — were crawling toward the latrine. I saw it but will not describe it.

In another part of the camp they showed me the children, hundreds of them. Some were only six. One rolled up his sleeve, showed me his number. It was tattooed on his arm. D-6030, it was. The others showed me their numbers; they will carry them till they die.

An elderly man standing beside me said, "The children, enemies of the state." I could see their ribs through their thin shirts. The old man said, "I am professor Charles Richer of the Sorbonne." The children clung to my hands and stared. We crossed to the courtyard. Men kept coming up to speak to me and to touch me, professors from Poland, doctors from Vienna, men from all Europe. Men from the countries that made America.

We went to the hospital; it was full. The doctor told me that two hundred had died the day before. I asked the cause of death; he shrugged and said, "Tuberculosis, starvation, fatigue, and there are many who have no desire to live. It is very difficult. . . ."

We went again into the courtyard, and as we walked we talked. The two doctors, the Frenchman and the Czech, agreed that about six thousand had died during March. Kersheimer, the German, added that back in the winter of 1939, when the Poles began to arrive without winter clothing, they died at the rate of approximately nine hundred a day. Five different men asserted that Buchenwald was the best concentration camp in Germany; they had had some experience of the others. . . .

There were two rows of bodies stacked up like cordwood. They were thin and very white. Some of the bodies were terribly bruised, though there seemed to be little flesh to bruise. Some had been shot through the head, but they bled but little. All except two were naked. I tried to count them as best I could and arrived at the conclusion that all that was mortal of more than five hundred men and boys lay there in two neat piles. . . .

I pray you to believe what I have said about Buchenwald. I have reported what I saw and heard, but only part of it. For most of it I have no words. Dead men are plentiful in war, but the living dead, more than twenty thousand of them in one camp. And the country round about was pleasing to the eye, and the Germans were well fed and well dressed. American trucks were rolling toward the rear filled with prisoners. Soon they would be eating American rations, as much for a meal as the men at Buchenwald received in four days.

If I've offended you by this rather mild account of Buchenwald, I'm not in the least sorry. . . .

Murrow's success during World War II was just the start of his career. His prestige and popularity as a broadcaster grew dramatically after the war. He was by far the most well-known broadcast journalist in the early years of television. With the best producer in the business, Fred Friendly, at his side, Murrow's TV programs were among the most popular in the 1950s.

"THE FAULT, DEAR BRUTUS"

One of Murrow's programs was "See It Now," a weekly 30-minute examination of often-controversial subjects. The most memorable episode was the one in which Murrow took on Senator Joseph McCarthy, who had established a national reputation with his anti-communist witch-hunt. McCarthy had charged that the State Department and Pentagon were riddled with communists. Murrow challenged McCarthy's tactics. At the end of the program, Murrow concluded with a biting attack on the senator:

No one familiar with the history of this country can deny that congressional committees are useful. It is necessary to investigate before legislating. But the line between investigation and persecution is a very fine one, and the junior senator from Wisconsin has stepped over it repeatedly. His primary achievement has been in confusing the public mind as between the internal and external threat of Communism. We must not confuse dissent with disloyalty. We must remember always that accusation is not proof and that conviction depends upon evidence and due process of law. We will not walk in fear, one of another. We will not be driven by fear into an age of unreason if we dig deep in our history and our doctrine and remember that we are not descended from fearful men, not from men who feared to write, to speak, to associate and to defend causes which were for the moment unpopular.

This is no time for men who oppose Senator McCarthy's methods to keep silent, or for those who approve. We can deny our heritage and our history, but we cannot escape responsibility for the result. As a nation we have come into our full inheritance at a tender age. We proclaim ourselves, as indeed we are, the defenders of freedom — what's left of it — but we cannot defend freedom abroad by deserting it at home. The actions of the junior senator from Wisconsin have caused alarm and dismay amongst our allies abroad and given considerable comfort to our enemies. And whose fault is that? Not really his; he didn't create this situation of fear, he merely exploited it and rather successfully.

Cassius was right. "The fault, dear Brutus, is not in our stars but in ourselves."

Because of Murrow's great popularity with the American people, his criticism of McCarthy is considered by many to be an important factor in the eventual downfall of the senator.

Murrow's influence on broadcast journalism was overwhelming. Eric Sevareid, one of the first "boys" to be hired by Murrow, was impressed by his boss from the beginning, and the admiration never ended: "He could absorb and reflect the thought and emotions of day laborers, airplane pilots, or cabinet ministers and report with exact truth what they were.... One can read his broadcasts now, years later, in the printed form for which they were never intended and find London all around—its sights and sounds, its very smells and feeling through the changing hours, all brought back."

Murrow, who died in 1965, would have liked that tribute. He probably would have replied that Sevareid was no "slouch" either.

ERIC SEVAREID:
WRITING
WITH CLASS

Many adjectives have been used over the years to describe the splendid writing of the late Eric Sevareid during his almost 40 years with CBS News. His writings have been described as "majestic," "magnificent," "elegant." His colleague Walter Cronkite spoke of Sevareid's "beautifully chosen words of wisdom," which made him "one of the finest essayists of the century."

*The late CBS News Correspondent
Edward R. Murrow on the set of an early
TV show, "See It Now"*
*HISTORICAL PHOTOGRAPH COLLECTIONS,
WASHINGTON STATE UNIVERSITY LIBRARIES*

There is no doubt that Sevareid's reports and commentaries stood a notch above most of the writing heard on the air. What he had to say was always important. Sometimes he expressed his strong feelings about the responsibilities of journalists, as he did in a commentary on the CBS Evening News on the night of his retirement. Here is part of that commentary:

```
Mine has been here an unelected, unlicensed, uncodified
office and function. The rules are self-imposed. These
were a few: Not to underestimate the intelligence of the
audience and not to overestimate its information. To elu-
cidate, when one can, more than to advocate. To remember
always that the public is only people, and people only
persons, no two alike. To retain the courage of one's
doubts as well as one's convictions, in this world of
dangerously passionate certainties. To comfort oneself,
in times of error, with the knowledge that the saving
grace of the press — print or broadcast — is its self-cor-
recting nature. And to remember that ignorant or biased
reporting has its counterpart in ignorant and biased read-
ing and listening. We do not speak into an intellectual or
emotional void.
```

In another commentary, speaking specifically of electronic journalism, Sevareid wrote:

It is a marvelous and frightening instrument, broadcasting, as part of this marvelous and frightening century. But ordinary men must use it as ordinary men have made this century what it is. Bad men can use it to their advantage, but in free societies, only for a time — and a shorter time, I think, than in previous eras. The camera's unblinking eye sees through character faster than the printed word.

And on the subject of democracy, Sevareid wrote:

Democracy is not a free ride. It demands more of each of us than any other arrangement. There can be no rights and privileges without responsibilities. My forebears here were at ease with the word "duty." They knew that self-denial was not just a puritanical test of character, but a social necessity, so that others, too, might have elbow room in which to live. They believed, as I do, that civilized life cannot hold together without these old and now sometimes derided values. The reason is simple: only people with a sense of personal responsibility can help others or, for that matter, be helped. There can be no final solutions. From solutions arise new problems, of lessened severity, we are entitled to hope. Time is life. If one uses it to ameliorate the problems, he has lived successfully.

No other people have that chance more than do Americans. The world still looks to this country as the critical experiment in the relations of man to man. This is a fabulous assignment history has given us. From what I have read of the past, and from what I remember of my own generation's beginnings, I believe we are not failing in this assignment, and will not.

At Sevareid's retirement, NBC's John Chancellor said, "With his colleague Edward R. Murrow, he [Sevareid] brought a level of excellence and distinction to broadcast journalism it had not enjoyed before."

CBS's Charles Kuralt added that Sevareid "was one of the better writers who ever worked around here, one I always admired and whose work I used to read." Kuralt added, "When I got to know him I discovered that he was never entirely comfortable with the lights and the cameras and the makeup and all of the things you have to put up with in television. He said working in television is 'like being nibbled to death by ducks.' "

Kuralt also said that once when Sevareid was "feeling particularly grumpy about television [Kuralt] heard him murmur, 'One good word is worth a thousand pictures.' "

GOOD THINGS FROM LOCAL STATIONS

All of the scripts that you have read so far have been by network journalists. Usually, they have more time to tell their stories than do their counterparts at local radio and TV stations. As a beginning journalist, you can also benefit from examining the work of fine local broadcast writers, who are working within the time constraints you will probably face in the early part of your career.

Well-written scripts do not have to be long. The challenge will be to tell your stories quickly without sacrificing quality. Here are examples of good writing from local journalists:

```
SLUG: GRANDMA 2
DATE: Wed Oct 30, 1991
REPORTER: NP
NEWSCAST: 5P
```

ON CAMERA

PARENTS OFTEN FIND THEMSELVES SHOULDERING THE BURDENS OF THEIR CHILDREN LONG AFTER THOSE CHILD-REN BECOME ADULTS . . . AND WHEN PARENTS BECOME GRANDPARENTS . . . THE EMOTIONAL LOAD CAN BE EVEN HEAVIER . . . IN OUR SERIES GRANDMA'S HANDS . . . WAFB'S NANCY PARKER REPORTS ON A GRANDMOTHER WHO'S TAKEN HER GRANDSON INTO HER HOME . . . WHILE <u>HIS</u> PARENTS ARE BEHIND BARS.

(*SOT PKG*)

Opening shot of C—
and grandmother walking
into prison

(V/O)

V/O

It's visiting day at Saint Gabriel Prison. D— H— and her 9-year-old grandson C— T— come here a couple times a month.

Nat sound up

(SOT)

Door slams shut as D— and C— sign prison visitors' book

	This is where C—'S Mother, U— T—, is serving time.
Dissolve to C—'s mother entering the room and nat sound of U— T— saying "C—" and hugging	(nat sound)
	The reunions are always sweet sweet for T— and her son. For three years now C— has been in his grandmother's care. His mother watches him grow, visit by visit.
SOT U— T—	(SOT) "Let me see how big you've gotten . . ."
V/O Mug shot of mother full screen	(V/O) U— T— and her son were seperated in May of 1989 when she was brought to Saint Gabriel on a drug distribution conviction, facing an eight-year sentence.
SOT Fade to T— bite, music up softly (love theme from "Dying Young")	(SOT) "I was arrested and they brought me to jail and I took it hard. The first thing that came to mind was where I was going to put my son. I'm going to be in prison the rest of my life."
	(V/O)
Full Screen Font: 530 INMATES	But she's not alone. St. Gabriel officials say of the 530 inmates

397 HAVE CHILDREN 12% OF CHILDREN IN FOSTER CARE 88% WITH FRIENDS AND FAMILY	at the prison, 397 have children. Twelve percent of these are in foster care, 88 percent are with friends and family.
Fade music out SOT Dissolve to Miss L—— bite	(SOT) "I pray a lot. I tell her mom to pray a lot, that she's gonna get out. I want him to be with his mother. He needs to be with her."
Fade to T—— bite	"She is the mother to him instead of me. Even when I was out she was a mother to him. I loved him and gave him material things. I didn't give him the mother's love, but she did."
Fade to Parker asking question and C—— responding Fade music down O/C Standup	Parker: "What's the worst part about not having your mom around?" C——: "I missed her." (O/C) C——'s grandmother not only has to raise him but she has to deal with his emotions as well. Not only is his mother in prison here at Saint Gabriel but his father is also behind bars.
SOT Fade to bite of grandmother Music up Nat sound of woman guard slamming jail door Dissolve and freeze and then slo mo of C—— and mother hugging and saying goodbye	(SOT) "I try to explain to him (music up) that they did something wrong and when you do something wrong you have to pay for it. But as long as she needs me, I'll be there. Even when she gets out, I'll be there for both of them."
V/O	(V/O) Nancy Parker, Channel 9 News, Baton Rouge.

The 50th anniversary of Pearl Harbor was a special occasion, so Executive Producer Rod Haberer of station KPNK-TV in Phoenix was given more air time than usual for this story, which he wrote and produced for anchor Kent Dana:

```
PEARL HARBOR


ANCHOR LEAD-IN:

50 YEARS AGO TONIGHT . . . MUCH OF THE WORLD WAS AT WAR.

BUT AMERICA WAS SITTING THIS ONE OUT. THAT IS, UNTIL THE

FOLLOWING MORNING. AMERICA'S ILLUSION OF PEACE WAS SHAT-

TERED ALONG WITH THE HULL OF THE BATTLESHIP ARIZONA. MORE

THAN A THOUSAND MEN WERE KILLED WHEN A JAPANESE BOMB EX-

PLODED ABOARD THE SHIP . . . DURING THE AIR RAID ON PEARL

HARBOR. KENT DANA REPORTS.

(SOT FULL RP)

(ALL GRAPHICS PRE-PRODUCED)

END TAPE 5:42  OUT: CALLED A MAN (FADES TO BLACK)

TOMORROW MORNING, AT 7-55 A-M . . . PRESIDENT BUSH WILL

BE ABOARD THE USS ARIZONA MEMORIAL . . . TO LAY A WREATH

OVER THE SHIPWRECK THAT STILL HOLDS AN ESTIMATED 900 MEN

ENTOMBED SINCE DECEMBER 7TH, 1941.

TAPE 29A  20:07                (NAT SOT EXPLOSIONS)

VG: LORRAINE MARKS           IN: On that day, 1177 men were
    USS ARIZONA              killed, the largest single naval
    HISTORIAN                disaster in United States history.

                             LORRAINE MARKS LIVES IN PHOENIX,

                             AND IS THE OFFICIAL HISTORIAN

                             FOR THE USS ARIZONA REUNION
```

ASSOCIATION. HER HUSBAND, WHO
DIED FIVE YEARS AGO, SERVED ON
THE ARIZONA. A SURVIVOR, ED
MARKS WAS ASHORE WHEN THE ARIZONA
WAS ATTACKED.

TAPE 29A   3:50   (SOT FULL)

MARKS   IN: In 1985 he went back to the
                        last reunion that he could
                        attend. And a television reporter
                        asked him why, after all these
                        years do you attend these re-
                        unions? And for the first time,
                        I saw him cry . . . because he
                        said we can't forget those guys.

TAPE 29B   3:07   (SOT FULL)

MARKS   IN: I know my husband suffered
                        all those years, he wouldn't
                        talk about it. There's a lot of
                        women I know who say their hus-
                        bands just won't talk about it.

TAPE 28A   5:40   (SOT FULL)

STRATTON   IN: Kind of a tough day.

STILL STRATTON   DONALD STRATTON, WHO NOW LIVES IN

TAPE 28B   26:30   YUMA, WAS ABOARD THE ARIZONA ON
                        DECEMBER 7TH, 1941, AT HIS
                        BATTLESTATIONS ON THE ANTI-
                        AIRCRAFT DIRECTOR ABOVE THE BRIDGE.

TAPE 28A   3:50   (SOT FULL)

STRATTON	IN: General quarters sounded and
VG: DONALD STRATTON	and everyone was on their battle-
USS ARIZONA BB39	stations as far as I knew.
TAPE 28A 4:44	(SOT FULL)
STRATTON	IN: When the bomb hit, it shook
	that 33-ton ship like you'd
	shake a piece of paper.
TAPE 28A 5:26 STRATTON	(SOT FULL)
	IN: The people in the number one
	and number two turrets and those
	manning stations to bring ammo
	from up below and all that, that
	was in the forward part, never
	had a chance.
TAPE 29B 1:00 MARKS	(SOT FULL)
	IN: The Japanese planes came,
	battlestations sounded, the band
	threw down all their instruments
	. . . and went to their battle-
	stations.
TAPE 29B 1:30 MARKS	(SOT FULL)
	IN: And their battlestations were
	in the bowels of the ship, passing
	ammunition and everyone of the
	that day were killed in the band.
STILL USS VESTAL	WHEN THE ARIZONA EXPLODED, THE
TAPE 26 16:12 & 17:00	U-S-S VESTAL WAS STILL TIED UP
	ALONGSIDE, AND THE VESTAL WAS THE
	ONLY WAY OFF THE ARIZONA FOR
	STRATTON AND OTHERS STILL STRANDED.

TAPE 28A   7:53   (SOT FULL)

STRATTON   IN: I would say 50-60 manned

                             that station, but there was only

                             six of us went across this . . .

                             as you know, the Vestal was tied

                             up alongside.

TAPE 29A   16:12   (SOT FULL)

MARKS POINTING TO   IN: This is the Vestal tied up

PAINTING   alongside . . . the repair ship

                             . . . and this is the ship that

                             threw a line over the aft

                             section of the mainmast where

                             Don Stratton was.

TAPE 28A   8:10   (SOT FULL)

STRATTON   IN: We pulled over the heavier

                             messenger line, and tied if off

                             to the Arizona, and we crawled

                             across to the Vestal.

TAPE 28A   8:54   (SOT FULL)

STRATTON   IN: I was burned over 60 percent

                             of my body.

                             STRATTON SURVIVED . . . BUT

                             SO MANY OTHER YOUNG MEN

                             DIDN'T. LIKE JAMES RANDOLF

                             VAN HORNE.

TAPE 29C   4:50   (SOT FULL)

MARKS   IN: He was a sophomore in Tucson

                             High School and he heard Admiral

                             Kidd, read Admiral Kidd, talk

                             about the navy.

TAPE 29C 5:18	(SOT FULL)
MARKS	IN: He quit school, and he joined the navy, both he and the admiral died just a few months later.
TAPE #1 17:43	(SOT FULL)

VG: PAUL STILLWELL
    AUTHOR/BATTLESHIP
    ARIZONA
	IN: I talked to the son of the admiral who was on board, and in 1942 his mother got a package from Hawaii that had in it her husband's naval academy ring, and that had been found fused to the conning tower right in front of the bridge, and apparently that was all that was left of Admiral Kidd.

STILL ROBERTS TAPE 29D 47:30	ANOTHER 17-YEAR-OLD KILLED THAT DAY . . . WAS WALTER SCOTT ROBERTS.
TAPE 29B 14:03	(SOT FULL)
MARKS	IN: The navy department deeply regrets to inform you that your son, Walter Scott Roberts, Junior Radioman First Class US Navy, is missing following performance of his duty and in the service of his country.
STILL BRITTON	AND 17-YEAR-OLD CHARLES EDWARD BRITTON OFTEN WROTE HOME . . . ON JULY 19TH, 1941, THIS NOTE TO · HIS MOTHER.

TAPE 29C 14:08   (SOT FULL)

MARKS   IN: I was not able to send you

                            the five dollars I got off

                            you . . . a 17-year-old boy

                            borrowing money from his mom.

                            PHOTOGRAPHS OF HER SON AND HIS

                            LETTERS HOME ARE ALL THAT CHARLES

                            EDWARD BRITTON'S MOTHER HAD TO

                            REMEMBER HER BOY. BUT SHE WOULD

                            BE PROUD, AND MOST LIKELY MOVED

                            TO TEARS, TO HEAR THE WORDS LOR-

                            RAINE MARKS HAS WRITTEN INTO THE

                            HISTORY BOOKS OF THE USS ARIZONA.

TAPE 29C 12:48   (SOT FULL)

MARKS   IN: Where his remains are now

                            are uncertain, but the soul of

                            this 17-year-old departed that

                            day, December 7th, 1941, from the

                            starboard side of the quarterdeck

                            of the burning and sinking battle-

                            ship USS Arizona BB39. His name

                            is engraved in stone along with

                            1176 of his shipmates on the wall

                            of the USS Arizona memorial that

                            spans the sunken hull in Pearl

                            Harbor, Hawaii. His service to his

                            country and ultimate sacrifice

                            earned him the right at the tender

                            age of 17 to be called a man.

Kris Kridel of radio station WBBM in Chicago
COURTESY OF WBBM-CHICAGO

Haberer was asked how he felt about doing all the work on the Pearl Harbor story, while Dana simply anchored the story. His reply: "It's the way TV has evolved recently. It's much more anchor driven than it used to be. People like the anchors and they want to see and hear more of them. It's our job to make the anchors look as knowledgeable and as strong as we can make them look." He said he accepts that the anchors are going to get credit for the work he does; "it's just part of the job." More on this in Chapter 18, "Ethics and the Law."

The following story was written by Kris Kridel of radio station WBBM in Chicago.

```
David Chereck Murder/Kris Kridel

[neighborhood traffic sounds]

In the three weeks since the murder of their son, Alan
and Esther Chereck's brick home in Skokie has been filled
with people: investigators and reporters, family friends,
and . . . most important to David's mother . . . his
friends.
```

Audio: His friends came. They just kept coming and they keep coming and, uh, and it just shows how much he was loved.

Kridel: Esther Chereck says David's friends sit in his room and talk about him.

Audio: More kids than I realized really knew and cared about David. The cards that we've gotten tell us memories of David and they fill in those blank spots that you don't share with your teen-ager.

Kridel: The Cherecks have learned, for instance, how David once helped a grammar school classmate.

Audio: One year she wouldn't have made her math class, if he hadn't helped her through it, she wouldn't have passed. He never boasted. We never knew these things about him.

Kridel: On the piano and in the nearby étagère in the Cherecks' living room are David's academic awards, his art-work, and pictures of him at all ages.

Audio: In fact, I put more of them up. Having him around, especially when I was sitting *shiva,* was a comfort. As you see, he has a bright smile and, uh, he's there with me. I don't think he'll ever leave us.

Kridel: It is a great comfort to the Cherecks that David's classmates at Niles West High School are organizing an art scholarship fund in his honor.

Audio: We just love them for what they want to do for David.

Kridel: David's parents are appealing to people who may have any information about his murder to step forward and help.

Kris Kridel, WBBM Newsradio 78

[neighborhood traffic sounds fade]

SUMMARY

No one expects you to turn out copy of the quality shown in this chapter right away. Working color into your stories effectively will not come easily or quickly. At the outset, the real challenge will be to write respectable broadcast news copy with speed. You will not have days (unless you are working on a documentary or special report) to write your story. Often you will be dealing in minutes and, at best, an hour or so if you are working on a TV script. But there will be enough time for you to write clearly and accurately while you are developing the skill of writing colorfully.

Don't wait until you are covering a story to develop your observation skills. Start to watch people and take notes about their appearance, how they talk and look, and anything unusual or different about them. Observe people the next time you go to the cafeteria or a ball game. Also start to develop your other senses. If you are in a crowded, smoke-filled room, think about how you feel. There are special smells just about everywhere: in a gym, in the corridors of a high school and a hospital, in a church. How many times have you entered someone's home and said, "Something really smells good . . . what's cooking?" Let all your senses work for you full-time, and put what they tell you into your copy.

1. List the various ways you can bring color to your copy.

2. Why do so many broadcast news professionals recommend that aspiring journalists read the works of Ernest Hemingway?

3. Give the names of other well-known non-broadcast writers who might help develop your writing style.

4. Why is the writing of Charles Kuralt so admired? Give some examples of sentences or phrases in his "On the Road" script that you particularly like, and tell why you like them.

5. What is it about the stories of CBS News Correspondent Roger Welsch that makes them so successful? Give some examples.

6. Give some examples of color in the writing of NBC's Bob Dotson. How would you describe Dotson's style?

7. Is color restricted to feature stories? Discuss.

8. Why is Edward R. Murrow's writing so well respected? Give some examples of the style that made him famous.

1. Examine one of the biographies of Edward R. Murrow, and summarize some of the statements made about his writing.

2. Listen to NPR's "All Things Considered," and make notes on stories that you think are colorfully written.

3. Watch a network newscast and the local newscast that precedes or follows it. Keep notes on the stories that you believe are well written, and why.

4. "Sunday Morning" on CBS is considered by many to be the best news program on the air. Watch it, and report on the stories that you like most. Explain why.

5. Describe, in as much detail as possible, your closest friend. Include the individual's physical appearance and any habits or mannerisms he or she might have. Tell what you like and/or dislike about the person and why you consider him or her to be your closest friend.

CHAPTER 6

WRITING FOR THE RADIO NEWSCAST

t is difficult to generalize about radio news operations and news programs because they seem to be constantly changing. One statement that can be made, however, is that newscasts on radio are getting shorter and less frequent.

There are still many radio stations, however, mostly in large- and medium-sized markets, that take pride in their news operations and maintain writing and reporting staffs of a dozen or more. Some of these stations, particularly those that provide "all news," may have staffs twice that size. In small markets, radio news is often the product of a one-person news staff. Many people who begin their careers in radio will probably work in that environment, which has some advantages. It's an opportunity to develop the skills that you learned in school: writing, reporting, interviewing, working with sound and editing. It also offers time to develop that most important of broadcasting skills, news judgment. But working alone also has some disadvantages. There will be no one there to correct and guide—to help you when you need it most.

This chapter discusses the factors you need to consider when preparing for and writing radio newscasts. Getting to know the audience is the first consideration.

YOUR AUDIENCE

One of the continuing debates in both print and broadcast news is whether the news should provide the kind of information that people *need* to know or the information they *want* to know. Most journalists agree that the answer lies somewhere in the middle. People must be informed, but it also makes sense to tailor the news for the audience. A station programming easy-listening music probably would not want to provide the same kind of news as a rock station. The rock station would have a relatively young audience, and the soft-music station would have an older audience. If you were the news director at the rock station, you would be looking for stories that might appeal more to young people. The writing style also would be lighter and less formal than it would be, for example, for the audience of a classical-music station.

The story selection also would be different for news delivered in urban and rural areas. Stories about the weather would be important in farm country, whereas stories about traffic congestion would be important in the city.

Although you need to consider all these factors, your main concern in covering the news is the news itself. A story of overwhelming importance, whether it is local, national or foreign, always must take precedence over the rest of the news.

**ORGANIZING
MATERIAL**

Before radio news writers decide which story should lead a newscast and which stories should follow, they must know what news they have to work with. A good way to start is to call the police and fire departments to see if anything is going on, then read the newspapers carefully. Newsrooms keep a file marked "futures" that alerts the staff to special events scheduled in the listening area that day and during the upcoming month or later. Check this file next. In a small community there may not be much going on, and, if that community is served by an equally small station, any material in the futures file was probably put there by the newsperson who will be covering the event.

Also check the news wires immediately. Of particular importance are the stories that the wires periodically move about events in the local area. After the copy has been ripped from the wires, you are ready to sort out the material.

Most newspeople working with hard copy like to use a ruler and a thick, crayon-like marker to write a one- or two-word slug at the top of every new story. After all the copy is cut, most writers make a number of piles: one for local news, another for national news and a third for international news. Some writers list on a pad all the stories they have to work with and try to figure out a tentative order in which the stories will appear in the script. Other writers simply go through the various piles of copy on their desk, sorting them so that the most important stories are at the top and the less important ones at the bottom. There is no right or wrong way to organize copy, so look for the method that is the most comfortable for you.

Anchor John Lynker of WTOP-Radio, Washington, reads a newscast.
COURTESY OF WTOP-RADIO

Writers using computers organize their copy in a variety of ways. Some move the stories they wish to consider for their newscast into a separate computer file. Later, when they are ready to rewrite the stories, they split the screen so that they can look at the wire copy on one side and use the other half, the blank side, to rewrite the copy in broadcast style.

Once that story is written it is saved, and the writer moves on to the next one, and so forth. When all the stories are written, the writer prints them out and puts them in the order in which they will be read on the air.

It is possible for a newscaster to read the copy right from the computer screen, and that is done on occasion, particularly when urgent material moves on the wire. But most newscasters find it uncomfortable to read entire newscasts from the computer screen.

**WRITING FROM
THE BACK**

One thing just about all news writers agree on is that the first stories they write are those that will not change. Working in this way is called *writing from the back* because the stories that are not likely to change are usually those that are read in the latter part of the newscast.

"Breaking" stories, as their name suggests, will probably change considerably before air time, so they should be written last.

THE LEAD STORY

The method for selecting the first story in the newscast—the *lead story*—may sound simple: Just pick the most important story. But how do you decide which story is most important? Should a local, national or international story be the lead? Does the time of day affect the decision? Will any of the stories affect the local audience in some way? The answers can help you determine which story should lead the newscast.

Most of a station's listeners will be more interested in what is happening in their community than in the rest of the world. There are exceptions, of course, as during the Gulf War when most Americans turned on their radio and TV sets to get the latest on the war.

But first, let's examine how we decide what's news to a local audience. News in a town of 5,000 is not necessarily news in a city of 50,000. What is considered news in that city may not be too important in a city of a million or more. Here are some story choices on a particular day at a radio station in the hypothetical town of Centerville, population 10,000.

1. The president says he is encouraged by South Africa's latest moves to end apartheid.
2. The Labor Department says unemployment rose another one-half of one percent.
3. The governor says he will make major cuts in services and state workers' jobs rather than raise taxes.
4. The wife of Centerville's mayor gives birth to triplets.

The story of most interest in Centerville, and the story that most listeners would be talking about that day, is the birth of triplets to the mayor's wife. But 100 miles north, in the state capital, the birth would be less important, and the governor's comments on cuts in jobs and services would be the top story. The network newscast would lead with the jump in unemployment because that story holds the most interest for a national audience.

Suppose we add another story to the list: a three-car accident on the freeway near the state capital. While the story may not sound too important, suppose the accident was at 8 in the morning, and those three wrecked cars had created a gigantic traffic jam. It most certainly would be the lead story on the 8 a.m. news for stations in the capital because that is "drive time," the highest-rated listening period for radio. The people listening to their radios on the way to work are more concerned about when they will get to the office than they are about the governor's comments on taxes and jobs.

How about the audience in Centerville? Because the accident took place over 100 miles away, the Centerville listeners would have no interest in it. The network radio audience would not even know about the accident because it would not be important enough to make the wires.

Keep in mind that when you start to prepare your newscast, you should not be overly concerned about which story will lead it. The chances are that what appeared to be the most important story an hour earlier may be overshadowed by a new story that broke before air time. That is the nature of the news business. On some very busy news days—unlikely in Centerville—a story that was considered the lead at one point may not even get into the newscast. That's why each story should be on a separate sheet of paper to allow for a quick reshuffling of the script.

THE REST OF THE NEWSCAST

You can use the formula you established for choosing the lead story to pick the rest of the stories in the newscast. Once you have selected the lead, determine which of the remaining stories would hold the most interest for your audience, then the next most interest, and so on. The stories would then be broadcast in that order.

However, there are important exceptions to this formula. Sometimes, it makes sense to place stories back-to-back because they have something in common. During the Gulf War, for example, it was not unusual for newscasts to carry a report of the fighting and then follow it up with a story from the White House or the State Department concerning some diplomatic aspect of the war. Frequently, those two stories were followed by a third that might have been a reaction-type story on the war from Congress or a poll of American opinion.

Another example would be the linking of weather-related stories. If part of the nation is suffering a drought and another section is in the middle of serious flooding, it would be logical to report those two stories together in the newscast. Without such logical connections, the rule is to report the news in its order of importance.

**LOCALIZING
THE NEWS**

When writing for a local station, always look for some local angle in national and international stories. If a British airliner crashes in Europe, the first thing to check is whether there were any Americans on board and, if so, whether any were from the local listening area.

During the Gulf War, local radio and TV newscasters were always interested in getting interviews with service personnel who were from their area. When there were casualties, it was the responsibility of news organizations to find out if any local men and women were killed or injured.

If a person wins a million-dollar lottery it's a good story, but if the person happens to be from the listening area, it's a "great" story.

STORY LENGTH

The length of a story is determined by the length of the newscast, the importance of the story and the availability of news at that particular hour. If there is not much news to report, the stories may have to be longer than they would be normally. If there is a lot of news, most stories should be short to allow sufficient time for the major stories.

You must determine how much time you actually have for news in a newscast before you start to write. In Chapter 1, you learned that most newscasters

ABC Information Radio network tape editor Carolyn Ripp edits an actuality.
COURTESY OF ABC INFORMATION RADIO

read approximately 15 or 16 lines of copy per minute. So, for a three-minute newscast, you would need approximately 45 to 48 lines of copy.

But is the newscast really three minutes long? Probably not. Let's say there are two commercials, each running 30 seconds, in the newscast, which leaves two minutes of news. If there is a 10-second weather report, five seconds for stocks and another five seconds to sign off, the two minutes have been reduced another 20 seconds. What is left is one minute and 40 seconds. If that time is converted to lines, you have about 25 lines in which to cover all the news. That is why you must learn to condense your stories. You may have as little as three lines to tell some of those stories.

ACTUALITIES

The voices of the news makers are called *actualities* or *sound bites.* They are the heart of radio news.

In the last chapter, you learned that color is often provided by the voices of the people in the story. A good writer can tell the story without the actual voice, but he or she faces a greater challenge. Even the best news writers would tell you that if given a choice, they would rather have the actual sound bite provide the color than their paraphrase of what was in the sound bite. Regardless of the writer and newscaster's talents, it's not possible to capture all of the nuances in a sound bite with a paraphrase and the newscaster's voice. How can anyone better express the remarks of New York City cab drivers than they themselves? And how would the newscaster make up for the missing sounds of the city in the background—the natural sound—without the tape? Good tape is essential.

WRAPAROUNDS

The combination of sound and words is known as a *wraparound.* This technique, as the name suggests, uses the voice of the newscaster or reporter at the beginning and end of a story or report and the voice of the news maker in the middle. You might want to think of a wraparound in terms of a sandwich. There can be more than one thing between the two slices of bread. Wraparounds frequently have more than one sound bite in the middle. The anchor or reporter may wrap several different pieces of sound with script. Here's an example:

```
A Conrail freight train today left the tracks near Center-
ville causing some major problems for passenger trains that
also use the tracks. Railroad officials say the locomotive
and eight of the train's 14 cars were derailed. They blamed
a broken rail.

Remarkably, there were only two injuries — to the engineer
and his assistant — and they were not serious. Engineer Bob
Potter spoke to us at the hospital.

                        (sound bite)
```

```
                         15 sec.

           Out-cue: ". . . I was plenty scared."
```

Conrail engineer Bob Potter. He's in good condition at Centerville General Hospital.

The train was on its way to Southern California with a load of steel and lumber when the accident took place shortly before midnight. Freezing temperatures — dipping into the teens — will make the job of cleaning up a very unpleasant one and will hamper efforts to get service back to normal. But Conrail spokesman Mark Florman is optimistic.

```
                      (sound bite)

                         20 sec.

      Out-cue: ". . . we will know more in a few hours."
```

Conrail spokesman Mark Florman.

He also said that Conrail passenger trains will be detoured, causing some delays probably for 48 hours.

LEAD-INS

Every sound bite, wraparound and report from the scene included in a news script must be introduced by a line or phrase known as a *lead-in*.

Here is one possible lead-in the anchor could have used to introduce the train wreck wraparound if it were done by a reporter at the scene:

```
A train wreck in Centerville during the night.

Reporter Cleo Allen has the details.

                   (Take wraparound)

                      Runs 1:10

      Out-cue: ". . . Cleo Allen reporting for KTHU Radio."
```

The most important thing to avoid when writing a lead-in is redundancy. One of the worst style errors is a lead-in that says exactly the same thing as the first line of the wraparound or sound bite. The way to avoid this problem is for the writer or anchor in the newsroom and the reporter at the scene to discuss in advance what each is going to say.

TEASES

The short sentences used in a script to hold the audience's attention just before a commercial break are called *teases*. The idea of a tease is to give the audience some reason to keep listening, rather than turning the dial. This is best accomplished by giving just a hint of what is to come after the commercial. The cleverer the tease, the greater the chance the audience will put up with the commercial.

If the train wreck wraparound were to follow a commercial, this is the way it might be teased:

Freezing temperatures add to the problems of a Centerville train wreck. That story after this.

(Commercial)

If the news is long enough, or being written for an all-news station, it's effective to tease two or more stories before going to a commercial. Such a tease gives the writer more opportunities to hook listeners. If they are not interested in the first story that is teased, they might go for the second or third one.

HEADLINES

Headlines are another form of tease. Headlines come at the top of a newscast and should reflect the most interesting and exciting stories to be covered in the up-coming newscast. Often, a headline for an offbeat story is an effective tease. Here is a sample:

A tornado rips through a small Kansas town, killing six people.

The cost of living climbs for the third straight month.

Governor Jones says he will veto legislation that would restore the death penalty.

And a pet cheetah scares a lot of people when he decides to take a walk down Main Street.

Those stories and more on the six o'clock news.

Good evening, I'm Bob Rene.

Stan Case reads the news in the CNN Radio anchor booth in Atlanta.

Some radio newscasts start with only one headline:

> Six people die in a tornado in Kansas.
>
> Good evening, I'm Bob Rene with the six o'clock news. The tornado ripped through Centerville, Kansas . . .

Many stations, particularly those that have shortened their newscasts, have eliminated headlines completely on the grounds that they are redundant and take up too much time. On many other radio stations, the only news *is* the headlines.

PAD COPY

Copy written for protection against mistakes in timing and unexpected changes in the newscast that could affect the timing is called *pad copy*. Most of the time, such copy will not get on the air, so the stories that are selected as pad copy should be relatively unimportant.

Because most radio newscasts are relatively short, pad copy normally consists of only a few short pieces totaling perhaps between 30 seconds and a minute. More pad copy might be written for longer newscasts.

Note that the chief reason for pad material is to avoid one of the scariest situations in broadcast news: running out of something to say before the program is scheduled to end.

BACK TIMING

Getting off the air on time takes some planning. If a newscast runs over, or is short, it can create problems for the programs that follow the news. This is particularly true if network programming comes after the newscast.

One way of guaranteeing that this does not happen is called *back timing*. The final segments in the newscast are timed and then deducted from the length of the newscast. Let's look at an example.

Suppose the last two items in a newscast are the stocks and weather. Both are timed. It will take 10 seconds to read the stocks and another 20 seconds for the weather. The standard close for the newscast takes another five seconds to read. The newscaster will need 35 seconds, then, to read the last three items. So, 35 seconds are deducted from the total time of the newscast. The newscaster now knows that he or she must begin reading those three final items at exactly 2:25 into a three-minute newscast.

The three final items should be placed in a separate pile within easy reach on the studio table. The time 2:25 should be written boldly on the top page of this back-timed copy. When the clock reaches the 2:25 mark in the newscast, the reader simply picks up the three pages and begins reading them, regardless of where he or she is in the newscast. Some stories may have to be dropped, and often they are, but that is the only way to guarantee the newscaster gets off the air on time.

SUMMARY

Working in a radio operation in a small market has always been a good way to break into broadcast news, although many people seem to find the glamour and the pay of TV more appealing. In radio, you *do* get a wonderful opportunity to learn how to do everything; you would be the writer, reporter, announcer and technician. In these days of automation, you might be the only "live" person in the building.

As the only member of the news staff, you would quickly learn how to organize your time and effort because you would have little or no help. Your news judgment would be tested every day. You would get an excellent opportunity to hone your writing and reporting skills. You would also be preparing yourself for the next job in a bigger market.

Even if your main interest is television, the things that you learned in this chapter are important because radio news provides an important foundation for work in television news. The principles of radio news writing also apply to television news, which is discussed in the next chapter. You will be required to make some adjustment because of pictures, but if you have absorbed the material in this chapter, you are well prepared to move along.

REVIEW QUESTIONS

1. Why is it important when you are writing broadcast news to know about your audience?

2. You are the only news person working at your radio station. When you arrive for work, you have two hours before you read your first newscast. Explain how you would get prepared.

3. Explain the meaning of the term *writing from the back*.

4. If you were writing news in Centerville, Kan., a market of 10,000, which story would you pick for the lead of your newscast? (a) United States forces drop emergency relief supplies to Kurdish refugees. (b) Ten thousand autoworkers go on strike in Detroit. (c) Centerville welcomes home ten of its soldiers who served in the gulf. Explain your choice.

5. If you were writing for a radio station in Ann Arbor, Mich., which of the stories in exercise 4 would you lead with? Why?

6. After you have selected the lead of your newscast, how would you determine the order of the rest of the stories?

7. What does localizing news mean? Give examples of how you could localize a story about a fire at a rock concert which caused some deaths and injuries and a story about the National Basketball Association draft.

8. If you were writing a two-minute newscast for radio, approximately how many lines of copy would you need?

9. If you have three commercials in the two-minute newscast, one of them 30

seconds and the other two 10 seconds each, how many lines of copy would you need to write?

EXERCISES

1. Using the stories reported on the front page of a newspaper, prepare headlines for a radio newscast.

2. Using those same headlines, write teases for two of the stories that will appear later in your radio newscast.

3. Read the front page of the newspaper, and decide which of the stories you would lead with in a newscast.

4. What other stories on the front page, and in the rest of the newspaper, would you use in your newscast, and in which order?

5. Go to a local radio station that has a news operation, and watch how they put a newscast together. Prepare a report on what you saw.

CHAPTER 7

WRITING FOR THE
TELEVISION NEWSCAST

he major difference between radio and TV news is, of course, pictures. When you write for television, pictures are always crucial to a story. In radio, you must create pictures in your mind—as did Edward R. Murrow and other great broadcasters who used the medium effectively—and then find the words to paint those pictures for your audience. In television, you can show the actual pictures.

COMBINING WORDS AND PICTURES

The battle over which are more important in television news—the words or the pictures—is endless. There is no doubt that words are vital and that some broadcast writers use them more effectively than others. Charles Kuralt is an example of a writer whose words rival the pictures for prominence in a story. But even Kuralt would be hard pressed to tell his stories without pictures. His talent lies in his ability to strengthen the pictures with words. *Great* pictures and *great* words make great television news.

The beauty of good pictures is that they do not need a lot of words—just some good ones. The challenge for TV writers is to avoid clashes with the video. Do not tell viewers what they are seeing. Instead, support the video by saying what the video does not or cannot reveal. Fill in the blanks, but do not overpower the video. Give your viewers time to savor the pictures.

Such advice assumes that you have good pictures to work with. If you don't, then the words do become crucial because they are needed to prop up the video. But because TV news is not about using poor video, stories with bad pictures are likely to be dropped for more appealing ones unless the messages they convey are too vital to be eliminated completely.

But if the pictures are poor, you can be sure you'll be asked to tell the story quickly. A frequent criticism of television news is that it relies on the pictures too much, but right or wrong the formula is not likely to change: poor pictures, short stories; good pictures, long stories.

SOUND BITES

As in radio, sound bites, the words of news makers, are key to telling a good TV news story. An advantage for TV writers is that TV sound bites feature the faces of the news makers as well as their voices. Good TV news writers weave their copy between and around the sound bites, much in the way that radio writers create wraparounds. This combination, called a *package,* is the best way to tell a news story on television. The reporting chapters will deal extensively with building packages.

THE TELEVISION NEWS WRITER

In television, as in radio, a writer's duties depend on the size of the newsroom. In a small market—and even in some medium-sized markets—no one is assigned solely to writing. The anchors, reporters, producers and perhaps an intern from a local college write the news. Television newsrooms in big markets and at the networks usually have a number of writers and perhaps associate producers who also write.

Television news writers have three basic writing tasks: read stories, voice-overs and lead-ins.

READ STORIES

Read, or *tell,* stories are read by the anchors without the use of pictures except for those that usually appear next to the anchor's head. Visually, read stories are the least interesting in TV news. They are virtually the same as radio copy. However, they are a necessary part of the TV newscast because they give the anchors exposure to the audiences. Anchors are paid well, and the audience expects to see their faces on camera at least part of the time.

Sometimes, read stories are used because no video is available. Read copy might even lead the newscast if it is about a breaking story that is just developing. We all are familiar with the phrase *film at eleven,* which usually indicates that it's too early for video, but it will come later.

Read stories are most often stories that are not important enough to require video or whose video itself would be dull. At the same time, read stories play a major role in the TV newscast—they break up the other types of material. Too much of anything tends to be boring, so the read stories provide a change of pace.

Finally, read stories are easiest to work with in a newscast because they are flexible. They are the putty that fills in the holes of the newscast. Read stories often play the same role as radio pad copy; they provide an opportunity to make adjustments that guarantee that the newscast gets off the air on time. If the TV newscast is long, the read stories are the likely stories to be dropped. If the newscast is short, more read stories are likely to be used.

VOICE-OVERS

The second type of assignment given to TV news writers is the *voice-over* (V/O), copy that the anchor reads while video or other graphics are shown. The video can either be silent or have a sound track that is kept low for natural effect, a technique referred to as *sound under* or *natural sound.*

*Anchors Bruce Kirk and Lin Sue
Shepherd of KPNX-TV in Phoenix
read scripts before going on the air.*
COURTESY OF KPNX-TV, PHOENIX

Remember that the copy must complement the video. It should not duplicate what is obvious to viewers. Avoid phrases such as *what you are seeing here* unless the video is difficult to understand. For example, if you are showing video of a train derailment, rather than tell your viewers "What you are seeing is the derailment of a Conrail freight train that left its tracks last night," you would say "A Conrail freight train left its tracks last night," and let the pictures *show* the derailed train.

To write voice-over copy intelligently, you need to look at the video and take notes. When viewing the video, use a stopwatch to time each scene. The cameraperson sometimes shoots a series of short shots that may require little editing, but individual shots are often too long to use without editing. Let's consider the train wreck story discussed in the last chapter.

The cameraperson shot a long, continuous *pan* of the wrecked cars that lasts about 30 seconds. There's another shot of a derrick hovering over the scene for 20 seconds and a third 20-second shot of railroad workers huddled around a hastily made trashcan fire to ward off the frigid weather. Finally, there's an additional 30 seconds of video that shows some of the train's wrecked cargo, an assortment of steel rods and girders and lumber. The total running time of the video is one minute and 40 seconds. The producer asks the writer for a 20-second voice-over. The writer, then, must lift an assortment of brief shots from the video that can be strung together in some logical order that will make sense when the narration is added. (In a small newsroom, reporters often write the script and edit the videotape. In a large operation, a tape editor follows the writer's or reporter's instructions.)

Now that the writer has notes on the length of each scene, she must decide how to *edit,* or *cut,* the video. (*Cut* is a film term that has carried over to video.

All editing is done electronically; the videotape is not physically cut.) The writer decides to use part of the long pan of the wreck scene first. The cameraperson held steady on the scene at the end of the pan, knowing that the writer might wish to use part of it. It is poor technique to cut into a pan, but it is acceptable to use part of it as long as it comes to a stop before the next shot. The writer uses eight seconds of the pan. Then the writer selects five seconds of the wreckage video that shows the steel girders and the lumber spread over the tracks and terrain. Four seconds of the derrick at work follow, and the voice-over closes with three seconds of the railroad workers around the trashcan fire.

The writer gives her instructions to the tape editor, and then returns to her desk to type out the script from her notes and wire copy. In preparing the script, the writer uses a format different from that used in radio.

THE SPLIT PAGE

In Chapter 1, you learned that TV scripts differ from radio scripts because they contain both the newscaster's words and an explanation of how the video is to be used. The format for a TV script is known as the *split page*. In Chapter 5, you saw examples of many such scripts.

The split page is divided vertically so that about 60 percent of the page is in the right column and about 40 percent is in the left. Many TV stations now provide their staffs with computers to write their scripts, which are then sent electronically to the teleprompters. However, typewriters are still used at many stations. The scripts are written on copy books, usually five or more pieces of typing paper separated by carbon paper. There must be enough copies of the script for the anchors, the director, the producer and the teleprompter.

The right side of the split page is reserved for the copy that will be read by the anchors, the running times (which also appear on the left) and the out-cues (final words) of any videotape that has sound. The anchors—and this is important to remember—will be able to see only the right side of the script on their teleprompters. It is also important that you write only in the column on the right side. If you write outside the column, the words will *not* appear on the teleprompter screens.

VIDEO INSTRUCTIONS

The left side of the script is set aside for the slug and for video and audio instructions and tape times for the director. Because of the limited space on the left side of the script, abbreviations are used for the various technical instructions. Here are some common ones:

1. O/C, "on camera," tells the director that at this point in the script the anchor will be on camera.
2. V/O, "voice-over," means the anchor is reading copy while the audience is seeing something else, such as silent videotape or graphics.

3. SIL indicates "silent" videotape and is used in combination with the V/O symbol.

4. SOT lets the director know that there is "sound on tape." It could be a sound bite with a news maker or a report from the field that was taped earlier.

5. ENG, "electronic news gathering," tells the director that the video is on a videotape cassette.

6. FONT, an abbreviation for the manufacturer Videfont, indicates that names, titles and other information are superimposed over videotape or graphics to identify news makers, locations and various other pictures appearing on TV screens. Many stations use the term *super* or the abbreviation VG (video graphic) instead of FONT.

7. SL, ESS or ADDA indicate that pictures or graphics of some sort will be shown next to the anchor. SL stands for "slide"; ESS refers to Electronic Still Storage, an electronic graphics and video computer system; ADDA is the name of a computer system that also provides electronic storage. If the word *box* appears next to any of these abbreviations, the graphic will be enclosed in a box next to the anchor, rather than fill the screen.

There are other technical abbreviations used by writers to help the director. You will learn them once you start working with video on a regular basis.

Here is the split-page script used for the train wreck story discussed earlier:

```
TRAIN WRECK 3/15 6pm tw                    SMITH

O/C Smith Box ADDA                  A Conrail freight train today

                                    left the tracks near Centerville,

                                    Kansas, causing some major

                                    problems for passenger service

                                    trains that also use the tracks.

V/O SIL (TRT: 40 sec.)                        V/O

                                    Railroad officials say the

                                    locomotive and eight of the

                                    train's 14 cars were derailed.

                                    They blamed a broken rail.

                                        Remarkably, there were only

                                    two injuries — to the engineer

                                    and his assistant — and they

                                    were not serious.
```

The train was on its way to
southern California with a load
of steel and lumber when the
accident took place shortly
before midnight. The wreckage was
scattered over a wide area.

Within hours a derrick was sent
to the scene to help clean up
the mess. Officials say the job
will take days.

Freezing temperatures — dipping
into the teens — will make the
cleanup difficult and unpleasant.

Smith O/C Tag   O/C

Railroad officials say that
while the wreckage is being
removed and repairs made to the
tracks, Conrail passenger trains
will be detoured. This probably
will cause delays for at least
48 hours.

If you examine this script, you will see that the slug *TRAIN WRECK* is in the upper left-hand corner along with the date, the time of the newscast and the writer's initials.

On the next line in the right column is *SMITH,* the name of the anchor. Because most newscasts have two or more anchors, the name of the anchor reading the copy must always be displayed at the top of the right-hand column.

On the next line at the left is *O/C Smith,* which lets the director know which anchor is on camera. Underneath that are the words *Box ADDA,* which tell the director that there will be a picture displayed in a box next to the anchor's head. In this case, it could be a generic train wreck graphic that TV newsrooms keep on hand along with scores of other such graphics. (It also could be a freeze-frame of part of the video that would be shown with the voice-over. But if that were the case, the writer would have to indicate it by typing *SIL/FF* ["silent/ freeze-frame"] next to *Box ADDA*.)

The anchor's script continues on the right side. Below the first sentence, you see the V/O symbol, which means that at this point in the script the video will be shown. The anchor continues reading, but the audience no longer sees his face.

The V/O symbol is also displayed in the left-hand column with the abbreviation for silent videotape, *SIL,* for the benefit of the director. In parentheses is the total running time of the videotape (TRT: 40 seconds), which tells the director that there are actually 40 seconds of wreckage footage on the videocassette. Since the V/O copy should only take about 30 seconds to read, this means the director has a 10-second cushion to avoid going to black, something of a nightmare for directors and their bosses. To avoid that problem, tape editors always "pad the tape"—cut more tape than the writer requests.

When the anchor has finished reading the V/O copy, he returns on camera (which is why we show *O/C* in both columns) to read a final sentence about delays in rail service brought on by the wreck. That final sentence is called a *tag,* and the writer of this script has added the word *tag* after O/C in the left column just to remind the busy director that this is the end of the story.)

SOUND ON TAPE

News writers must also learn to write voice-over scripts that include sound on tape (SOT). Because the voices and pictures of news makers are a vital part of TV news, a great deal of the sound on tape will be provided in the middle of reporter packages and is of no real concern to the news writer. But sound is often worked into the anchor's script without the help of the reporter, and that *is* the news writer's function.

Let's go back to the train wreck story and suppose that there is some sound on tape of one of the workers trying to keep warm around the trashcan fire. The writer decides to add that sound on tape to the script at the end of the voice-over before the anchor comes back on camera. A sound bite used at the end of a voice-over is abbreviated *VO-SOT* or *V-SOT*. The script would look like this:

```
SOT :15                     TRACK UP

FONT: Mark Florman          Out-cue: ". . . get any warmer."

      Railroad Worker       Time :15


O/C Smith                                       O/C

                             Railroad officials say that

                             while the wreckage is being

                             removed and repairs made to the

                             tracks, Conrail passenger trains
```

```
                                        will be detoured. This probably

                                        will cause delays for at least

                                        48 hours.
```

The sound on tape symbol and the time appear in the left column to indicate that sound on tape will be used at this point in the script. The director now knows that when the anchor reads the last words of the voice-over, "... difficult and unpleasant," it is time to bring in the sound on tape.

The terms *Track Up* and *Time :15* also appear in the right column along with the out-cue, the final words of the sound bite. This lets the anchor know that a 15-second sound bite comes up before he returns on camera to read the last sentence in the story. The abbreviation *FONT* in the left column means that the name and identification of the railroad worker is to be superimposed over the lower portion of the screen while the railroad worker is speaking. The director will signal the font operator to punch up the information approximately three seconds into the sound bite.

After the sound bite instructions, the symbol O/C is written on both sides of the script to indicate that the anchor returns on camera to wrap up or "tag" the story, or to begin a new story.

LEAD-INS

The third common scripting chore for the TV news writer is preparing *lead-in* lines for sound bites and reporter packages. Writing television lead-ins is similar to writing lead-ins for radio wraparounds, but is slightly more complicated. As with radio lead-ins, the information in the first line of the report or sound bite cannot be repeated in the lead-in.

Unlike radio lead-ins, those for television require some additional instructions for the director because while the anchor is leading into the report or sound bite on camera, some visual is usually shown in a box next to the anchor.

```
        TRAIN  WRECK  3/15  6pm  tw

        O/C Smith                                    SMITH

                                    A Conrail train has derailed

                                    in Kansas and we have a report

                                    from the scene from our reporter

                                    Frank Coakley.


        SOT :55                                  TRACK  UP

        FONT: Frank Coakley          Out-cue: ". . . Frank Coakley

                                     reporting." Time :55
```

The writer used a soft lead-in because she knew that Coakley would provide the hard-news lead. He started his report this way:

> The engine and eight cars of the Conrail train left the tracks around midnight near the town of Centerville. Fortunately only two people were injured slightly.

This lead-in is effective because it allows the reporter's opening words to build on it as he tells the rest of the story.

HEADLINES AND TEASES

Depending on the size of the news operation, headlines and teases usually are turned out by the writer, the editor or the producer.

As always, the major difference between headlines for television and those for radio is that headlines and teases on television are normally supported with pictures. Some network newsrooms forgo the traditional headline approach, preferring to have the anchors talk briefly about the top story before going to a reporter for details. But local news almost always leads the newscast with headlines, which are most effective when used with flashes of video. Here's a sample of how one local news room scripts headlines:

```
HOWARD (GAIL)                           (HOWARD)
                               Coming up on Action News
                               at Six . . .

V/O # 5 (liquor store)         Police search for two men who
                               killed a liquor store owner
                               during a holdup.
RUNS :04
WIPE TO V/O #3                           (GAIL)
(Mayor shaking hands)          Mayor Thompson honors a citizen
                               who rescued a child from a
                               burning building.
RUNS :04
WIPE TO V/O #2                          (HOWARD)
(Unemployment office)          And unemployment in Center City
                               reaches a new high.
RUNS :03
O/C Howard (Gail)              Good evening, I'm Howard Bass.
                                         (GAIL)
                               And I'm Gail Lawson. Those
                               are some of the stories
                               we're covering on tonight's
                               Action News.
```

In the left column, *HOWARD* indicates that one anchor reads the opening line of the newscast and the first headline, while *(GAIL)*—note the parentheses—indicates that the other anchor is also on camera.

Both anchors quickly disappear from the screen, but Howard is heard reading the first headline over video showing the scene of the liquor-store holdup. The video runs about 4 seconds. After the first headline, the video wipes to a shot of Mayor Thompson shaking hands with a hero while Gail reads that headline. The second voice-over also runs 4 seconds. The video wipes a third time to a three-second shot of workers standing on line at an unemployment office. Howard reads that headline, as indicated, over the video. Then both anchors return on camera as Howard says "good evening" and identifies himself. Gail does the same and reminds the audience that the stories just teased would be covered in the upcoming newscast.

The numbers next to the voice-over symbols indicate which playback machines will be used in the control room, information that is vital to the director. If the director or his or her assistant calls for the wrong machine, the wrong video would appear, and the newscast would get off to a confusing start. Some stations give numbers to the tapes instead of the machines. In that case, the tape numbers would be placed on the scripts so that the director could call for the proper one.

Later in the newscast—before the commercials—teases will be used in an effort to hold the audience. The same voice-over technique used in headlines is used for teases. Many producers also include fonts over the video to give it extra punch. For example, these words might appear at the bottom of the appropriate video:

Police hunt killer . . .
Hero honored . . .
Unemployment climbs . . .

The point of such teases is to hook viewers, to keep their interest in the news during the commercial. Teasing three stories increases the chance that your audience will be interested in at least one of the upcoming stories.

A TEAM EFFORT

As you can see, writing television news is more complicated than writing radio news. Although one individual writes the television story and may even edit the videotape used in the story, the final product involves other people in the newsroom.

In radio, writers usually pick the stories they wish to tell their audience. In television, those who write the stories are told what to write and how long the stories should be. In radio, one person may do it all—record interviews on the phone, cover a news conference and include in the newscast some of the tape he or she has edited. There are no one-person newsrooms in television, although at small stations you may be expected to play more than one role.

As in radio, there will be opportunities in television to learn how to do a lot of different jobs. Writers frequently go on to other positions, often as reporters, anchors and producers. Some move over to the assignment desk, where the people "find the news," a subject discussed in Chapter 9.

SUMMARY

This chapter introduces a variety of terms used in television news, such as split page, voice-over, package and font, and describes a television writer's most common writing assignments.

In carrying out these assignments, you need to learn to work with both words and pictures. Broadcast news professionals have very strong views on which is more important, the words or the pictures. The truth, of course, is that *both* words and pictures are critical to a successful TV news script. Television is a visual medium, and the pictures must be effective, but if the words that go with those pictures are unclear, confusing or contradictory, the story will fail because there will be no true communication.

Choose your pictures carefully, and do the same with your words.

REVIEW QUESTIONS

1. What is the major difference between writing for radio and writing for television?

2. How will poor pictures affect TV news stories?

3. How important are sound bites to a TV news script? Why?

4. What is a read story?

5. Why are read stories important to a TV newscast? List the different ways they are used.

6. What is a voice-over? Describe what the audience sees and hears during a voice-over.

7. Describe some of the things to remember when writing for pictures in a voice-over script.

8. Is it better to have too few or too many words in a voice-over? Explain.

9. Explain the steps that a writer takes in selecting videotape to be used in a voice-over.

10. Explain the term *split page,* indicating the dimensions and how the page is used.

11. Why must you be careful in observing the margins on the split page?

12. Explain the purpose of fonts and give some examples.

13. Explain the following abbreviations: *SL* and *ADDA.*

14. What does *SL Box* in a script mean?

15. What does *TRT* mean, and why is that term important for a director?

16. What is an *out-cue,* and why is it important to the director and anchor?

17. What is the most important thing to remember when writing a lead-in to a sound bite or a correspondent's report?

EXERCISES

1. Take a story from the wire or a newspaper, and rewrite it on a split page as a read story. It should be 20 seconds long.

2. Using the same piece of copy, prepare a V-SOT. Suppose that you have a sound bite from someone who is involved in the story. Use the split page, indicating the proper symbols and time for a 10-second sound bite. You have 30 seconds for the entire story.

3. Suppose that you have a reporter covering a story about a tornado hitting Centerville, Kan. Three people have been killed, and another dozen have been injured. Write a lead-in for a live report, indicating also what the reporter's first sentence will say.

4. Using wire copy or the front page of a newspaper, script three headlines for a TV newscast.

5. Using the same copy, script two teases that will come before your first commercial break.

6. Go to a local TV station and observe who is doing the writing. Talk to either a writer or a producer on how the writing is assigned, and report on what you discover.

CHAPTER 8

DELIVERING THE NEWS

any of you have hopes of anchoring news. How long it takes you to end up at the anchor desk depends mostly on two factors. The first one is talent—your ability to deliver the news. The second consideration is the size of the market in which you begin your career.

If you have talent and start working in a relatively small market, you may reach the anchor desk quickly. You will still, however, have to prove you are ready for that job by impressing the news director with your reporting ability. Also remember that not all reporters become anchors; some good reporters do not have the special talent required to anchor news. Similarly, some anchors make awful reporters. This chapter discusses the qualities you need to anchor or report in front of a camera or microphone.

CREDIBILITY

Ask news directors what they look for in reporters and anchors and most will tell you *credibility*. They want people who are believable: people who come across as knowledgeable about and comfortable with what they are doing.

Jeff Puffer, a voice coach for one of the nation's major broadcast consulting firms, Frank Magid Associates, says he knows many "reliable anchor-reporters with good potential who just don't seem comfortable in the anchor chair. In person they're spontaneous and charming. But on the air they're wooden, with unnatural speech rhythms and awkward inflection."

Puffer says that when he's instructing anchors and reporters, he expects them "to show two qualities in their reading: intelligence and genuine sensitivity." He says he looks for "emotion that is appropriate for the story, the person and the occasion. I want them to demonstrate that they know what they're reading and that they're thoughtfully weighing the facts as they speak." Puffer says, "I always want them to say it with feeling, not artificially, but with sensitivity and maturity."

It is not always easy for anchor-reporters to accomplish these goals, and those who coach people in delivery techniques use a variety of methods. Puffer says he doesn't concentrate on speech pathology material such as breathing, diction and resonance. "We're involved in matters relating to interpretation, making the voice sound spontaneous and conversational, like an ad-lib."

Puffer admits that his methodology could be called "unconventional or unorthodox" but, he says, "given what we have been finding in neuro-science research, we know that the whole of human intelligence is not just the left side of the brain, the intellectual side. It's also intuition, artistry, abstractions, pattern recognition, and the like."

ONE-WAY COMMUNICATION

Puffer says the difficulty in broadcast training is the "non-interactive environment." He points out that there is "no give and take, it's largely one way. The result of that strained environment is that the communicators do not automatically use all their self-expression when looking into a camera or speaking on mike as they would in a face-to-face dialogue." Puffer adds, "What we try to do is restore that quality and feeling in the delivery. We try to trigger that part of the brain that is responsible for artistry, abstraction, etc."

Puffer also notes that he's not trying to make a person's voice sound like someone else's. "We all have developed and cultivated a wealth of knowledge regarding what is appropriate inter-personal communication over the years," he says. "We all know the tools; we know how loud to speak; how to emphasize and articulate our words; how to use our face and eyes with accompanying gestures; no one has to tell us how to do these things. The idea," Puffer adds, "is to tap into those resources and help bring them into the environment that is not interactive, like the broadcast studio."

GETTING HELP WITH YOUR DELIVERY

If you are having problems with your voice, diction and delivery, it's a good idea to deal with the problems while you are in college. Speech and debating courses sometimes help, but if you have serious problems, you may need a voice coach.

Former CBS News Correspondent Walter Cronkite was among the most respected anchors in TV news.
COURTESY OF CBS NEWS

Voice coach Carol Dearing advises students intent on being in front of a microphone or camera to "do all they can to prepare themselves *before* they leave college." She says that without professional help, some students "fall into habit patterns that will work against them."

DIALECTS

Traditionally, station managers and news directors look for people who speak "standard American speech" when they hire on-air personnel. That's another way of saying they like Midwestern voices, which are considered "neutral."

Don't count yourself out if you were not born and reared in South Dakota. Some dialects can be eliminated with good coaching. If they cannot be corrected, it's still possible to work in an area where your dialect is the primary one. "If you have a Southern dialect you can work in the South," says coach Dearing, "but you are not likely to get on the air in Chicago." She said that same rule applies to people who were born and reared in Chicago. "If they have a strong big-city dialect they are not likely to make it in Dallas."

Mary Berger, a speech pathologist at Columbia College in Chicago who works with young people, says it's important to let students know, if they have a dialect that reflects a minority racial or ethnic background, that there is "nothing wrong with them. Many have been told that they are stupid because of the way they speak. Once you tell them that you do not intend to change the dialect but develop a new 'style' for use in the work place, they relax." Berger explains her methods in her book "Speak Standard, TOO."

Like Jeff Puffer, Berger says many of her colleagues may consider her approach to speech problems "unorthodox." She recalls that she was asked by Columbia College to design a course after the college got feedback from graduates indicating that they were having trouble finding work because of voice problems.

"What we find in our classes," she notes, "are a lot of students with high-pitched, nasal-sounding, unpleasant voices not acceptable for air. We don't try to correct those problems in the traditional way, working on pitch and inflection, etc. What we do is give them an 'indirect hint' that says, 'Your voice is different but *you* can change it without too much help from us.'"

Berger says the first thing she has the students do is record their voices and then listen to them. "They detect immediately the high pitches and other things that they would like to change. Then we say, 'OK, now pretend that you are someone else, like newscaster Bill Curtis or a general giving orders to troops.' Amazingly, their voices suddenly get deeper."

Berger stresses that there are times when students obviously cannot change their readings. "When their voices are straining, for example, when they try to change their pitch, we direct them to people who deal with such problems."

Voice coach Carol Dearing says that pitch *is* one of the most troubling problems for young people. "Young ladies," she says, "usually have too high a pitch. When they read their copy, it sounds as if they are much younger and less credible than they really are." But Dearing warns young women that trying to

*Jeff Puffer, a consultant for Frank N. Magid Associates, Inc.,
confers with a client.*
COURTESY OF JEFF PUFFER/FRANK N. MAGID ASSOCIATES, INC.

change the pitch of their voice dramatically without professional help can be dangerous.

Dearing says another common problem is articulation. She says many people going into broadcasting have a minor lisp. But Dearing says this problem is easily correctable and should not prevent anyone from moving forward as a reporter or an anchor.

LISTENING TO YOURSELF

In the style chapters, you learned that it is always a good idea to read your copy aloud because your ear catches mistakes and detects poorly constructed copy that your eye misses. Similarly, reading aloud will alert you to any problems you have with pronunciation, articulation and awkward speech patterns.

**GETTING
PRONUNCIATION
HELP**

News broadcasters should avoid using words that are difficult to pronounce. The mind understands the meaning of many words, but sometimes it has trouble relaying the pronunciation to the tongue, which causes newscasters to stumble over their copy. Tricky words and phrases invite trouble.

There will be times when writers and anchors have no choice, however. Proper names, for example, cannot be changed. Spelling them correctly does not guarantee that they will be pronounced correctly. It is the responsibility of the writer of a newscast to identify the correct pronunciation of any difficult names in a script. Reporters should ask the people whom they are interviewing for the proper pronunciation of their names. Names of towns also should be checked if there is any doubt. For example:

Biloxi in Mississippi is pronounced Bi-lok'-si.

Acadian in Louisiana is pronounced E-kay'-di-en.

Kankakee in Illinois is pronounced Kang'–ka-ke.

Cairo in Illinois is pronounced Ka'-ro.

If a job takes you to a new part of the country, it is a good idea to seek out someone who has lived in the area for some time. Colleagues who have been working at the station will be able to help, and someone at the local library or historical society will probably be happy to answer questions about the pronunciation of nearby towns or local family names.

The wire services send out pronunciation guides to their customers (see Figure 8–1). These are particularly useful when covering national and international stories. If your news operation is computerized, these guides should be stored for future use.

In cities large enough to have a wire service bureau, the staff will help its clients find the proper pronunciation of a name or place in the city or state. The wires also have a phonetics desk that helps with hard-to-pronounce names in national and international news stories.

In Chapter 1, you learned that it is not always necessary to use the names of foreign dignitaries. If you do use them, it is a good idea to refer to the dignitaries by their titles during the rest of the story, particularly if the names are unusually difficult to pronounce.

When using difficult names, write them phonetically in the copy to help the person who will be reading the script. (See Figure 8–2 for an example of how to spell phonetically.) The phonetic spelling can be given after the word or written above the word. Writers working on a newscast should ask the anchors which style they prefer. Here are examples of the two methods:

Cayuga (Ka-yoo'-ga) Indians still live on the land.

(Ka-yoo'-ga)
Cayuga Indians still live on the land.

Dictionaries, which give the proper pronunciation of words as well as their meanings, are invaluable tools. There also are a number of dictionaries of pronunciation on the market, and most news rooms keep copies at hand. If you are unsure about the pronunciation of a word, look it up.

PACING

What else can you do to improve your delivery? CBS News Correspondent Charles Osgood says *pacing* is important. Osgood advises using a pause to get attention when you want something you just said "to sink in. . . . A pause can be very telling, provided you know something." He says the "most remarkable

NEWS
Hanan Ashrawi: hah'-nahn ash-row'-ee
Hafez Assad: hah'-fez ah'-sahd
Azerbaijan: ah-zur-by-jahn'
Bosnia-Herzegovina: bahz'-nee-ah hurts-uh-goh-vee'-na
Ciudad Juarez: see-yoo-dahd' wah'-rehz
Alberto Fujimori: foo-jee-moh'-ree
Moammar Gadhafi: moo'- ah-mahr gah-dah'-fee
Yegor Gaidar: yay'-gohr gy'-dahr
Hans-Dietrich Genscher: hahnz'-dee'-trihk gen'-shur
Guantanamo Bay: gwan-tah'-nah-moh
Inuit: en-yoo-it'
Alija Izetbegovic: ah-lee'-yuh ee-zet-beh'-goh-vitch
Kabul: kah'-bool
François Mitterrand: frahn-swah' mee-teh-rahn'
Hosni Mubarak: hahs'-nee moo-bah'-rahk
Jorge Muniz: hohr'-hay moo'-nyees
Nagorno-Karabakh: nuh-gohr'-noh kah-ruh-bahk'
Najibullah: nah-jee-boo'-lah
Nunavut: noon'-uh-vuht
Turgut Ozal: toor-guht' uh-zahl'
Sarajevo: sehr-uh-yay'-voh
Tanjug: tahn'-yoog

SPORTS
Danielle Ammaccapane: ahm-uh-kuh-pahn'-ee
Bill Koch: kohk
Mario Lemieux: leh-myoo'
Liselotte Neumann: lee'-suh-lot noy'-muhn
Bob Plager: play'-gur
Brian Sutter: sut'-ur

Figure 8–1. An AP pronunciation guide.

pacer in our business is ABC newscaster Paul Harvey. You can drive a truck between Paul Harvey and 'Good day.' He's doing that for a reason."

Osgood recalls times when he's been traveling with a news crew and there's all sorts of conversation until Harvey begins broadcasting. "When Paul Harvey comes on the radio," Osgood says, "everybody stops [talking] and listens to Paul Harvey. You cannot not listen to that man."

-A-
AY for long A (as in mate)
A for short A (as in cat)
AI for nasal A (as in air)
AH for soft A (as in father)
AW for broad A (as in talk)

-E-
EE for long E (as in meat)
EH for short E (as in get)
UH for hollow E, or schwa (as in the)
AY for French long E with acute accent (as in Pathe)
IH for middle E (as in pretty)
EW for EW dipthong (as in few)

-I-
IGH for long I (as in time)
EE for French long I (as in machine)
IH for short I (as in pity)

-O-
OH for long O (as in note or though)
AH for short O (as in hot)
AW for broad O (as in fought)
OO for long double O (as in fool or through)
OW for OW diphthong (as in how)

-U-
EW for long U (as in mule)
OO for long U (as in rule)
U for middle U (as in put)
UH for short U (as in shut)

CONSONANTS
K for hard C (as in cat)
S for soft C (as in cease)
SH for soft CH (as in machine)
CH for hard CH or TCH (as in catch)
Z for hard S (as in disease)
S for soft S (as in sun)
G for hard G (as in gang)
J for soft G (as in general)
ZH for soft J (as in French version of Joliet)

Figure 8–2. A phonetic pronunciation guide from UPI.

ABC News Commentator Paul Harvey prepares for a broadcast in Chicago.
COURTESY OF ABC NEWS

Osgood says, "You can hate him. You can think he's terrible. You can disagree with him completely as far as his politics are concerned. But you can't not listen to him, because he has got you. He has found out how to say, 'Hey, shut up. I'm talking now.' "

Here's an excerpt from a "Paul Harvey News" broadcast aired on June 3, 1992:

```
What happens . . .
When galaxies collide . . . ?
Our Hubble Space telescope . . . reveals that
two galaxies have collided, the resultant "starburst"
is spawning new stars at a furious rate . . .

Primary day in six states . . .
And all said the same thing.
Voters have now given more than enough votes
to Bush and Clinton . . .
but they have given their hearts to Ross Perot.
Exit polling in all six states indicates that
in a three-way race Perot just might win.

Americans are disgusted with politicians in
general . . . And Ross Perot is something else.

Last night was a big night for women . . .
When they'd counted your ballots . . . you California
democrats had nominated two women to the
United States Senate. Iowa democrats may
```

```
send a woman to the Senate. Montana may elect its
first-ever woman governor. The next House of
Representatives could include several women.
North Carolina has a chance to send two black
women to Congress. Ohio nominated Mary Rose Oakar
for a ninth term.

California Republicans nominated for United
States Senator conservative TV commentator
Bruce Herschensohn. Palm Springs Mayor Sonny
Bono struck out.

Residents of Los Angeles voted an amendment
to their city's charter. It would LIMIT the
terms of future police chiefs. And it would
enable the mayor to hire or to fire them. The
yes vote was two-to-one.

Dan Quayle may yet have the last word. One
source says . . . Producers of Murphy Brown
have decided she will re-marry her ex-husband . . .
so her baby will have a father.
```

Osgood says that when he writes for himself, he uses a lot of ellipses (series of three dots). "I want to remind myself that that is supposed to be a pause. I will also capitalize certain words . . . because I want to hit that particular word for it to work."

The CBS news correspondent also says it's important to remember when you are on the air that "you're talking to somebody, which means that you have to be conscious at all times that there's somebody there." Osgood notes that you can't assume people are listening; you "have to get their attention, you don't automatically have it."

MARKING COPY   Most newscasters mark copy in one way or another to help them remember when to pause or to emphasize certain words. They mark the copy as they read it aloud, which also helps them control their breathing. Long sentences require extra breath, so newscasters must either pause more often or rewrite the sentence. Otherwise, they sound as though they are running out of breath. Often, inexperienced newscasters try to speed up their delivery when they realize that they might have trouble getting through a complicated sentence, but that's a poor solution. If you find yourself leaning toward this solution, rewrite your copy until you can read it at a normal pace.

Here is an example of copy marked by a newscaster.

B)

    THE SALT RIVER PROJECT'S

WEST VALLEY SERVICE CENTER/

HAS BEEN CLOSED AFTER TESTS

SHOW THE PRESENCE OF

LEGIONNAIRES' DISEASE . . .

TAKE 1/2″ VO :00   S-R-P CLOSED THE CENTER

. . . AT 79TH AVENUE AND VAN

BUREN . . .(AS A SAFETY PRE-

CAUTION.)

VG: 79TH AVE &   THAT'S AFTER THE PRESENCE

VAN BUREN SRP   OF A WATER-CARRIED BACTERIA/

CENTER CLOSED   THAT CAUSES LEGIONNAIRES'(WAS

FOUND.)

    THE COMPANY <u>DID</u> <u>NOT</u> <u>WANT</u> TO

ENDANGER ITS 200 EMPLOYEES AT

THE CENTER ./. . SALT RIVER

SAYS IT EXPECTS TO REMOVE THE

BACTERIA AND RE-OPEN THE

END TAPE :20   BUILDING TUESDAY.

    LEGIONNAIRES' IS A RARE DIS-

EASE NORMALLY FOUND IN HUMID

CLIMATES . . . BUT THERE WERE

17 CASES REPORTED IN ARIZONA

Bruce Kirk, an anchor at KPNX-TV in Phoenix, who marked the example script, uses slash marks to indicate pauses and underlines words that he wishes to emphasize. Some anchors use a double underline for words that require extraordinary emphasis. Other anchors use all caps for words they wish to stress. Some anchors use ellipses to indicate pauses, and still others use dashes. Some anchors like their scripts typed in all caps while others prefer upper- and lowercase (which, according to studies, is easier to read).

Christine Devine, an anchor for KTTV in Los Angeles, who marked this next example, says she doesn't always have time to mark her script, but when she does "it results in a better show." Devine uses a bracket to let herself know she's starting to read a new paragraph and a new thought, and after a sound bite so she doesn't lose her place. She uses an ellipsis to signify the end of a phrase, but not the end of a thought.

Devine underlines key words for emphasis, which seems to be standard practice among anchors. She also routinely underlines *not*. In addition, Devine says she underlines for contrast when, for example, contrasting Republicans and Democrats.

ANCHOR	(CO)
I-DEADLY FIRES	<u>TWO</u> PEOPLE ARE DEAD TO-NIGHT AFTER <u>SEPARATE FIRES</u> IN <u>TWO</u> SOUTHLAND CITIES.
	A BLAZE SWEPT THROUGH A <u>HOME</u> IN <u>ORANGE</u> EARLY THIS MORNING . . . FATALLY IN-JURING AN <u>ELDERLY</u> WOMAN AND LEAVING HER <u>HUSBAND</u> <u>CRITICALLY INJURED</u>.
	OFFICIALS SAY THE FIRE WAS SPARKED BY A <u>NATURAL</u> <u>GAS</u> <u>EXPLOSION</u> IN THE COUPLE'S KITCHEN.

SUMMARY

If you wish to report or anchor for radio and television, you must analyze your voice as soon as you can. One of your instructors may be able to tell you if you need help and where you can get it. If speech courses are not offered in your journalism program, seek out the speech department. Consider the help of a coach if you have some special problems with your voice or diction.

Remember that a regional or cultural dialect will not necessarily eliminate you from contention as a reporter or anchor. Many of those problems, if they can't be eliminated, can at least be modified sufficiently for you to work in the area where you were born and reared.

If you have a good voice, learn to use it properly. Get accustomed to reading your copy aloud before you go in front of a microphone. In addition to alerting you to grammatical errors or awkward phrases you may have missed, reading your copy aloud will help you discover that certain words and names in the copy are hard to pronounce. If so, add the phonetic spellings next to or above the difficult names and places. Last, reading your copy aloud gives you the opportunity to determine what words you want to emphasize and how you can use pacing effectively.

REVIEW QUESTIONS

1. Name some of the talents you must develop if you wish to become a radio reporter.

2. What additional talents will you need if you wish to report or anchor for television?

3. If you are having troubles of any kind with your voice, how soon should you get an evaluation?

4. If you have problems with diction, breathing or dialect, what kind of help can you get?

5. What are some of the approaches to solving voice problems?

6. Two of the voice coaches quoted in this chapter say some of their techniques might be considered unorthodox. Discuss.

7. The wire services offer some pronunciation assistance to their clients. What kind of help?

8. Why is Paul Harvey so effective in getting and holding an audience's attention?

9. Why do anchors mark their copy? What are some of the symbols they use?

EXERCISES

1. Read a few newspaper stories silently and then read them into a tape recorder. Make a note of things that you discovered were a problem in the copy *only* after reading it aloud. After making appropriate changes in the copy, read it into the tape recorder a second time, and note any improvements.

2. Write a one-minute radio script based on information from a newspaper or newspaper wire. Then read the script into a tape recorder. Listen to the recording, and make notes on anything that you did not like about your reading, such as inflection, breathing, pitch or pace.

3. Do a second reading, but this time mark your copy before doing so. After reading, note whether there was an improvement in your delivery.

4. Go through a newspaper or newspaper wire copy, and find words that are

unfamiliar to you. Look up the words in a dictionary for meaning and pronunciation and in a pronunciation guide if one is available. Write the words
phonetically along with the rest of the sentences, and read them into a tape
recorder. Then replay the tape for other members of your class, and note
whether they understood the meaning of the words.

5. After you have noted the words that fellow students did not understand,
find synonyms for them and rerecord the sentences with the new words. See
if the students understand the copy this time.

CHAPTER 9

FINDING THE NEWS

ost national and international news comes into a newsroom from the wire services. Most local news comes from a combination of sources and activities, including the police and fire departments, the courts and various other municipal institutions, and community and business organizations. Local news also is generated by the routine follow-up of the leads and tips that pour into the assignment desk on a continuing basis from beat reporters, tipsters and even non-news personnel who work for the station. This chapter and Chapter 16, "Other Methods of Collecting Information," examine all these sources of news.

THE WIRES

The term *wires* is still used to describe the services offered by news-gathering organizations such as The Associated Press, United Press International and Reuters, a British firm.

The word *wires* refers to the telegraph cables that were originally used to transmit the news to newspaper clients. Today, AP feeds news to some 6,000 radio and TV customers, more than three times the number of newspapers receiving its services. The news is distributed not by wires but via satellite to machines that print as many as 1,200 words a minute. Although most broadcast newsrooms still use printers, many radio and TV stations have converted to systems that allow the news to be fed directly into computers in the newsrooms and at the anchor desks. Writers, producers and anchors can print out stories that interest them, and if they wish, the anchors can read the material live from the video screens at their desks.

Most small-market radio stations make use of the AP or UPI broadcast wires that transmit hourly summaries of the news. The broadcast wires are designed for those stations with little or no news operation. The broadcast wires are popularly referred to as the "rip-and-read" wires because that is the way they are most often used at stations lacking staff to rewrite news copy; the stories are designed to be read without any rewriting. The major problem, of course, is that the newscast will sound the same as that of any other station using the material.

Radio and TV stations also may subscribe to a UPI or AP newspaper wire, called the A Wire. There also are wires devoted to state news, financial news, sports, agriculture and a variety of other special topics. The A Wire provides considerably more detail about national and international news than the broadcast wires because A-Wire stories are written primarily with newspapers in mind. The A Wire also moves many more stories than the broadcast wires. Because the A-Wire stories are written in newspaper style, however, they are virtually impossible to read on the air without a rewrite (see Chapter 6). So, there is little purpose in subscribing to the A Wire unless there is someone to rewrite the copy.

The wires also provide *splits* on the broadcast and main wires throughout the day and night. Splits are stories of state and regional interest sent to radio and TV customers from bureaus in your state and surrounding states.

In addition to the various wires, AP also provides a variety of audio feeds via satellite, including news on the hour and the half-hour, special reports on the hour's major stories, and an hourly feed of actualities and natural sound. AP also provides scripted national and international news, agricultural reports, business news, sports, entertainment news, special features and a headline service designed for what AP describes as stations with "a limited news appetite."

AP also provides a number of photo and graphics services, including an interactive data base that supplies thousands of head shots, maps and images of breaking news and a high-speed, digital photo network that delivers color photos to TV stations in less than three minutes.

UPI, which has been in serious financial difficulty for a number of years, was acquired by Worldwide News, Inc. in 1992. Its parent company, Middle East Broadcasting Center, Inc., based in London, produces TV programs in Arabic and distributes them to Europe, North Africa and the Middle East.

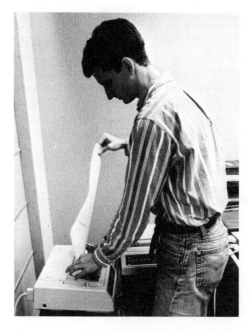

WAFB-TV Producer Marc Bitner checks the news wires.
PHOTO BY JAMES TERRY

UPI operates domestic and international news wires, two radio networks, a news photo service and specialized services that deliver business, financial and sports news scripts for broadcast. It has bureaus in 33 cities in the United States and 47 bureaus in other countries.

Steve Geimann, a spokesman for UPI, said the new owners have the resources that UPI has needed for years. He said "they are making investments in staff, equipment and communications so that UPI can once again be competitive in the information marketplace." Geimann said the previous owners had allowed UPI to stagnate by reducing funding, staffing and salaries. He added that the new owners were "putting in place a fairly ambitious rebuilding campaign."

TELEVISION SATELLITE FEEDS

Television stations also receive a steady stream of sound bites and reports via closed-circuit feeds, usually referred to as *newsfeeds,* by the networks and various independent producers. While satellite technology has changed the way newsfeeds are transmitted, the networks have been feeding local stations with news for years.

Among the newsfeed services is NBC's News Channel, which is located in Charlotte, N.C. The CBS newsfeed operation, Newsnet, services its clients from six regional centers throughout the country. CNN's newsfeed service, Newsource, is based in Atlanta.

The most active of the non-network groups is Conus, which gathers material from local stations and feeds it back to subscribers. In addition to regular newsfeeds, the Conus Satellite News Cooperative provides live feeds of breaking news stories. It describes itself as "a clearing house for information as well as a source of delivery." More than 100 stations were participating in the cooperative in early 1993. Conus distributes eight daily national feeds, each 15 to 45 minutes long. Additional feeds are distributed by Conus regional cooperatives located throughout the United States.

OTHER SATELLITE NEWS SERVICES

There are a variety of other companies using satellites to feed news. Here are the top ones:

Visnews International: An international TV news agency with camera crews and bureaus throughout the world. Owned by Reuters and the British Broadcasting Company.

Independent Television News: A full-service news and entertainment bureau specializing in domestic and international satellite transmission.

Worldwide Television News: An international news-gathering agency with crews and facilities in many parts of the world. Owned by ABC and TV groups in Britain and Australia.

Assignment Editor David Koors of WBRZ-TV, Baton Rouge, checks video being fed from a microwave truck.
PHOTO BY CHRISTOPHER J. ROGERS

The All News Channel: This service offers half-hour custom-made newscasts 24 hours a day, 7 days a week.

Radio and TV stations also can buy satellite-delivered information about health and medicine, finance, weather, sports, music, consumer news and scores of other subjects. Multiply the paid syndication services by 10 and you probably have a figure close to the number of organizations and companies that dump *free* information on satellites each day. It's free information because it's promoting an organization or a cause. Among those making use of satellites are associations representing the chemical, gas, sugar and scores of other industries; the American Legion; the FBI; various religious and health-related organizations; public relations companies; and a variety of universities. Some of the free material is produced as a public service, but most is pure public relations.

VIDEO NEWS RELEASES

TV stations are being inundated with satellite feeds of public-relations material known as video news releases (VNRs). As the phrase suggests, VNRs are pre-packaged public-relations news releases designed to look like *news* stories. This multimillion-dollar business provides additional video material for TV stations, but many newsrooms have banned it. Although many VNRs are of high quality (produced at a cost of $30,000 or more), they are "pushing" something.

The underlying message is often subtle—VNRs with subtle messages are the most effective and those most likely to be aired—but their news value is questionable.

Most VNRs are used by TV stations in relatively small markets, but they sometimes are aired in moderate-sized and even large markets, particularly on news-scarce weekends, in place of soft features.

NEWSPAPERS   Many broadcast news managers do not like to admit it, but they often rely on newspapers as a source of news. Because they have much larger news staffs, and more room for news, newspapers frequently have stories that broadcast newsrooms miss or do not bother to cover.

Some stations rely on newspapers more than others. A station with enough reporters to do a good job covering the local scene will be less dependent on newspapers than stations with small news staffs. Some stations are constantly playing "catch-up" because they cannot compete with the newspaper's beat system.

Broadcast newsrooms often find themselves trying to figure out ways to take a good newspaper story and *advance* it. Advancing the story, finding some new development to make it appear new or at least fresh, is often considered a justification for "borrowing" the information developed by the newspaper. However, it's important to remember that if a newspaper is the *only* source for a story, it is ethically proper, and a necessary protection in case the information is not accurate, to attribute the story to the newspaper. Remember also that most newspapers copyright their material. Few papers object when their stories are broadcast, as long as credit is given. Some news directors take the position that once the accuracy of information first disclosed in a newspaper has been independently verified by the station, it is no longer necessary to credit the paper.

Although good broadcast news operations should rely as little as possible on newspapers for story ideas, papers should be mandatory reading for everyone in the broadcast newsroom. Broadcast editors and writers find it is often a good way to double-check the facts in a wire story. Also, it is not unusual for national papers such as The New York Times and The Washington Post to have details or new angles on a story that are not in the wire versions.

MONITORING RADIOS   Every newsroom should have radios that monitor police and fire department channels, which broadcast every fire or police call that is being answered in the station's immediate area. Someone should monitor the radios constantly. The station that ignores the radio gets scooped by the competition.

Scanning devices on radios can monitor police and fire channels at the same time. The scanners hop back and forth, pausing whenever anyone starts to speak. The chatter is difficult to hear at times, but with practice it becomes easier to decipher, particularly if you learn the special codes used by authorities.

One of the most common systems used by police is known as the *10-code*, which uses *signal codes* that vary from city to city. For example, in New Orleans, 10-55 means a police officer needs assistance. In Baton Rouge, that message is a signal 63. A robbery in progress in Baton Rouge is a signal 42, but in New Orleans it's a 65. Some cities, including New Orleans, use the state's criminal code numbers. A signal 30 is a homicide, a DWI is 599, and a hit-and-run is 100. Because cities use different systems, you'll need to learn the codes when you enter a new market. They should be posted near or on the radio.

Neither of these sources—the radios and the teletype messages—is ever to be used alone in writing a story for broadcast. They must be checked out by phone. Often the police and fire reports turn out to be unfounded or less serious than one might expect from the code or teletype message. It is also a violation of FCC regulations to rebroadcast any material heard on police, fire, or ham radio broadcasts.

MAKING PHONE CALLS

Unless a station has someone on duty overnight, which is not that common except in very large markets, the first member of the news staff to arrive at the station each day should call police and fire department headquarters. Large cities provide a special phone number and public-relations staff just to handle the media. But for the most part, reporters will be dealing with the police and fire dispatchers.

News staffs, particularly in medium-sized and large markets, routinely make other telephone calls: before and during rush hours, they check on auto traffic and commuter train and bus service to see if there are any major delays. During bad weather, such information becomes more critical. Trains and buses may not be moving. The roads may be treacherous. School officials may call in to report closings; that information is important in *every* market.

During bad weather, the news staff also takes calls from the PTA, the Rotary Club, the YWCA, the local theater group and scores of other organizations that may cancel events because of the weather.

The newsroom should have a complete list of emergency telephone numbers on rotary files, clipboards or in the computer. The local gas and electric companies will have information on disruptions of service and potentially dangerous situations brought on by snowstorms, tornadoes and earthquakes.

A serious snowstorm turns a routine weather report, normally read near the end of a newscast, into a lead story. News staffs check with the local weather bureau at least every hour, perhaps more often, during a potentially disastrous weather situation.

STRINGERS

Many stations—both radio and television—have working relationships with *stringers*, people who are not on the payroll but are paid for stories that they develop, or who cover breaking news at night when no one is working at the station. Stringers often help a station avoid the embarrassment of missing a story that breaks overnight.

Some stringers have their own camera gear, and some TV stations provide gear to stringers who are productive. In large markets, particularly where crews belong to unions, stringers often cause resentment among full-time employees.

Many news directors also have arrangements with firefighters or police officers on duty overnight who agree to call the news director at home if an important story breaks. Some stations encourage viewers to submit stories shot on home video recorders if the stories have news value. But such video must be aired with extreme caution because of the potential for deception, libel and other problems.

TIPSTERS

Most stations also encourage people to call with news tips. Some even pay for such information. It is surprising just how much news is generated this way.

All tips should be taken seriously. Many are about breaking news stories—a shooting heard from the listener's bedroom window or a fire spotted by someone walking the dog. Other tips come from people who are upset for some reason. It may have to do with something going on in local government or at the plant where they work. If possible, get the caller's name and phone number. Frequently, tipsters refuse to identify themselves, but assignment editors should not make the mistake of thinking that most people who call a radio or TV station are cranks. There will be lots of crank calls, but newspeople must consider every phone call to be potentially important.

One of the news producers for a network investigative unit made the mistake of telling a tipster to "write a letter," one of the worst ways to deal with someone who calls with information about a story. Instead of writing a letter, the tipster called another network, which assigned a producer to check out the information. The story attracted national attention when it was broadcast.

There will be more on tipsters in Chapter 17, "Developing Sources."

EMPLOYEE INPUT

Story ideas often come from people on the news staff—reporters, producers, anchors, desk assistants and others—and some ideas originate with secretaries and people in the mail room.

People working in news seem to develop a sense that alerts them to news in all sorts of places. A producer waiting to cross the street near a bus stop suddenly got a blast of soot in her face. As she recovered, she noticed that a passing city bus continued to emit a steady stream of pollutants as it moved down the block. Standing next to the angry producer was a police officer. "Did you see that?" yelled the producer. "What?" replied the officer. "All that pollution!"

The police officer looked a little confused by the observation and shrugged his shoulders as if to say, "So what?"

The producer could not wait to get to the newsroom to share her experience with the assignment editor. The editor listened intently and agreed that there might be a story here. A couple of telephone calls later, the assignment editor strolled over to the producer's desk and said, "The reason that cop gave you a blank stare is because we don't have any anti-pollution laws in this city."

That was the start of a good series on pollution.

Everyone on the staff should be encouraged to develop story ideas. One news director uses the station's newsletter to encourage non-news employees to stop by the assignment editor's desk if they should see or hear anything that might make a news story.

Assignment editors *do* listen to a lot of stories, and some of the stories *do* generate news. But assignment editors do more than just listen. They are in charge of collecting and organizing most of the source material that comes into a newsroom.

Sometimes the assignment desk is very modest. There may be one person in charge of assignments, and then only during the daytime. Assignment editors are found mostly in TV newsrooms, but some large radio news operations in major cities also employ them. At many radio stations, and some small TV stations, the news director or perhaps an assistant news director will function as an assignment editor but will not have that title. Large-market TV stations normally have at least two assignment editors—one for the morning and one for the evening. In the largest newsrooms, the assignment desk operates around-the-clock.

Almost everything starts at the assignment desk because that is where all the

Assignment desk at WTVJ-TV, Miami
COURTESY OF WTVJ-TV, MIAMI

information enters the system. Assignment editors are the "keepers" of the news wires. They monitor the wires constantly, looking for stories that will be of interest to producers who are responsible for putting newscasts on the air. Some of these stories will be assigned to reporters. Others will be given to writers for read stories or, perhaps, to be used for V-SOTs. Still others will need follow-up by the assignment editor. In a breaking story, that follow-up will be immediate.

SOUNDING THE ALARM

A desk assistant is the first to hear the fire department advisory. It's obviously a bad one. He tells the assignment editor, and she listens for about 15 seconds, long enough to know that she has to get people moving on it. She calls the crew room. As she waits for an answer, she calls to the reporter who is listening to the radio, "Frank, let's go." Frank heads for the door.

By the time Frank reaches the microwave truck, the assignment editor has figured out exactly where the fire is and the best way to get there. She gives the information to the cameraman on the two-way radio and turns up the volume on the scanner.

The producer of the 6 o'clock news notices all the sudden activity and is quickly informed that a reporter and a photographer are already on the way to a major fire.

On a fire story, especially in the middle of the afternoon, the microwave truck is used for a variety of reasons: to get some live reports on the air before the evening newscast, if warranted, and to go live from the scene during the newscast.

As soon as the truck arrives at the scene, the cameraman sets up the microwave rod to make sure he can get a picture back to the station. A monitor is set up at the assignment desk, as well as in master control, where the actual feed comes in, so that the assignment editor will know if it's possible to get a live shot. The producer will also be waiting for that information.

Meanwhile, the assignment editor and her desk assistant are working the phones. The wires have caught up on the story, and they report there have been some deaths and injuries. The desk assistant says he caught something on the scanner about two hospitals, City General and St. Joseph's.

Another reporter has been waiting at the assignment desk for orders, and now she gets them: "Go to City General Hospital." Another photographer is already sitting in the station's other microwave truck, waiting to roll.

And so it goes for the rest of the afternoon and into the late evening. A third reporter, who has been covering another story, is pulled off it by the assignment editor and sent to the second hospital. The assignment editor and her desk assistant get as much information about the fire and deaths and injuries as they can from the scanner and the telephones to support what the reporters are finding out at the scene.

There is an almost continuous conversation among the reporters and those at the assignment desk as they all share this information. The assignment editor and the desk assistant also take notes for the producers and writers on everything from font information to the number of deaths and injuries and the status of the fire.

The assignment editor's desk is also the clearinghouse for exchanges between the reporters and the producers. After the first report is finished at the top of the 6 o'clock news, the producer may tell the assignment editor he wants an update in 20 minutes. That information is relayed to the microwave truck, and in a few minutes the producer is told, "You got it!"

As things settle down, there's an advisory on the wires. Fire officials suspect arson and will hold a news conference in 20 minutes. There is an unconfirmed report that someone may already be under arrest.

The assignment editor tries to reach the reporter at the scene to verify the information, but the reporter is out of touch. Next, the editor is on the radio with the crew at St. Joseph's. "Break down and get to Fire Department headquarters immediately for a news conference. Tell John [the reporter] that I will talk to him when you get rolling."

Meanwhile, the desk assistant has tried to get more information on the advisory. A call to fire department headquarters confirms the report on the news conference, but the official refuses to say anything about an arrest.

"Tell the writer," says the assignment editor, and the desk assistant takes off. Within minutes, the writer has the new copy on its way to the anchor desk. The newscast will be over before the news conference gets under way, but the anchor reads the new copy and promises, "We'll have details on the news conference at eleven o'clock and, of course, we'll break into our regular programming with any new details on the fire as soon as we receive them."

DEVELOPING STORY IDEAS

Fires and crimes do get a lot of coverage on local newscasts, but assignment editors have to look for other, non-breaking news to fill an hour-long newscast. To accomplish the goal, they must be part journalist and part detective.

They must examine every wire story to see if there is any possible angle that can be developed into a good local story. Chapter 6 mentioned how important it is to look for a local angle in national and international stories. This search is constant at the assignment desk. For example, if the unemployment figures out of Washington are bad, the assignment editor tries to develop a story about local effects. Have the local unemployment figures gone up too, or did the community do better than the rest of the nation? What are the opinions of the people at the unemployment office— those on line and those behind the desk? How are shop owners doing? If local unemployment has worsened, has it had an effect on their businesses?

What about inflation? If Washington reports a dramatic increase, how has it affected shoppers? The assignment editor might send a reporter to a supermarket. The manager might admit that prices have been going up, and you can bet the people at the checkout line will speak out.

The assignment editor also looks for ways to update a story. The fire story

Assignment Editor Sam Moore of WBRZ-TV, Baton Rouge
PHOTO BY CHRISTOPHER J. ROGERS

detailed earlier presents lots of opportunities. There will be interviews at the hospitals with the injured as their condition improves. The arson investigation will provide updates, and if someone is arrested, that would provide another update.

INTERACTION   Assignment editors probably interact with more people than anyone else in the newsroom, which is why they are so essential to a good news operation.

In the fire story, you saw the assignment editor's interaction with producers, photographers and reporters. There must be a close, harmonious working relationship between those at the assignment desk and all these people. During a breaking story, the assignment editor must control the coverage of the story firmly from the start. The news director usually keeps a close eye on what is going on, but more often than not he or she allows the assignment editor to run the show.

When things are quieter, more dialogue is likely to take place between the producer and those at the desk. The producer often influences assignment decisions on non-breaking stories. If the producer is not very interested in a story, the assignment editor may think twice about giving it to a reporter. But many assignments have to be made before the producer even arrives in the newsroom. The producer has to accept the assignment editor's judgment in covering stories. Once reporters have been assigned to stories, it is the producer's responsibility to try to work most of them into the newscast. Otherwise there would not be enough material for the newscast.

As you saw earlier, once reporters are on the road, it is the job of the assignment editor to keep the producer informed on their progress. Some stories may not work and will be killed. A reporter may inform the desk that his story is not as strong as it first appeared and so will be shorter than anticipated. Another reporter may say her story will be longer. Producers must know all this in planning for the newscast.

Interaction with the camerapeople also takes much of the assignment editor's time—and tact. A good relationship is vital.

Generally, local stations assign just a photographer to a microwave truck. When a story is breaking, as in the case of the fire we just discussed, a station will sometimes assign a two-person crew (if an extra person is available) so that the photographer can shoot without worrying about setting up and monitoring the live shot. This is particularly true if the story breaks just before air time. Some stations in large markets, and at the networks, have unions that sometimes determine the size of the crew.

An important part of the assignment editor's job during a breaking story, as you saw earlier, is to get the reporter and crew to the scene as soon as possible. The assignment editor also needs to schedule reporters and crews so that they arrive on time for non-breaking news conferences and other planned events. The assignment editor must provide accurate street and room numbers and the names of contacts.

Like many people in the newsroom, crews often work long hours and are under a great deal of pressure. They may miss lunches and dinners and be required to work overtime at the end of an already full day. Showing them the respect they deserve usually motivates tired crews more than do screams and demands. So, assignment editors, who are under a lot of pressure themselves, need to keep their cool. They also need to be organized.

INSIGHTS

Assignment editors play a major role in determining what the newscast will look like. Although the producers have the responsibility for making the final decisions on what goes into newscasts, they must rely on the judgment of the assignment editors in the collection process. That process works best when it is organized.

Earlier sections of this chapter discussed the responsibility of the assignment editors to go over the wires carefully and to check the newspapers to see if there's something going on that the wires might have missed. The assignment editors must also look through the *futures* file discussed in Chapter 6. The file contains information about news conferences and other events and feature stories that are set up in advance.

Once all this has been digested, the assignment editor must prepare a *menu*—sometimes called *insights* or *outlooks*—of all of the news possibilities for the day, along with evaluations and recommendations as to which stories should be assigned to reporters and which should be covered only by a cameraperson.

This document is distributed to the entire news editorial staff and discussed at a meeting, usually scheduled in mid-morning, that is attended by the news director, various producers, writers and any reporters—especially beat reporters—who have not already been sent out on stories. The meeting determines the "battle plan" for the day. As with any battle, it is impossible to predict how it will turn out. What appears to be news in the morning may not be so in the middle of the afternoon. That is the nature of news.

ASSIGNMENT BOARDS

In addition to the written assignment outlooks, the assignment desk staff must maintain an *assignment board* that lists all of the stories that have been assigned for that day. The board shows the names of the reporter and crew, the location of the story, the time it is scheduled and, usually, the time the crew is expected back. There also should be room for additional notes on the progress of the story.

A chalk board or a white plastic board with soluble markers is used so that changes can be made throughout the day. Because the board is usually right behind or to the side of the assignment desk, it should be big enough so that producers, reporters and others do not have to crowd around it to read the information. Keeping up the board is usually the responsibility of the desk assistant.

DESK ASSISTANTS

Desk assistants answer the phones, distribute copy to anchors and teleprompters and do many other chores that are asked of them as they gain experience working in a newsroom.

The job is one of the best ways to get started in broadcast news. Desk assistants who work hard and impress the staff and bosses soon find that they are given more responsibility that may include writing an occasional story and going out on assignments with reporters.

SUMMARY

If news staffs didn't know where to look for news and how to gather it, there would be little news on radio and TV. Most of the collecting is done by assignment editors, while the gathering is the responsibility of reporters.

The assignment desk is where most information enters the newsroom. The assignment desk staff monitors the news wires, the police and fire radios, and the telephones and receives an endless assortment of news releases by mail, wire and telegram. Assignment editors also look for story ideas from reporters, particularly those with beats, as well as from stringers, tipsters, and other newsroom employees. The assignment editor, who may be the news director as well in some markets, makes the initial decisions on which of this material should be considered for coverage. He also assigns reporters and photographers to stories.

Assignment editors and news director also rely heavily on the rest of the news team, especially producers. The producers select material and decide what goes on the air; they are responsible for the look of the news. Many newsrooms hold daily meetings to plan the newscast and also maintain assignment boards to keep staff members apprised of their duties for the day. Broadcast news is very much a team effort. Without harmony and togetherness the newscasts will not succeed, and the ratings will fall. That's bad news for everyone because when ratings fall, owners usually look for a new team. The team that works together will live to see another "sweeps."

REVIEW QUESTIONS

1. What are the names of the most widely used news wire services?

2. Which wire is used most often by small radio stations? Why?

3. What is the A Wire, and what kinds of stations usually subscribe to this service? Why?

4. What other kinds of products do the wire services offer radio stations? Describe them.

5. TV stations have access to feeds from the networks and other sources. How do they arrive at the TV stations? Explain how material is used.

6. What are video news releases? Who uses them? Why are they controversial?

7. Why are there special radios in broadcast newsrooms? How are they used? Are they important?

8. It is routine for many broadcast news staffs to make certain telephone calls each morning. What kinds of calls? Why are they important?

9. Who are stringers, and what do they do? Why are they important?

10. Explain why the assignment desk is an integral part of a news operation.

EXERCISES

1. Part of the assignment editor's job is to look for updates on stories. Look at the wires or your newspaper, and pick stories that have potential for being updated. Explain how you would update them.

2. The assignment editor is always looking for local reaction–type stories to national and international developments. Look at the wires and newspapers for stories that might provide local reaction. Tape a reaction from someone.

3. If there is a news wire bureau in your area, visit the office, and write a report on what you observed. If there is not, visit your local newspaper office, and see how the wires are used by the staff. Then write a report.

4. Visit a local radio or TV station and see who is monitoring the police and fire radio. Take notes on what you heard, and turn in a report.

BROADCAST NEWS REPORTING

ood reporters first must learn to write, which is why the first part of the book was devoted mostly to writing. But just being able to write well does not guarantee that a person will make a good reporter. Many additional skills and abilities, unrelated to writing, are required.

While print and broadcast reporters need many of the same skills, broadcast news reporters face challenges not encountered by their print counterparts, or even by broadcast journalists of the recent past. Electronic news gathering (ENG), which relies on videotape and microwave technology, places demands on TV reporters that were unknown when reporters filmed stories and had the luxury of writing their scripts while the film was being developed. Broadcast journalists today need to think faster and to prepare their reports more rapidly, often while the story is still going on around them. They also need to learn about the different types of assignments they are likely to cover and the best means of carrying out those assignments.

The next several chapters describe these needs and offer suggestions for developing skills to meet them. This chapter begins with the basic skills required of successful reporters.

BASIC SKILLS
As Chapter 1 noted, the most important skill a reporter needs to develop is accuracy. At first this may not appear to be a skill, but being accurate requires a lot of attention—checking and double-checking information demands concentration. Errors usually creep into copy when reporters become too relaxed. Nothing should be assumed or taken for granted. If information cannot be confirmed, it should not be used without some kind of attribution.

Reporters also must develop news judgment. They must understand what news *is* and be able to recognize that certain stories are more important than others. That skill sometimes takes time to develop. Later in this chapter, professional journalists offer you their views and advice on what makes news and how you can develop news judgment.

Reporters must also be curious, showing an interest in everything and everyone making news, whatever the reason.

Reporters must be concerned, sometimes alarmed, often angered and always caring about the major problems that face the community and world in which we live. Reporters often can do little to correct injustice or unfairness, or the misery, suffering and critical problems of certain segments or groups in our society, but they should have a desire to do so. Their weapons are enlightenment and information.

Reporters must be determined and persistent in their search for facts and details. Reporters must be aggressive, walking a thin line between tenacity and belligerence.

For many people entering journalism, some of these characteristics seem to come naturally, while others need to be developed. Let's look at these qualities in detail.

ACCURACY

Accuracy requires hard work. Every detail in a news story must be checked and rechecked. For example, names. Remember how embarrassing it was the last time you introduced a new acquaintance by the wrong name? Reporters must develop a habit of making sure they have a person's name right, not just the spelling but the pronunciation as well. Other routine information, such as addresses and ages, also need to be checked for accuracy, as do all other pieces of key information.

It does not matter how well a story is written or whether it has a clever lead or a snappy ending if it is not accurate in every detail. News managers have little patience with reporters who cannot get the facts straight. Inaccuracy can end a reporter's career quickly.

No one is perfect, of course, and journalists do make mistakes. But the responsibility for accuracy demands that such mistakes be kept to a minimum. When they are made, they must be corrected as quickly as possible.

NEWS JUDGMENT

In the Introduction, the idea that news judgment is something "you are born with" was dismissed. It can be developed. But how?

First, perhaps news judgment should be defined, which isn't easy. Even professional journalists have difficulty explaining the term. ABC "Nightline" Correspondent Jeff Greenfield says people have different news judgments, which he believes is desirable. He noted that "Nightline" anchor Ted Koppel is a "foreign policy freak" and tends to "see more value in an international story," while he himself is a "political freak."

Greenfield said that if a relatively unknown politician announced he or she was running for president, Greenfield might suggest that it was time to examine the whole field of candidates, while Koppel might still prefer a foreign story. Greenfield commented, "Does that mean that Koppel is without news judgment? I think not. Does it mean that I am without news judgment? I think not."

Greenfield said news judgment can also be related to the audience you are trying to serve. "The editors of The New York Times and The [Washington]

ABC "Nightline" Correspondent Jeff Greenfield
CAROL HALEBIAN/GAMMA-LIAISON

Post will see news differently," he said. "They each will ask, 'Is this a story my readers will care about and want to know about?' "

Greenfield cited as an example the story of Kimberly Bergalis—a woman who died from AIDS after being infected during oral surgery performed by her HIV-positive dentist. "Why is that a news story?" asked Greenfield. "Because something terrible happened to her. She never used drugs and never had sex of any kind. Yet, this beautiful young woman was dying of the disease."

The ABC correspondent said it was a news story for two reasons. First, he said, "We resonate to the story . . . it's a 'there but for the grace of God' story." Second, he added, "It raises a public-policy debate. Should medical professionals have to be tested for HIV?"

Greenfield said that while people react differently to that story, news judgment dictates, "We've got to cover it."

NBC News Correspondent Bob Dotson says that when he thinks of news judgment he thinks of fairness. He believes reporters must ask themselves if there is more than one side to a story and try to give them all. Dotson says he views ethics as an important part of good news judgment.

CBS News Correspondent Richard Threlkeld believes news judgment is "in the eye of the beholder. If you are going to put on a newscast and want people to watch it," he says, "you have to give them stories that they ought to know—important developments overseas and how the mayor and governor are doing their jobs at home. They also want to know if there was a bad fire in the neighborhood. News judgment comes into play in giving the public the proper mix of things they should know and want to know."

Dotson says one of the best ways to develop news judgment is to learn from one's mistakes and try to avoid them in the future. He remembered working as a young newsman in Oklahoma City and being asked to do a story about the anniversary of Pearl Harbor.

"I was only 22 at the time and didn't know a heck of a lot about Pearl Harbor," Dotson recalled, "but I had a handout film that had sprockets on both sides of the film. I had a master's degree in cinematography," Dotson said, "but I forgot to check which side was up. So during the newscast the planes attacking Pearl Harbor came in upside down."

Dotson said that because he didn't know any better, he thought maybe the Japanese had actually done it that way. "But when the flag came on upside down I knew I was dead meat," said Dotson. "The news director always had a critique after the news, and he would tell you what you did wrong and often make you do it over again. Well," Dotson continued, "you didn't do that too often before you started thinking of ways to improve what you were doing."

ABC News Correspondent Morton Dean says he developed news judgment "by just working in the field . . . by doing it and working with some very good people and learning from them. You have to pay attention to people around you, and if you are fortunate enough to have good, solid, professional people to work with when you start out, that's a great help. It's like being in a perpetual classroom." Adds Dean, "It's important in this business to keep your eyes and ears open all the time. . . . You can always learn new things, not only about the world but about yourself. It's important to look at yourself and listen to yourself to pick up on whatever communication problems you have."

NBC Correspondent Roger O'Neil notes that when he was a local reporter he "always paid attention to every network correspondent on the air." He "studied them, analyzed what they said and learned a lot."

CBS's Richard Threlkeld also says reporters always have to remember—regardless of their age—to be concerned about things that are of interest to people outside their age group. "Young reporters just starting out," he notes, "must realize that there are people out there who are over 35 and have different interests and concerns." Threlkeld adds that even he has to keep asking himself, "What are my daughters, who are in their 20s and 30s, interested in? What would they want to watch? The same goes for people who are my seniors. Is this a story that would interest them?" Threlkeld advises reporters to remember that broadcasting is "mass media, and that means everybody—little kids, and old people, and black and white and brown people. They're all watching, and they all deserve the best that you can give them."

CURIOSITY

For curious people, one of the rewards of reporting is the joy of discovering things. Discovering something "first" is the best reward of all. But discovering information is not always as exciting as it is depicted on the TV programs based on broadcast news. To hold a network prime-time audience, these programs must come up with some imaginative story ideas each week. In the real world, few reporters get caught up in the kind of sensational situations and intrigue depicted on sit-coms and TV dramas.

Most reporting assignments are fairly routine. Reporters spend a great deal of time covering murders, lots of fires, plenty of elections, more news conferences than they would care to remember, accidents of all kinds and hundreds of feature stories. That is the *real* world of broadcast news.

But just because most reporters may not deal with crooked politicians, track down terrorists or go to bat for someone on death row who they are convinced is innocent does not mean that reporting is dull. There is an endless assortment of stories to satisfy most people's curiosity, and there are opportunities to explore previously unknown subjects. Getting the answers, finding out about things—and learning and growing along the way—are part of the excitement of reporting. They are also some of the reasons that the profession is so compelling.

When reporters arrive at the newsroom for work, they never know what stories they will be covering, and that in itself is an exciting concept for curious people. Most reporters will tell you that they could not imagine any kind of work that they would rather do. CBS News Correspondent Betsy Aaron agrees. "It keeps you young. We're in this business because we are nosy, and curious, and angry and we want to change the world. If you lose this edge," she says, "then it's hard to put in the 90 hours a week and mess up your family life and the other things that go along with it."

CONCERN AND CARING

There is never a shortage of news about people who need help. People in many parts of the world are dying of hunger and disease. Thousands are dying as a result of civil and political strife in various countries. At home, unemployment, homelessness and poverty continue to be major problems. Tuberculosis, a disease that at one time was thought to have been eradicated, at least in the United States, has again become a threat. AIDS is not only a serious medical emergency but a subject of national debate over whether the government is doing enough to combat the disease.

These are just a few of the tragedies and distressing stories making news. All such stories raise concern, as they should, for those hearing the news. Those reporting the news must be equally concerned. Part of the job of reporting such stories is providing information that may enlighten the audience. There may be little that a radio or TV reporter can do about the plight of civil war or famine victims except to report the story in a thoughtful and caring manner. But in the case of domestic problems such as homelessness, AIDS and unemployment, a reporter often can provide information that may help those affected deal with the problem or may call others' attention to it.

PERSISTENCE

A good reporter hates taking "no" for an answer. Learning how to get people to talk to you when they may not want to is a skill. Getting them to tell you things they don't want to requires even more skill.

ABC News Correspondent Barry Serafin says that he usually does take "no" for an answer when someone does not wish to speak with him, but he says that he also mentions in his report that the individual refused to be interviewed. Serafin says that the situation is different when a public official is involved. "Then," he adds, "I try not to take 'no' for an answer."

Serafin's colleague at ABC, Correspondent Jeff Greenfield, has a similar view. "If it's a private individual who doesn't want to talk to you," he advises, "get out. But if it's a public or government official, you are entitled to keep banging on the door as much as you like. It's not a privacy issue."

Greenfield notes it takes a "combination of aggressiveness and guile" to get someone to talk when they are reluctant. He says he has had some success by telling people: "Look, I can't really force you to talk to me, but I am not out to prove a point or make a case. There is an issue at stake here, and your side is important to us. It is absolutely up to you whether you will talk to us."

Greenfield says he also makes this promise: "I'll give your side of the story fairly." He adds, "I then ask the person, 'Exactly what is it that you are most afraid to discuss with me?' Sometimes it works, and sometimes it doesn't."

AGGRESSIVENESS   Most reporters seem to agree that they try to be aggressive without being obnoxious. They criticize reporters who shout and shove microphones into people's faces, demanding answers to their questions. Unfortunately, some news directors insist on such behavior—they expect to see microphones with

Louisiana Governor Edwin W. Edwards meets with journalists.
PHOTO BY JAMES TERRY

the station call letters on the 6 o'clock news as much as possible even if the only voices heard on the microphones are the reporters'. News directors also listen to hear if their reporters asked questions, which is a reasonable expectation.

But these scenes can get ugly. Hollywood filmmakers have portrayed reporters as rude and arrogant—and often stupid—in movie scripts for decades. The Hollywood stereotype of the dumb reporter has been overdone but not entirely.

Most politicians, police officials, lawyers and others who deal with the media on a daily basis are accustomed to a certain amount of badgering from the press. They would probably be disappointed and feel neglected if the news corps was not surrounding them when there's a story to tell. But the reporter who runs down the street after a news maker's car and shoves a microphone into the open window is out of line. More than one reporter has lost a microphone that way when the irritated person rolled up the window.

FAIRNESS

It is often argued that it is not possible to be completely objective. This may be true. Everyone has certain biases and prejudices, but reporters must learn to leave out their personal feelings when they start writing or delivering news. Objectivity for a journalist really means "fairness"—it means honestly giving both sides of an argument, controversy or debate.

Reporters can tell when their report on a controversial issue has been successful: both sides of the issue accuse them of being partial to the other.

STAYING WELL-INFORMED

Reporters cannot function well unless they are well-informed. Being well-informed does not just mean having a good education, it means taking the time to know what's going on around you. Journalists must constantly add new material to their knowledge. One of the best ways to stay well-informed is to read.

Reading the news wires extensively is an immediate way to know what is going on. Reporters should read the local newspaper (or all of them if they work in a city with more than one) and at least one national paper every day. Weekly news magazines are a useful source of additional information, as are books—particularly nonfiction best sellers.

It also is a good idea to observe the competition. Reporters who watch and listen only to their own station's newscasts miss an opportunity not only to find out what the competition is saying but also, on occasion, to improve on their own techniques.

RESEARCH

All good reporters do research because they want to know as much as possible about a story before trying to cover it. Large radio and TV stations usually have good libraries and *morgues*, which store back issues of newspapers and magazines and tape of video and audio news stories recorded over past weeks, months and even years.

Well-equipped newsrooms also have a library of good research books, including encyclopedias, the Congressional Directory and, perhaps, special publications such as Standard & Poor's financial reports. If the news operation is small, reporters may have to spend a lot of time at the public library.

It also is a good idea to get on mailing lists. Many organizations are happy to add a reporter's name to their lists, and just getting on some mailing lists automatically places your name on many others. Much of the information distributed by these groups has limited news value because it is public-relations material, but it is useful for alerting you to the positions certain organizations take on issues. Many of the groups are dedicated to worthwhile causes.

MANNERS AND SENSITIVITY

Reporters must often cover unpleasant stories. They are expected to interview people who are involved in a variety of tragedies—to talk, perhaps, to the parents or relatives of a homicide or accident victim. It is important for inexperienced reporters to learn how to handle such interviews with tact and sensitivity.

There have been so many bad examples of tactless interviews that the question "How do you feel about your daughter being murdered?" has become a stereotype of the insensitive reporter. It *is* an insensitive question. News directors should quickly discipline reporters who display such bad taste.

NBC News Correspondent Bob Dotson says part of the problem is that "people don't want you there, and *you* don't want to be there." Dotson recalled covering a tornado story in Small Town, S.C., where there had been a number of fatalities. "It was the day after the tornado struck, and we made sure that we got there before 9 o'clock in the morning," recalled Dotson, "because anyone who is affected by a hurricane or tornado is not going to be at home later. They are either going to be at the hospital checking on loved ones or at the mortuary. So we got there before 9 o'clock because the one thing people always do in tragic situations is come back and look for pictures. They don't care about stereos or TVs," Dotson noted, "but they are looking for pictures."

Dotson recalled that they found a man and his son digging through the rubble. "The son came up to us and jumped in my face, and rightfully so, and said, 'What are you guys here for . . . you're vultures,' and so forth. And I looked at him and said, 'You know it's Sunday morning, and there are a lot of folks getting up and asking themselves why . . . why did this happen?' And that is all I said, I didn't ask him a question. And then the father came over and he said to me, 'I'll tell you why.'

"Well," Dotson said, "we started shooting what he had to say. But he became overcome with grief thinking about the loss of his wife and daughter, and he walked away. Then—because of the kind of person he was, and because he said he would tell us—he came back and finished the story."

Dotson said the story ran on NBC News—including the 10 or 12 seconds when the man walked away to compose himself and then walked back to the camera. "A week later I got a letter from him, and he said he had received thousands of letters from people around the country saying that he had helped them put tragedy into perspective, and he thanked me. And then I got a Christmas card from him. So," Dotson observed, "it doesn't necessarily mean that just because you are working on an emotional edge you are not going to be able to handle that situation properly."

He added that it is important in such situations to make it plain that you are representing yourself and not your company, and "If that means not having your camera rolling when you walk up, then so be it. If someone is experiencing great grief and doesn't want you there, fine, there's another story somewhere. But nine out of 10 times you can stay if you come along and talk to them as an individual first and don't ask questions—just commiserate. Then," Dotson added, "if they take a liking to you, someone will stop and tell you, and that's when you turn the camera on. But," Dotson stressed, "you never go up to someone who has great grief and act like a stereotypical journalist or you are going to go out on your ear, or worse."

ABC News Correspondent Morton Dean says, "You have to think carefully about what you are going to ask. You can't rush into it. Ask yourself, 'What would make me react the best way if, God forbid, I were in a situation like this.' I sometimes say, 'This has got to be a terrible moment for you,' and I know there are people out there who, having heard that question, will say, 'No kidding, dummy, of course it's a terrible moment.'" But, Dean adds, sometimes those "dumb" questions have to be asked. He recalled that when he returned from reporting in the Persian Gulf, friends and even relatives frequently asked, "How could you people ask so many dumb questions at those news conferences? You know they are not going to answer a question about when the ground war is going to start."

Dean said his response was, "I've made a career out of asking dumb questions. I mean that's our job—not to prove how smart we are but to elicit answers, and I think you sometimes have to ask what appears to be a dumb question. I am not out there to impress the audience that I have brilliant questions all the time. I am old-fashioned enough to believe that the idea is to get some news at the other end of the question."

REPORTER IMAGE   As was said earlier, many Americans have a negative image of the news media. According to a Gallup poll, journalists ranked 10th on a list of those most trusted by the public. People trust druggists most. Police were seventh, funeral directors were eighth and bankers were ninth.

A poll conducted by Times Mirror and Gallup found that a majority of Americans believe that the news media as a whole is biased and negative, influenced by powerful organizations and unwilling to admit mistakes.

Former "CBS Evening News" anchor Walter Cronkite sees the negative view of the media, or "media-bashing," as a "normal fallout from [the media's] doing a much better job than they've done in the past. The press, for the most part," he says, "is more responsible than it's ever been before." He says it's a more intelligent and better-educated work corps.

Cronkite also says that "newspapers and to a degree, TV, are doing a much better job of investigative reporting than they used to. With each of these [investigative] stories," he says, "we alienate a portion of the population. They fail to understand the importance of a strong, tough-minded press."

Cronkite says that if reporters do not do investigative reporting, "our democracy is in much greater danger than it would be even from an irresponsible press." He says it would be much worse if the press didn't have "the guts and determination" to report the truth.

There will be more on the responsibility of the press in Chapter 18, "Ethics and the Law," and Chapter 19, "More Legal and Ethical Issues."

WORKING WITH COLLEAGUES

Reporting the news is a team effort. Getting along with colleagues is essential. Young reporters just beginning their careers should watch and listen to the seasoned staff members. Seeking their advice lets them know that they are appreciated. When that happens, there is little that they will not do to help a reporter, which is important when the reporter needs a cameraperson to skip lunch or a tape editor to spend an extra 30 minutes in the morgue looking for "just the right file footage" for a story.

It is also important to remember that reputations follow reporters from station to station. News managers like team players. They hire reporters who have demonstrated in previous positions that they are cooperative and eager to learn and grow.

SUMMARY

This chapter describes the skills and character traits of a good journalist. While few reporters have *all* of the qualifications, the most successful ones strive toward them.

Here is a list of those skills and character traits:

accuracy	fairness
news judgment	good research habits
concern and caring	aggressiveness
curiosity	sensitivity
persistence	

Developing such skills will make your life, as well as your career, more interesting and rewarding.

REVIEW QUESTIONS

1. What is the most important skill required of a reporter?

2. News judgment is a difficult concept to express even for veteran journalists. How would you explain it?

3. Can news judgment be developed? Explain.

4. What other character and personality traits should a reporter possess?

5. How aggressive should reporters be when they are trying to get a story?

6. Reporters should always strive to be fair when they are covering stories. What does that entail?

7. Reporters are sometimes accused of being insensitive. How should reporters ask questions of someone who is involved in a tragedy?

EXERCISES

1. Switch from station to station at the top of the local news, and note whether the stations are leading the news with the same or different stories. Which story would you have led with? Defend your choice.

2. Accompany a radio or TV reporter on a story, and observe how he or she handles an interview and works it into the story.

3. Interview a radio or TV reporter, and find out how he or she prepares for an assignment before leaving the newsroom.

4. Visit a newsroom, and find out what kind of research books, audio or video morgues, and computer resources are available for writers and reporters looking for background information. Turn in a report on your findings.

CHAPTER 11

REPORTING ASSIGNMENTS

eporters spend most of their careers covering *spot news,* which dominates the contents of all radio and TV newscasts. Spot news includes fires, accidents, holdups and other incidents that occur every day, with varying frequency, in every city and town in the nation.

As Chapter 9 mentioned, reporters learn about most spot news stories from the police and fire radio advisories. Tips from viewers and listeners can also provide the first word on a spot news story.

This chapter discusses the most common type of spot news stories, and Chapter 12, "Covering Planned Events," examines a variety of other typical assignments. The purpose of these two chapters is to describe the various types of assignments and to highlight the things that reporters must remember to do in covering them.

Most of the discussion focuses on editorial decisions. Remember, however, that television is a visual medium, and the success of reporting for television depends to a large degree on the pictures taken by camerapeople. Establishing a good working relationship with a cameraperson is also discussed in this chapter.

FIRES

The decision on whether to cover a fire usually is based on the amount of destruction it is causing. Sometimes a relatively small fire can have tragic results if it occurs in an occupied house, particularly in the middle of the night when people are asleep.

These are the considerations on the news director's or assignment editor's mind when news of a fire first breaks. In a large city such as New York, there would not be enough reporters to cover other news if reporters were assigned to every fire. There are just too many of them. A cameraperson may be sent to cover a burning, empty warehouse, and the video may provide 20 seconds on the 6 o'clock news. In the same city, such a fire may not even be mentioned on radio newscasts unless the blaze lasted for hours or caused some tie-up in traffic or injuries to firefighters. In a small town, a fire of any kind may be a major story and call for a reporter at the scene. A fire in a residential area is almost always news, regardless of the size of the community, once it has been determined that the dwelling is occupied and lives are in jeopardy.

Once at the scene, the radio and TV reporters look for the same kind of information: Are there any injuries or deaths? Are there any people in the building? If it's an industrial building, what is burning? Is the material hazardous? How many firefighters and pieces of equipment are at the scene? How did the fire start? And finally, is there any question of arson?

Reporters get most of this information from the fire official in charge. The official doesn't always know the answers to some questions, but they must be asked anyway. The radio reporter gets the answers on a tape recorder, and the TV reporter's cameraperson videotapes or beams the interview back to the station via microwave or satellite. Because of new technology, radio reporters also can go live from a scene without depending on the phone or two-way radio in the mobile unit. Using a cellular telephone, the reporter can move about at the scene and file the report whenever it's ready. By plugging a tape recorder into the phone jack, the reporter has the ability to go live with a previously recorded interview or to isolate an actuality for use in the middle of a live open and close (wraparound).

The radio and TV reporters at the fire scene also look for other people to interview—those who escaped from the building, those who might have seen the fire start or, in the case of fatalities, friends or relatives of those who died in the building. The radio reporter also records the natural sound of the fire and the battle to put it out, and the TV cameraperson does the same on videotape.

Station WISC-TV in Madison, Wisc., won the 1992 Radio and Television News Directors Association first-place award for spot news for its coverage of a most unusual fire. Here's the station's 10 o'clock news report on the fire, which was still in progress at the time.

A fire in this warehouse in Madison, Wisc., caused tens of millions of dollars in damage and kept broadcast news organizations busy for days.

PHOTO BY KATHY OZATKO. USED BY PERMISSION OF THE CAPITAL TIMES.

	(Beth V/O)
WIDE LIVE SHOT	An enormous four-alarm fire is still raging on Madison's east side, seven hours after it began. The warehouse owner came home from vacation tonight:

SOT	SOT
Kenny Williams	"I just can't believe it. It's
Warehouse Owner	taken a lifetime of work."
RUNS :03	
TWO SHOT	(Beth O/C)

Good evening everyone. Dozens of firefighters are still trying to put out the fire at the Central Storage Warehouse on Cottage Grove Road.

(John)

And tonight they're having limited success.

FILE TAPE #1009   The three buildings are the size of two football fields. Tonight two of them are ruined and dozens of firefighters are battling to save the third.

The blaze broke out when a fork-lift battery exploded in mid-afternoon. It set off what likely will go down in history as this city's costliest fire, in the tens

of millions of dollars for the
building alone. That doesn't count
the 51 million pounds of food
stored inside that is causing environmental concerns.

New Three's Joel DeSpain begins
our coverage.

Package   (SOT)
Font: Joel DeSpain
      Reporting

Font: 4309 Cot-
tage Grove Rd.

                                 (Package outcue: Standard)
O/C TWO SHOT   John O/C
                             The fire isn't the only huge con-
                             cern tonight . . .

                                         Beth
                             There's also a big environmental
                             impact, and it deals with a river
                             of food washing down the street.
Key Live/Remote   News Three's Roger Putnam joins us
                             live with the story.

Remote   (Roger remote)
                             City crews are keeping waist-deep
                             grease from clogging city lines.

Package   SOT
                                  (standard outcue)
Question after   Roger, how are they doing battling
package   this melted butter and hot dog
                             problem?

```
Roger remote con-              (Roger remote)
tinues
O/C                                John O/C

                          At least two Madison-area companies

                          had products in the warehouse. Oscar

                          Mayer lost about four million dol-

                          lars worth of meats but says the

                          loss won't have much of an impact.

                             Certco, a grocery delivery com-

                          pany, had frozen foods stored there —

                          it's not known how much. And Swiss

                          Colony has used the warehouse be-

                          fore, but it wasn't confirmed that

                          products were there today.


O/C                                (Beth)

                          Several accidents tonight as a re-

                          sult of the fire, but nothing seri-

                          ous.


V/O (NAT/SOT)                      (V/O)

                          Stoughton Road was blocked off for

                          more than four hours. Debris from

                          explosions at the fire was falling

                          onto Stoughton Road creating a

                          safety hazard. Dempsey and Atlas

                          Roads were also congested.
```

WISC-TV continued its coverage throughout the night.

ACCIDENTS   Accidents are another common type of spot news stories. Reporters cover a variety of accidents during their careers. When people talk of accidents, they tend
to mean traffic accidents, which certainly do provide a lot of news. But there are
many other accidents that occupy a reporter's time: trains jump tracks, cranes

fall at construction sites, children fall out of windows, small planes collide and buildings collapse. Most of the time, such accidents—and many others—call for reporter coverage.

But traffic accidents do get the most attention, even when they do not result in deaths or injuries. A chainlike collision involving a dozen or more cars on a snow-covered major highway is certain to attract reporters. Radio reporters know that drive-time audiences will be interested because of the effect such a pile-up may have on getting to and from work, and TV reporters and crews want to be at the scene for pictures and interview possibilities. TV audiences, at least in the minds of news directors and assignment editors, are fascinated by the sight of a dozen cars wrecked on a highway. Fortunately, most of those chainlike accidents produce more totaled cars than deaths and injuries. The drunk-driving accidents are the deadly ones, and reporters find little joy in covering them.

CRIME

The police radios chatter endlessly in all newsrooms. The information these radios provide sends reporters to many traffic accidents and also to the scene of holdups, gang battles, homicides, drug busts and scores of other incidents that require police attention.

The crime that gets the most news coverage is homicide. Americans kill one another more than people in any other country, and the great majority of these homicides seem to be reported on radio and TV newscasts. It is not unusual in a major city to have more than one homicide to cover at the same time. As macabre as it sounds, assignment editors sometimes have to decide which homicides to ignore and which to cover.

Reporters working nights frequently get burned out covering murders night after night. The scripts all tend to sound alike after a while. Reporters talk to police in an effort to find out what happened and, more often than not, the word *drugs* is in the sound bite. There are sound and video of crying relatives, questions to witnesses and shots of the body bags.

Crimes other than murder are also news. The decision whether to cover other crimes, such as holdups and gang battles, depends to a large degree on the circumstances, the size of the market and what other news is going on at the same time. In a large city, a holdup would only bring a reporter to the scene if people were seriously injured or taken hostage or if an enormous amount of money was involved. In a small community, even an injury-free holdup of a convenience store might attract a broadcast reporter to the scene.

It may sound obvious, but reporters must always remember that a person charged with a crime is considered innocent until proved guilty. The fact that someone is charged with a crime does not mean he or she is guilty; police make mistakes. It's up to a judge or jury to decide whether someone is guilty or not guilty. It is important to remember that many accused people walk out of court free.

Before the courts reach a verdict, a reporter must always say the defendant is "accused of" or "charged with." A reporter must never take on face value what a police officer or detective says at the scene of a crime. A reporter may be told that John Doe was stopped in his car and a pound of heroin was found in the trunk. It is irresponsible reporting to go on the air and say: "Police find a pound of heroin in a Center City man's car trunk. Details in a moment." The words *police say* or *police charge* are critical, even in a headline. It is the reporter's job to make sure the defendant is treated fairly in any broadcast about a crime.

POLICE-MEDIA RELATIONS

Most of the time, the media and police cooperate. There are times when police complain that the media do not treat them fairly. The now-famous Los Angeles case in which a video camera showed police officers beating motorist Rodney King received national media attention, and the acquittal of the police officers of the charge of using excessive force brought on riots in Los Angeles and other parts of the nation.

Before the trial, police charged that the story had received too much attention and that the media had smeared the entire Los Angeles police force because of the actions of a few. The media started looking more closely at the actions of police departments in other cities, and police in those cities started to feel that they, too, were attacked because of what happened in Los Angeles. The result was an overall strain in relations between police and reporters. But journalists have a job to do, and what happened in Los Angeles deserved the media attention it received. Whether it was blown out of proportion is debatable.

While police and the media usually *do* get along, police can make jobs tough for reporters who do *not* "get along" with them. Tempers are lost sometimes, but the Hollywood detective movie stereotype of the police and reporters constantly at one another's throats is much overworked. Many detectives and reporters become friends because of their working relationships, and those relationships are invaluable.

THE COURTS

Those arrested by police wind up in criminal court unless the defendants are under 16 years old; people under that age are handled by the juvenile courts. Domestic relations courts also get some cases involving marital disputes.

A second court system, the civil courts, handles noncriminal matters—civil suits between individuals, between individuals and corporations and other institutions, and between two or more companies. These suits, for the most part, are about money. Someone wants payment for damages. It could be for libel, an unpaid bill, shoddy workmanship, an auto-accident injury or scores of other reasons.

There also are federal courts to deal with matters that in one way or another involve the federal government or federal laws.

This section concentrates on the courts that most reporters cover—criminal and civil.

CRIMINAL COURTS

Depending on the state, city or town involved, there are a variety of court procedures before a defendant comes to trial. In small communities, a defendant may appear first before a justice of the peace, or he or she may appear in a county court. The defendant could be released on bail or remanded to jail to await a court hearing. In minor cases, a judge may hear the case and render a verdict unless the defendant requests a jury trial.

In cities, the defendant usually is brought first to a police station where he or she is *booked*—formally charged, photographed and fingerprinted. Depending on the time of day of the arrest and booking, the defendant appears in court the same day or the next, where he or she enters a plea and is released on bail or sent back to jail to await arraignment and the setting of a trial date. More serious crimes are sometimes turned over to a grand jury, which examines the evidence and decides whether the accused should be indicted and stand trial or be released.

If the defendant is a celebrity, radio and TV reporters usually cover the court appearances even if the charge is relatively minor. More serious crimes—such as rape or homicide—draw a crowd of reporters in many instances. Because there are so many killings in large cities, radio and television reporters virtually ignore many of them. Assignment desks send reporters to homicide arraignments only if there is something unusual about the killing or if the defendant or victim is well-known.

In smaller cities such as Richmond, Va., and Baton Rouge, La., which have unusually high numbers of homicides in proportion to their size, every homicide is big news. Each one gets complete coverage along with a reminder of the standings: "The city's 64th homicide of the year was reported tonight."

REPORTER ACCESS

Although many courts are easing restrictions on cameras and recorders in courtrooms, many still bar such equipment. When they are allowed, it usually is on a pool basis. Some courts allow reporters with cameras and tape recorders to question lawyers, prosecutors, defendants and others in the corridors, while others restrict the media to remaining outside the courthouse.

Good reporters attend the court hearings and trials even if the equipment is barred. They take detailed notes on what goes on for use in their reports. The reporter not only looks for important remarks and choice quotes from the judge, prosecutor, defense counsel and witnesses but also makes note of facial expressions and other signs of emotion. If it's a jury trial, the reactions of the jury members are particularly important because they may give some clue as to how the case is going.

When cameras are not allowed in the court during an important case, an artist is usually assigned along with the reporter to do sketches of the principal figures.

CIVIL COURTS

When people believe that they have been damaged in one way or another by individuals, professionals or companies, they may seek redress by suing in civil court. The suit may be for libel, malpractice, failure to live up to a contract or to pay a bill, or divorce (just to name a few). The loser in civil court usually ends up paying money. No one goes to jail as they once did when debtor prisons existed. However, refusal to pay court-ordered alimony or child support would be considered contempt of court, and *that* could put the guilty party in jail.

Radio and TV newsrooms do not assign reporters to many civil court trials or hearings because most of the cases tend to be dull and relatively unimportant. However, an unusual malpractice case involving millions of dollars or a class action suit against an auto company for allegedly building an unsafe vehicle attracts the broadcast media to the courthouse. Reporters also cover civil cases when celebrities are seeking damages for libel or are involved in a scandalous divorce or paternity suit.

As far as reporting assignments go, the rules are the same as those for covering the criminal courts. Attend the hearings and trials, take notes (particularly if you can't use equipment inside), and try to speak with both sides outside the courthouse.

DEMONSTRATIONS The right to demonstrate is one of the freedoms we enjoy in the United States, and hundreds of thousands of people, maybe more, take advantage of this freedom each year. Radio and TV reporters do not cover every demonstration, but if the organizers know their business, they can almost always orchestrate a demonstration to guarantee media coverage. Regardless of the nature of the demonstration, the primary responsibility of the reporter is to avoid being "used."

With the possible exception of issues of civil rights and U.S. involvement in the Vietnam War, the battle over abortion has brought out more protesters than any other controversy. Americans on both sides of the issue are dedicated to their cause, and they spend a great deal of time defending, or trying to close, abortion clinics. The picture and sound possibilities are always good at such demonstrations, so a high percentage of them will get radio and TV coverage. The right-to-life demonstrators are likely to have their children in tow and an assortment of picket signs accusing abortion clinics of murder; often they may be carrying a fetus in a jar. The pro-choice advocates have their share of signs and are extremely vocal in pleading their case that a woman should have control over her body.

Reporters cannot allow themselves to get caught up in all this frenzy. Once the media arrive at the scene, the crowd gets louder and more agitated; the arrival of the TV cameras brings the noise to a peak. If you see this happening, wait until the crowd gets back to normal or near normal. Turning the camera off, and moving away from the crowd for a few minutes, is often effective.

The reporter should find a spokesperson in the group and get a statement. It is *not* the reporter's role to debate the merits of the controversy with the individual. The reporter should also knock on the door of the clinic and try to talk with someone inside.

Quite frequently, both sides will show up at the same site. That makes the reporter's job of being fair even easier. Remember that regardless of what the demonstration is about, the reporter must always get the views of both sides.

RIOTS

Demonstrations sometimes get out of hand and turn into riots. And sometimes riots just break out on their own—in prisons, among workers involved in a strike, or on city streets following a racial incident. The most sensational rioting in recent years followed the verdict in the Rodney King trial in California.

There are special rules for covering such events. The most important one: reporters should *never* put themselves or the crew in unnecessary danger. It is impossible to determine, or even guess, what an unruly mob will do, and it could just as easily as not turn its anger on the media.

Nighttime is particularly dangerous. Camera lights invite trouble, and most news directors tell their crews not to use them. Today's cameras do a credible job with just street lights. News managers suggest that crews use telephoto lenses if the situation shows the least sign of becoming dangerous.

Helicopters have eliminated some of the danger. All seven VHF-TV stations in Los Angeles had helicopters in the air videotaping the looting and rioting that followed the Rodney King trial verdict.

Reporter Christine Devine of KTTV-TV in Los Angeles conducts an interview during the rioting that followed the acquittal of police officers charged in the beating of Rodney King.
PHOTO BY MIKIHOLO

DISASTERS

A disaster, according to the dictionary, is any unfortunate event that happens suddenly; a calamity or catastrophe. Hurricanes and tornadoes often produce disasters. A plane crash or the sinking of a vessel is also a disaster, if many lives are lost.

Some reporters never experience a disaster. But those working in tornado or hurricane areas and in cities with major airports will probably cover one eventually. The horror of disasters creates an emotional and trying experience for reporters.

Although it's often difficult, reporters covering a disaster *must* get the facts straight. That may sound obvious, but because of the magnitude of a disaster, there is a lot of confusion. All sorts of people will be talking to reporters, and it often is difficult to tell which version is accurate. A reporter must check and double-check all information. If something sounds suspicious, it should be reported with specific attribution. If there are two versions of casualty figures, for example, the reporter should give both figures, with attribution, and advise the audience of the discrepancy. This is better than trying to guess which figures are accurate and running the risk of having to make a correction later. The key point: When in doubt, be cautious.

TRAGEDIES

A tragedy is a form of disaster on a smaller scale. But for the friends and relatives of a couple and five children killed in a fire, the event is no less a disaster.

For reporters, tragedies are often more painful to cover than full-blown disasters because they become more personal. Regardless of how tough a reporter

Victims of Hurricane Andrew leave what remains of a trailer park in Homestead, Fla.
AP/WIDE WORLD PHOTOS

thinks he or she is, the sight of five small body bags being removed from a burned-out building has a strong emotional impact. Reporters can cry, and sometimes do, alone. But they must report such stories as dispassionately as possible and move on to the next one.

For some the emotion is too strong. More than a few will quit.

KEEPING IN TOUCH

The news director and the assignment editor always must know what's going on "out there." If, for example, a demonstration is getting out of hand and is turning into a riot, the newsroom must be told. Any changes in stories, even the routine ones, should be reported. There is nothing that irritates an assignment editor more than a crew and reporter who "disappear."

A reporter must keep the desk informed as much as possible on the status of a story. Is it running late? Is it falling apart? Is the video poor? All of these things and more must be shared so that those working on the newscast in the newsroom know what to expect. They also have the right to expect the reporter and crew to return early enough so that the story can be edited and aired on time. The team in the field should figure out a *cut-off* time—the time at which they must stop shooting and start to pack up their gear and head for home.

WAR REPORTING

Most journalists will never be required to cover a war or other military action, so offering advice on how to do so might not seem necessary. The journalists who reported from Vietnam and Korea and during World War II would probably say there is not much advice they could give, other than the obvious about reporting accurately and objectively, because the rules have changed. They changed in Grenada and then even more drastically in the Persian Gulf during Desert Storm.

Historically, war correspondents have been permitted to walk onto beaches with U.S. Marines and to sit in the belly of a bomber on a run over an enemy target if they wanted to risk their necks in such endeavors. Many did, and some died. That kind of reporting allowed the people at home to know firsthand how the war was progressing and what was happening to their loved ones. But during the Vietnam War, the first to be brought into American homes via television, something else happened. Americans saw more dramatically than ever before what war was really like. And they would eventually see, despite the efforts of the military and various administrations to keep it from them, that the United States was losing the war.

Many generals and politicians still blame the media, particularly television, for the withdrawal of U.S. forces from Vietnam. Many journalists maintain that the military learned a lesson in Vietnam: never again to allow the media the kind of unrestricted reporting they were permitted in Vietnam.

The invasion of Grenada was virtually complete before the media were allowed to report from the island. National security was cited as the reason for the secrecy. As for Desert Storm, Doug Ramsey, of the Foundation for America

Communications, said there were "two great victories in the Gulf War: the allies decisively defeated the Iraqi military and the American military decisively defeated American news organizations."

Ed Fouhy, a 25-year network news veteran, said that as a result of Vietnam, the military not only instituted pool coverage of wars, but they also "sent their officers to charm school, and to make sure the briefers were people with stars on their shoulders—not bars as they were in Vietnam." Fouhy said the Pentagon made a political decision to control information.

The chairman of the Radio and Television News Directors Association, Jeffrey Marks, said the military engaged in "news management." He said, "We were maneuvered away from the stories we wanted to cover. Trips into the field were orchestrated to show only what the military wanted America to see and hear. . . . Reports were censored for reasons of pride, not security."

NPR Correspondent Deborah Amos, who reported from the battlefield, said the ability to report was "personality driven." She said, "If you had a decent public affairs officer, it got done. If you had an officer who was suspicious of the media, then your life was hell."

Former CBS News Anchor Walter Cronkite told Congress that "with an arrogance foreign to the democratic system, the U.S. military in Saudi Arabia is trampling on the American people's right to know."

A group of news organizations was so disturbed by the censorship in the gulf that it filed a suit in U.S. District Court in New York against the Defense Department, charging the department with imposing unconstitutional restrictions on the media during the Gulf War.

CBS News Correspondent Robert McKeown, who was the first journalist to report live from the front lines on the night the ground war began and the first reporter to report live from Kuwait City (arriving even before allied troops), said there was "greater manipulation of the press than there had ever been before." But he said it didn't affect his reporting a bit because he and some others

NPR News Correspondent Deborah Amos prepares to report from Kuwait during the Gulf War.
PHOTO BY NEAL CONAN

"decided to be illegal from the beginning and not to be part of the press restrictions and pool."

But McKeown said the censorship affected the networks overall and the war was covered "to only a fraction of what it should have been, given the technology."

McKeown was able to scoop many of his colleagues because he was equipped with a mobile satellite dish. He said CBS decided to invest millions of dollars in the rolling dishes because it wanted to be ready when the ground war came. He said the network ran into delays of four or five days in getting material broadcast during the air war, and the network "wanted to make sure that wouldn't happen when the ground war started."

McKeown disputed the Pentagon's claim that pool coverage was necessary because of national security. He said that he saw many things in the desert that could have presented a security problem if he had reported them, but that he didn't even though he had the ability to go live at any time.

The CBS news correspondent said, "It is not our job to compromise national security. The system always has been built on a system of checks and balances and a responsible press. A responsible TV reporter would not report stories that jeopardized national security, and we didn't."

CNN's Peter Arnett, a Pulitzer Prize winner for his reporting in Vietnam, was the subject of much controversy for his reporting from Baghdad after all other Western correspondents were forced out of the Iraqi capital. Arnett's reports were censored by the Iraqis, which troubled many people who felt his reports could not be trusted and might help the enemy.

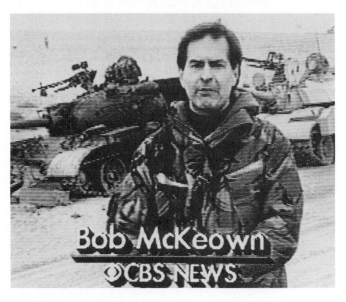

CBS News Correspondent Bob McKeown reports from Kuwait during the Gulf War.
AP/WIDE WORLD PHOTOS

In defense of Arnett, New York Times TV critic Walter Goodman said that Arnett "was doing what any journalist would do." He noted that the other networks would also have liked to have had a reporter in the city if they could have managed it.

Goodman added: "The notion of American correspondents reciting reports approved by the enemy is uncomfortable, but noncoverage is not an attractive alternative. The best the journalist can do in enemy territory is to make plain to viewers and readers the conditions under which he or she is permitted to operate and try to slip in more information than the minders have in mind."

The TV critic stressed that while he could not fault Arnett for staying in Iraq, "the question nags" whether he and other reporters in Baghdad "adapted too readily to their host's scenario, whether they might not have found more ways to talk to viewers over, behind, beneath, and around those friendly minders."

BEATS

During their careers, reporters cover most of the types of spot news stories just discussed. Some reporters may have one particular type of story assigned to them as their *beat*.

Unfortunately, not too many radio and TV newsrooms use the *beat* method of reporting, which was developed by—and is still a tradition at—newspapers. Most broadcast managers argue that they do not have the budgets that would allow them to assign reporters to beats. They note that news is only a small percentage of what is viewed on television every day, while newspapers devote most of their attention to it. Many people believe broadcast news suffers because it does not have enough beat reporters.

The networks and some large-market stations, however, do have beat reporters—journalists assigned to special areas such as the environment, medicine or business. A firm believer in the beat system is Marty Haag, vice president, news, for the A.H. Belo Corporation, which owns five TV stations, including KHOU in Houston and WFAA in Dallas. Haag says he uses a beat system at WFAA. He has reporters assigned to politics, medicine, courts, police, education and city hall. One reporter is also assigned to features and another to consumer issues and problems. WFAA also has bureaus in Austin, the state capital, and in Washington, D.C. Haag has 23 reporters.

WFAA's beat reporters devote all of their time to beat reporting, while beat reporters for the other stations in the Belo group split their time between beat and general assignment reporting. Haag says he believes in the beat system because "the world is too complicated. The beat reporter knows what he's writing about; you have someone who is familiar with the players."

Haag says the beat system also allows WFAA "to compete with newspapers. We don't want to be clipping stories out of the newspapers and then covering them," he says. "We want to be ahead of them not behind them."

Another believer in the beat system is Ed Godfrey, news director of WAVE-TV in Louisville, but his reporting staff numbers only 11, half the number Haag has in Dallas. Of course, Louisville is much smaller than Dallas. Godfrey,

The newsroom at WFAA-TV, Dallas
COURTESY OF DON WALL, WFAA-TV

a former president of the Radio and Television News Directors Association, has beat reporters cover city hall, the state capitol, medicine and consumer news. He says beat reporters give a news operation two important advantages: They can enterprise stories and cultivate sources.

But Godfrey says there are some disadvantages to beat reporting. Sometimes, he says, the reporters "get too close to their beats and wind up with stories not interesting to a general audience." Another problem, he says, is that beat reporters sometimes "get too close to their sources and can lose their objectivity." But he quickly adds that the advantages of beat reporting "far outweigh the disadvantages."

In Phoenix, KTSP-TV News Director Dave Howell wishes he had "the luxury of enough reporters to work on beats full time." His newsroom, he says, is like most: "You wind up with a hybrid, part general assignment and part beat reporter." KTSP does have a full-time health reporter because, Howell says, research shows that more people are interested in health than in any other area except the weather.

There will be more on beat reporting in Chapter 20, "Specialty Reporting." Both general-assignment reporters and beat reporters need to be concerned with two aspects of broadcast reporting: advancing the story and avoiding the pack.

ADVANCING THE STORY

If news were a commodity, it would be a bad investment because it doesn't last long; it's perishable. So, reporters must keep looking for new angles to try to update, or *advance*, it. Chapter 4 discussed the need to update the lead of the story so that the news sounded fresh even if it were not.

Updating a story—putting a new lead on it—is only part of what is involved in advancing a story. A new lead reporting, for example, that the death toll in an air disaster climbs from 100 to 115 does advance the story, but it is a rather routine update for such a story. In the more traditional sense, this story could be advanced if, for example, the cause of the crash was determined or it was suddenly discovered that a famous person was on the plane. The story also could be advanced if a reporter learned that this particular type of aircraft had been involved in a series of similar crashes in recent months or if a reporter discovered that the FAA was about to ground all planes of the same make as the one that crashed.

AVOIDING THE PACK

Good reporters are always looking for an unusual angle for their stories. Sometimes it is difficult to report a story differently from other reporters because the lead seems so obvious. But finding a new twist to a story is what distinguishes some reporters from the rest of the pack.

ABC News Correspondent Morton Dean says he tries to get "an edge" on his colleagues by doing research before he goes out on a story. "I try to get as much background and history as I can," says Dean. "I try to find my own sources. I try to make an extra phone call. One way or another I try to find a nugget of information that might give me an edge."

CBS News Correspondent Robert McKeown notes that "good reporters aren't to be found" in the pack. They are out seeking people other than officials. He also says it's important to "know the beat and become familiar with it so that you sound like you know what you are talking about when a story develops. You should have a sense of what is really happening."

ESTABLISHING RAPPORT WITH THE CAMERAPERSON

The beginning of this chapter mentioned that a good relationship between a reporter and cameraperson is essential. Here are some suggestions and observations on establishing that relationship.

ABC News Correspondent Morton Dean says it is always a good idea "to discuss with the cameraperson what you are looking for, what your expectations are, and what you plan to do with the story."

CBS News Correspondent Robert McKeown gives much of the credit for his successful reporting during the Gulf War to his cameraman, David Green, and his satellite technician, Andy Thompson. McKeown and his crew had a high-tech mobile unit that allowed them to set up a transmitter that sent a live TV signal to a satellite, which relayed the signal some 23,000 miles to CBS studios in New York. McKeown says most people are not aware of the cooperative effort that goes into the news that they see on their screens.

NBC News Correspondent Bob Dotson advises a reporter to look for help and advice from the cameraperson. "They should have a shorthand, kind of like what a married couple would have," he says. "If you have this sort of camaraderie, the cameraperson is going to think, maybe for the first time in his life, that somebody thinks what he's doing is important."

Dotson credited Tom Zannes, a free-lance cameraman for NBC, for the outstanding video used in Dotson's excellent package about a woman trapped in a cavern in Carlsbad, N.M. (The script for this package appears in Chapter 5.) Zannes was in the cavern with the team that was exploring it for the Encyclopaedia Britannica when a member of the team slipped and broke her leg. When Dotson arrived at the scene to cover the story, Zannes was still in the cave. Dotson said Zannes was allowed to remain there during the rescue because he is a world-class caver and because "he knew when to take pictures and when to put the camera down and help with the rescue."

Former CBS News Correspondent Ben Silver says that if there is not a close working relationship between the reporter and the cameraperson, each may go off in a different direction, and they won't end up with a good product. "If you want camerapeople to get good video for your story," he says, "they have to know where you're going with the story."

Silver, now professor emeritus at Arizona State University, says reporters should remember that camerapeople frequently have journalism backgrounds and have good ideas too. "Two sets of eyes are better than one," he says, "and three sets of eyes are even better." Moreover, Silver notes, when reporters are working on a story, strangers will sometimes approach them with information. "Listen to them," Silver advises, "they may have seen something you and the cameraperson missed because you were busy doing something else. You always have to keep an open mind."

SUMMARY

Most of the reporting jobs in radio and television are general-assignment positions. Reporters with these jobs cover everything they are told to cover; most of their stories are spot news stories. Spot news deals with everyday breaking stories—fires, accidents, crimes, disasters and so on. Some stations and the networks use beat reporters—reporters assigned to specific topics, such as education, politics and health.

Whether you cover general assignments or a beat, remember that good reporters learn how to advance a story—find new information to keep a story fresh—and how to find a new angle from which to develop a story.

REVIEW QUESTIONS

1. What are spot news stories? Give some examples.

2. What factors are taken into consideration when a decision is made on covering a crime or a fire?

3. Journalists must be especially careful with stories about defendants in a criminal case. How is that done?

4. Why does an assignment editor or news director decide to cover some court cases and pass up others?

5. What precautions should reporters and crews take to ensure that a demonstration is covered fairly?

6. What precautions should reporters and crews take in covering a riot?

EXERCISES

1. Arrange with a news director or assignment editor to follow a reporter when he or she is assigned to a breaking news story. Report on what happened at the scene and how the reporter covered the story.

2. Attend a pro-life or pro-choice demonstration, and report on how the media covered the story. Make note of the radio and TV reporters who covered the demonstration and monitor their wraps and packages to see if the reports were balanced and fair.

3. Check the local newspaper(s) to see how the demonstration was covered by print reporters. Write a report comparing the print and broadcast coverage.

4. Monitor a local TV newscast, and see how many spot news stories were reported. What other types of stories were in the newscast?

CHAPTER 12

COVERING PLANNED EVENTS

here are literally thousands of corporations, politicians, special-interest groups, nonprofit organizations, government agencies and other individuals and groups looking for exposure on network and local newscasts. Assignment desks are inundated with news releases and telephone calls from public-relations firms and publicists working for these various groups. Many stations also have a special public-relations wire in the newsroom that allows organizations to get their releases to the assignment editor more quickly.

Every one of these publicists tries to persuade the assignment staff that there is something special or important about the product, company, issue or individual they represent. The assignment desk rejects most of these news releases and telephone calls for a variety of reasons—usually because they are too commercial or have little or no news value, or because there just isn't enough air time available to go around. But some of these releases and telephone calls alert the assignment staff to events that are important, and they warrant coverage.

NEWS CONFERENCES

Gathering a crowd of journalists with tape recorders and cameras in one room is a triumph for anyone working in public relations. The number who attend such news conferences depends on what is being "sold." Make no mistake about it, that is what we are talking about—"selling."

It makes no difference whether the news conference is called by a government official, a Broadway producer, a major corporation or the Red Cross; each news conference has a message that it wishes to sell to the American people. For example, the district attorney may call a meeting with the news media to announce the arrest of several organized-crime bosses. The arrest is news, of course, but the district attorney also wants to let everyone know what a good job he or she and the department are doing.

The Broadway producer is betting that the media will turn out to hear about a new show because the release just happens to mention that the chorus line will be there in full costume.

The Red Cross is hoping for the best but knows that not too many broadcast reporters will show up at its news conference to discuss a blood shortage because it's not likely to provide good pictures for television or exciting sound

Setting up for a news conference
PHOTO BY JAMES TERRY

bites for radio. The conference may get a 20-second read story on the 6 o'clock news. You might wonder why a blood shortage is not considered an important story. It is, but it probably will get more attention from newspapers than from radio and television. It just isn't a "good" broadcast story—a point of view that brings on a lot of criticism of broadcast news, much of which is justified.

That same morning, General Motors is holding news conferences in the convention center in your city and in various key locations throughout the country to display its new line of cars, including, as its news release boasts, a compact car that gets 40 miles to the gallon and supposedly will "recapture the market dominated by the Japanese." As you might expect, every radio station, TV station and newspaper as well as a score of magazines will send reporters, and the story will make every local news program and network newscast.

How do reporters get ready for news conferences? Let's look at a reporter preparing for the news conference being held by the district attorney. The reporter starts with the newspaper clip file and video morgue to see what's available on the arrested organized-crime figures. If there is video of them, she asks for it to be pulled. She reads carefully the newspaper clips on the arrested men. Before she leaves for the news conference, she also might make a quick check with other reporters in the newsroom to see if they have any additional information they gathered while covering other stories involving the men.

The reporter and her cameraperson arrive at the news conference early because it will be crowded and she wants to get a good position for the camera and herself. When the conference begins, the DA makes a prepared statement. The cameras and tape recorders will be rolling, though little of the statement—and maybe none of it—will get on the air. The question-and-answer period following the opening statement usually produces the best sound bites.

The reporter keeps notes on the statement, in any case, so she will know where the best bites are if she decides to use any of them. She does the same when the question-and-answer period begins, keeping track of the time when the best comments are made.

While she was reading the clips in the newsroom, the reporter noticed that the organized-crime leaders were arrested five years before. The DA—the same one—got a conviction, and the men were sentenced to 10 to 15 years in prison. The reporter hopes that no one else beats her to the question she is ready to fire at the DA: "How come these guys aren't still in prison? It's only five years since you grabbed them and put them away the last time." The question would surely be provocative; perhaps the answer would be one of the highlights of the news conference. In all likelihood, the DA would respond with something like, "I just convict them, ask the judges and the parole board why they are back on the street so quickly." The DA, who had been critical of the judiciary on a number of other occasions, provided anchors with the headline, "DA criticizes judge and parole board."

Sometimes it is important to ask tough questions. News conferences should not be just a forum for those calling them. It's also important to ask follow-up questions, particularly when the individual holding the news conference is evasive or unclear. Techniques for asking good questions are discussed in detail in Chapter 15, "The Interview."

Many broadcast reporters like to interview individually the person holding the news conference when the conference is over. ABC News Correspondent Morton Dean says he does this if he doesn't hear what he wants during the news conference or if he wants to go in a different direction. "Otherwise," he says, "I'll pull a bite from the news conference."

Frequently, reporters call in advance to arrange an interview with the person *before* the news conference. Some people agree; others refuse because they know it sometimes irritates other members of the media. This is particularly true when the reporter is still conducting the interview when the rest of the news corps arrives in the room. Other broadcast reporters, seeing what's going on, tell their camerapeople to set up and start shooting. Suddenly, there's a mini–news conference going on before the regular one starts. Such occurrences are particularly offensive to the print reporters, who must then wait for the scheduled news conference to begin. Once the broadcast people have their interviews, it is not unusual for them to pack their gear and be on their way, leaving the person holding the news conference with just the newspaper people. Many broadcast reporters cover news conferences this way because their assignment editors tell them to be in and out of the news conference quickly so they can move on to other stories.

Doing an interview before a news conference does have its risks. Another reporter may know something important that the early reporter missed in the one-on-one. Or a confrontation may occur when one of the print reporters asks an embarrassing question that catches the news conference host by surprise. The early reporter who came and went will not have this confrontation on tape.

**LOCAL
GOVERNMENT**

The work of city and town government is extremely important, but it also can be one of the dullest assignments radio and TV reporters must cover. The problem for broadcast reporters is that the deliberations of the city council, the board of supervisors and other local officials often take hours. The debated issues, however, often affect a great many people. An increase in local taxes, a curfew for teen-agers or a company's effort to locate a waste-disposal plant in a community brings out a big crowd and lots of journalists. Because such meetings can go on for hours and days, what do radio and TV reporters do?

Let's suppose that the Centerville town supervisors are considering an out-of-town company's offer to build a waste-burning incinerator in the town. The company claims that the facility will employ 100 people and that it will be completely safe. Centerville could use another 100 jobs. Basically a dairy-farm community of about 5,000 people, Centerville is hurting because of the recession and, as many believe, because the price of milk is not high enough for farmers to survive.

But these people are farmers because they appreciate the earth and clean air, and they are suspicious of anyone or anything that might damage the environment. A local newspaper has already reported that the company wants to burn medical waste.

More than 100 people show up at the high-school auditorium to hear exactly what the company has in mind. There is a radio station in town but no TV station. A TV reporter from a nearby city shows up along with a local radio reporter and print journalists. TV cameras and tape recorders are rolling as town officials introduce a spokesperson and an engineer from the waste-disposal company. After some lengthy statements by the two representatives—complete with charts and statistics—a heated debate begins. The broadcast reporters take detailed notes, keeping a record of who is speaking and when.

A local real estate agent says the plant would hurt property sales. "People escape the city to get away from pollution. They won't buy here if you build the plant," the agent says.

A parent questions the effect of toxic fumes on the town's children.

The company official tries to reassure the crowd, which clearly is reacting negatively to the idea of putting this plant in town. "There is absolutely nothing dangerous about anything we will be burning," the spokesperson says.

A man stands up holding a newspaper clipping. "Wasn't your company cited for not burning things right in the Carolinas?" he asks. "This story says your company left a real mess around and you were burning all sorts of dangerous things improperly."

The company official tries to explain away the story, saying, "We had a few workers who weren't doing their jobs the way they should have, but they've been replaced and things are all squared away now."

The man with the paper is still standing. "And this story says that you only employ about a dozen workers at that Carolina plant. You claim the plant here would mean 100 jobs for our town."

The debate went on for two hours, but the story prepared by the TV reporter would probably last no more than 90 seconds, maybe a little longer if the meeting took place on a slow news day. The local radio reporter would devote more time to the story because the issue is big news in Centerville. The radio reporter might do a special in-depth wrapup of the meeting in addition to some one-minute wraparounds during newscasts throughout the day. There is no local daily newspaper, only a weekly, so the townspeople are anxious to hear as much as they can on the debate.

The cameraperson with the TV reporter picked up the heated debate and stopped shooting during the dull periods. After a while, a cameraperson develops a sense for knowing when to start and stop shooting a story like this. Because the cameraperson knows that less than a minute of sound bites will make the news, it is unnecessary to shoot continuously.

After shooting the highlights of the debate, the reporter and cameraperson moved outside and interviewed some people as they left the building. Everyone they spoke with was opposed to the incinerator. In an effort to be as fair as possible, the reporter continued interviewing until she finally found a man who said he was "keeping an open mind on the matter" until he heard more. If there really would be an extra 100 jobs, he said, "I'd want to think about it."

The reporter decided they had enough material. She would have liked to do a separate interview with one of the company representatives, but there was no time. The debate had run almost two hours, and the ride back to the station would take 40 minutes. She decided to use part of the official's remarks for balance and to include some of the debate along with the interviews she conducted outside the building. She also decided to use some of the crowd shots to go along with the sound bites. The company had provided her with a video of the South Carolina plant.

The reporter opened her package with a sound bite—a *cold open.*

```
SOT Woman yelling              SOT runs :04
at meeting
                        "I'm not going to let you put any-

                        thing in my backyard that's going

                        to poison my children. . ."

V/O Crowd debating                   V/O

NAT SOUND UNDER          This woman was one of almost 100

                        people who showed up at a meeting

                        in Centerville tonight to listen

                        to a proposal that would establish

                        a waste-burning incinerator in

                        this predominantly dairy farm com-

                        munity of five thousand people.
```

SOT MAN TALKING IN CROWD. HE'S WAVING A NEWSPAPER	SOT :12
	"I don't trust your company. This story says your company left a real mess around and you were burning all sorts of dangerous things improperly. . . "
V/O SHOTS OF S.C. PLANT	The company that this man is referring to is the Medvac Waste Disposal Corporation out of Greenville, South Carolina. And there have been published reports that Medvac was fined for not properly disposing of medical waste at its plant outside Greenville.
SOT	SOT :06
FONT:BOB SMITH CEO, MEDVAC WASTE DISPOSAL	"We did have some trouble for a while, but we've corrected all those problems."
	(protest from crowd)
	(V/O)
V/O ANGRY CROWD	There was no doubt about the sentiments of most of the people assembled here tonight. These are farm people and the environment –
Video of farms and rolling hills	the land they work and the air they and their cows breathe — is precious to them. But many young people have left the farms and are desperate

	for work in Centerville. Medvac claims it would hire 100 people at the incinerator it wants to build.
SOT ANGRY MAN	SOT :08 "And what about these 100 jobs you're talking about? This story says that you only employ about a dozen workers at that Carolina plant."
V/O CROWD LEAVING HALL	V/O The debate lasted almost two hours and we only found one man who had anything positive to say about the proposed plant.
SOT O/C TWO SHOT	SOT :05 "Well if it's true that the plant would bring 100 jobs to town I'd want to think about it."
V/O VIDEO OF TOWN OFFICIALS AND OTHERS TALKING OUTSIDE HALL	V/O Town supervisors told Medvac that they would have a decision for them within 30 days. But from the tone of tonight's meeting it seems unlikely that the project will be approved. This is Laura Wright reporting from Centerville.

This package is a good example of the proper way to cover a local government meeting. Unfortunately, many local reporters cover such stories from the back of the meeting room or on the steps of city hall. In such stories, the opening shot shows the reporter and then the camera moves from the reporter to the members of the city council or other governing body. In dull fashion, the camera pans from one member to another while the reporter voices the report. There usually are no sound bites in the story, just the voice of the reporter and the nameless faces and voices of the town officials. Former CBS News Correspondent Ben Silver calls such reports "video clichés."

To avoid such uninteresting stories, the reporter covering local government meetings should find out in advance what is going to be discussed and select the most interesting subject—one that lends itself to video footage. For example, let's consider a story about the extension of sewers to a certain part of town. Before the debate, the reporter and cameraperson should go to the location, take pictures of the area and speak with some residents. Some might like the sewer idea, but others might oppose it because it would mean higher taxes.

Now when the reporter attends that public meeting and reports that the town supervisors voted to extend the sewer system, she can say, "Earlier in the day we spoke to some residents of that area and here's what they had to say." The taped comments and video of the area make better news than pictures of the reporter announcing the supervisors' decision and shots of the members voting.

The first of three presidential debates during the 1992 campaign, this one held on Oct. 11, 1992, in St. Louis, Mo. The candidates, Ross Perot (left), Bill Clinton (center), and George Bush, are responding to questions by a panel of journalists.
AP/WIDE WORLD PHOTOS

POLITICAL CAMPAIGNS

People are running for something just about everywhere. Most reporters find themselves covering a political campaign early in their career. Even relatively small communities hold elections—for mayor, sheriff, town supervisor and a number of other positions. Reporters also cover the campaigns of candidates for the state legislature, for congress and for the presidency when those candidates visit the area.

The most important requirement for reporting on politics is remaining neutral. Regardless of how reporters feel personally about the candidates, they must maintain their objectivity. Assignment editors and news directors are not going to ask reporters what their politics are when they're assigned to cover the campaign of a state assemblyperson. The reporters are expected to report fairly, without any bias, even if they think poorly of the candidate. On the other hand, it is not unusual for reporters to find that they like some candidates after they have been on the road with them. However, reporters need to watch that this admiration doesn't creep into their script. When it does, the reporter might not even be aware of it, but sometimes it is visible to the audience and other journalists.

ABC News Correspondent Barry Serafin says it is a challenge sometimes to hide personal feelings when assigned to cover one candidate. "After a while the candidate will be calling you by your first name and so will his wife. It is particularly difficult to maintain your objectivity," says Serafin, "when you like the person. It's not so bad," he adds, "if you don't like him because all your training automatically comes into effect and all the safeguards drop down. If you like him it's harder but you absolutely, positively have to keep that arm's length—that journalistic objectivity."

Serafin recalled covering Ronald Reagan during two campaigns. "I got to know him better than any other candidate, and afterwards I was happy when some of the people around him said, 'We didn't always like the stories you did but we think you were fair. We never thought you cheap-shotted us.'

"I decided that if after two campaigns they didn't like every story I did and thought I was fair, then I probably didn't do a bad job," said Serafin.

ABC "Nightline" Correspondent Jeff Greenfield also notes that a reporter runs the risk of getting to like the candidate he or she is following and sometimes "has a professional reason for wanting the candidate to do well—including taking him to the White House with him." But Serafin says that danger has been minimized because the networks now tend to rotate their political reporters.

PUTTING COMMENTS INTO PERSPECTIVE

When covering a candidate on the campaign trail, a political reporter should not just parrot the candidate's speeches. If the candidate says the same things every place he or she goes, it would be appropriate for the reporter to point that out. It would be equally important for the reporter to note when candidates change their positions on the issues depending on the kind of group they're addressing.

CBS News Anchor-Correspondent Dan Rather interviews HUD Secretary Jack Kemp at the 1992 Republican Convention in Houston.
COURTESY OF CBS NEWS

The reporter should also tell the audience things about the location of the speech and the crowd. Was the candidate speaking in a predominantly Republican or Democratic area? Was the crowd mostly white-collar or blue-collar? Obviously, if the candidate was Republican and he was addressing a crowd in an affluent area of the city, his reception could be expected to be warmer than in a ghetto. And the opposite could be expected if the candidate was a Democrat.

The crowd's reaction is important. Was it enthusiastic or relatively quiet? Was the crowd large or small? If the weather affected the turnout, that should be noted. Did people challenge the candidate's remarks? Did they seek out the candidate to shake his or her hand?

CNN Correspondent and Anchor Bernard Shaw suggests that the broadcast media should be doing more to put political statements and claims into perspective. He questions whether radio and TV stations really want to stop "attack ads." He notes that millions of dollars in ad revenue are at stake and that sales departments "are loaded with people who have never seen an ad they didn't like. But isn't there a higher calling? A higher need?" asked Shaw.

The CNN correspondent says attack ads have become news stories, and it is the responsibility of news directors to point out the distortions and to expose candidates who "work harder at ducking than discussing issues."

Shaw also suggests that the news media should let candidates know that the voters are not more interested in a "staged picture than a thousand words of discussion of issues on their minds." He speaks of the "arrogance of the candidates and their managers and their media manipulators who fly into an airport, speak for five minutes, pose for pictures for 10 minutes and get back in the plane and move on to another location."

Shaw says that when a candidate does that, there is nothing wrong with leading the newscast that night by saying, "Democratic candidate Tom Harkin thought enough of San Jose voters to spend 22 minutes at the airport today before going on to a Los Angeles fund-raiser tonight. The senator said nothing he did not say before but he did note that our weather was the best he had seen in days."

He cites another way to put a political story into perspective:

President Bush took his campaign for re-election to the Prairie View nursing home for the elderly today, promising that Democrats would tamper with Social Security over his dead body. But when he left, President Bush used a side door and his motorcade went the wrong way on a one-way street apparently to avoid some two thousand unemployed workers whose benefits had run out—benefits the president has repeatedly refused to fund, citing budgetary reasons.

Shaw says audiences are "keen for those kind of reporting distinctions. They need them for perspective on the sleights of hand that they are subjected to by politicians lusting for votes but lacking in so many ways."

Shaw also attacks some "sins" committed by politicians, citing as an example the arrogant refusal to answer reporters' questions on the issues. "But worse than the candidate's refusal to answer the question," he says, "is the news

CBS News Correspondent Charles Osgood
COURTESY OF CHARLES OSGOOD/CBS NEWS

media's complicity by generally failing to point out and underscore that the politician did not answer the question."

The CNN anchor says that every time this happens it reinforces "the politician's misguided belief that he can get away with it and voters don't care." Shaw believes it's time to stop the exploitation of the news media by politicians. "If what politicians are saying and doing is not news, why put it on the air?" he asks.

FEATURE STORIES   Covering hard news—whether spot news or planned events—is the meat and potatoes of broadcast journalism. Feature stories are the dessert. Those are the stories that often bring a smile to our faces and sometimes a tear.

CBS News Correspondent Charles Osgood is a master of the feature story. He says he gets many of his ideas from unimportant-sounding stories on the wires. For example, he once found a three-line story about the Navy's considering a change in the rank of admirals. Osgood said, "You just suck the rest of it out of your thumb." His thumb gave us this:

> The U.S. Navy wants to establish a new rank to distinguish one-star rear admirals from two-star rear admirals. They thought about it and thought about it and the proposed name for the new rank that they've come up with is "rear admiral lower half." Now if President Reagan approves "Rear Admiral Lower Half" then "Rear Admiral Lower Half" it will be. Let's consider if this is such a good idea.

> Military ranks are sort of baffling to the layman to begin with. We all know that generals and admirals are big deals, but there are many gradations inside the general and admiral category; and these are not always what you would think they would be. Major outranks a lieutenant, but a lieutenant-general outranks a major-general. A very model of a modern major-general only has two silver stars. A lieutenant-general has three. Both of them are outranked by the just plain general who has four silver stars. All three are addressed as "general" and so is the brigadier-general who has the one star. These are a dime a dozen at the Pentagon, as are admirals, of course. And there are different kinds of admirals, too. The admiral who corresponds to a four-star general is called an admiral. The admiral who corresponds to a three-star or lieutenant-general is called a vice admiral. And the one who corresponds to a major-general is called a rear admiral. The next naval rank down corresponding to a brigadier or one-star general is now called a commodore.

The U.S. Navy has now decided that its commodores should be admirals too, just as the Army's brigadiers are generals, and so the Navy has proposed a new rank called, "rear admiral lower half." You would address such an officer as admiral so-and-so, not rear half so-and-so, by the way. The abbreviation for the new rank — they have thought of everything — would be "R.A.D.M. lower half," not "R.A.L.H.," as you might think. Too bad, because then if your first name was Ralph you could be R.A.L.H. Ralph. Sort of like Major Major Major in "Catch-22."

I'm sure "Rear Admiral Lower Half" is very nautical and a great naval tradition and all of that, but what I question is whether "Rear Admiral Lower Half" brings the right sort of image to mind. The concept of rear is already somewhat puzzling, since the aft section of a ship is not called the rear, but the stern. There are a lot of stern admirals. Some of them are rear admirals and some are not. Once our attention has been called to a rear, it seems an unfortunate added indignity to specify that one is referring specifically to the lower half thereof.

How about you? Would you rather be called a commodore or a rear admiral lower half? Commodore is a little dated, admittedly. Even the Hotel Commodore isn't called the Commodore anymore. No, it isn't the Hotel Rear Admiral Lower Half either. It is now the Grand Hyatt Hotel. How about grand hyatt for the name of a new rank? Instead of rear admiral lower half so-and-so, the officer would be grand hyatt so-and-so. Grand hyatt has a certain brassy Gilbert and Sullivan flair to it. "Captain Jones, you're being promoted to the rank of grand hyatt." None of that stuff about rears and lower halves. You see what I mean?

Osgood said the nice thing about writing such stories is that "you don't have to know a lot. . . . I go to the almanac and find the different ranks in the Army and Navy and how they correspond to one another. I don't know that stuff," he added, "but you can get your hands on it easily and it's right there in the newsroom."

Features also receive a lot of attention on NPR's "All Things Considered" and "Morning Edition." Reporter Cokie Roberts wrote and produced a feature about Congressman Morris Udall for "Morning Edition." Here's the way the anchor led into the report:

Cokie Roberts reporting for ABC from the Republican National Convention in Houston in 1992. In addition to working for ABC, Roberts is a news correspondent for National Public Radio.
MARIA MELIN/CAPITAL CITIES, ABC NEWS

Anchor: One of the most respected and best-loved members of the House of Representatives is expected to announce his resignation today. Arizona Democrat Morris Udall has been suffering from Parkinson's disease for many years but in January a serious fall incapacitated the 68-year-old Congressman, leading to his likely resignation. NPR's Cokie Roberts reports:

Roberts: Mo Udall came to Congress 30 years ago as a reformer out of the West, ready to take on the structures and seniority of what was then a hidebound House of Representatives. He leaves as a senior statesman who earned the admiration and affection of his political friends and enemies through his hard work and, especially, through his humor. Mo Udall is not only a very funny man himself, he is a connoisseur and custodian of American political humor, compiled a number of years ago into a book.

(sound bite)

Udall: I was doing a chapter the other day on
           politicians' mixed metaphors and bloopers. I'll
           share a few with you today as a sort of preview if
           I can push the book a little bit (laughter). I'll
           start with Gerry Ford, who said in that famous
           speech on the House floor, "If Lincoln were alive
           today he would be turning over in his grave." And
           somebody said, perhaps it was I, "we honor Lincoln
           because he was born in a log cabin which he built
           with his own two hands." (laughter)

Roberts: The occasion of this spate of storytelling was
           Udall's 1984 announcement that he would not run
           for president again. He said the presence of other
           liberals in the race made his candidacy unneces-
           sary but, in fact, Udall was already suffering
           from the Parkinson's disease that has made the
           last several years so difficult for him. The deci-
           sion not to make the run was a tough one because
           Udall had long before been attacked by the politi-
           cal malady of presidentitis. He went for the White
           House in 1976 but after coming in second in seven
           straight primaries, Udall concluded that he drew
           more laughter than votes, causing columnist James
           Kilpatrick to declare the Arizona Democrat too
           funny to be president. That eventually became the
           title of Udall's book which was finally published
           in 1988. When NPR's Scot Simon interviewed the Con-
           gressman on his collection of political anecdotes,
           Udall — as usual — praised John Kennedy and Adlai
           Stevenson as the masters of the political quip.

(sound bite)

Udall: Stevenson had a natural sense of humor — a sense
          of the ridiculous. A good example: Stevenson went
          to one of the women's colleges up in New England
          and made a big hit and as he was leaving this
          woman shouted, "great going, Governor Stevenson,
          you got the vote of every thinking person," and he
          said, "it's not good enough, I need a majority"
          (laughter).

Roberts: It could have been his own story. Udall was never
          able to attract a majority for president or for a
          House leadership position although he ran for
          Speaker in 1969 and for majority leader in 1971.
          But he did wage a successful attack on the House
          seniority system, pushed through a landmark cam-
          paign finance bill, and as chairman of the Inte-
          rior and Insular Affairs Committee he shepherded
          several major environmental measures through Con-
          gress, including the Alaskan Lands Act. Udall suc-
          ceeded legislatively by pulling together sometimes
          impossible coalitions, often using humor as his
          thread. To Udall, the ability to amuse was essen-
          tial for a committed politician.

(sound bite)

Udall: Politics used to be entertainment. If you lived in
          a little town in South Carolina 100 years ago, you
          never saw a Presidential nominee on TV or other-
          wise. They were names in a newspaper and when the
          politicians came to town, they were expected to
          make two-hour speeches that would entertain the

troops, and now we have speech writers and gag writers in great profusion. The mere act of hiring a gag writer says I don't understand myself and the issue enough to make people laugh legitimately, I have to hire somebody to give me a false line.

Roberts: Today's generation of politicians, lamented Udall in his book, "is less seasoned, more serious, richer and less humorous. The ability to deliver a riveting speech, rich in substance and leavened with humor and anecdotes, is a declining art in Washington today."

It would have died a lot faster had Mo Udall not been here for the last three decades, savoring his stories and telling his tales.

(sound bite)

Udall: I grew up between the Navajos and the Apaches. I worked on Indian problems all my life and the Indians really appreciate this story: a politician goes to an Indian village and gathers the Indian voters around and says, "you like me, you vote for me and we get schools and hospitals for little Indian children" and they shouted "gooma, gooma" and he said, "you vote for me and we will put gas heat in every tepee," and they shouted, "gooma, gooma" and the chief said, "you white man great friend of Indian, you must come down to the corral where we are going to give you an Indian pony, but," he said, "be careful you don't step in the gooma, gooma" (laughter).

Roberts: (music under) Arizona Democrat Morris Udall, retiring today. I'm Cokie Roberts.

Features also are a basic part of local TV news, and to a lesser degree, to network TV news. Every local news producer schedules a variety of features throughout the newscast to give it balance. Viewers like, and expect to see, some feature stories to help break up the stories on crime, fires, Congressional debates, the rising price of gasoline, inflation and the seemingly never-ending issue about whether to raise or lower taxes.

TV producers try to place some sort of feature in most sections of a newscast. Features frequently come just before a commercial, but long, in-depth features sometimes lead off the portion of a newscast just *after* a commercial break.

SUMMARY

Reporters spend much of their time covering planned events. Unlike spot news, which is unpredictable, most planned events are known about by the assignment editors days and weeks in advance. These events fill part of the newscast almost every night.

A good percentage of planned events are news conferences. Because news conferences are called by people trying to "sell" something, reporters must be prepared to ask tough questions; they cannot allow themselves to be used.

Other common planned events are those provided by the workings of government—town and city council meetings and, in state capitals, meetings of the legislature. Research is important. Reporters must be familiar with the issues under discussion and be ready to ask intelligent questions about them.

Planned events are not always exciting; frequently they have few or no picture opportunities. But they are an important part of covering the news, even if they wind up as a 20-second voice-over.

Another type of non-breaking story is the feature story. Feature stories give reporters more opportunity to display their creative talents.

Every reporter has his or her favorite type of story, but you must remember that you have to learn how to cover them all, not just the colorful and exciting ones.

REVIEW QUESTIONS

1. Name some of the planned events that broadcast reporters cover.

2. How do assignment editors determine which planned events they will cover?

3. What are the chief reasons that people and organizations call news conferences?

4. How does a reporter prepare for a news conference?

5. What is the best way for broadcast reporters to cover a town or city-council meeting?

6. What is the worst way to cover such a meeting?

7. What are the most important things for you to remember when you are covering a political campaign?

EXERCISES

1. Cover a city-council or town meeting with a tape recorder or video camera. Prepare a wrap or package.

2. Attend a news conference, and prepare a wrap or package.

3. Attend a morning news meeting at a TV station, and write a report on how decisions were reached on which stories would be covered that day.

CHAPTER 13

REPORTING LIVE

hapter 10 mentioned some of the differences between broadcast reporting and newspaper reporting. This chapter discusses one of the most profound differences, the ability of broadcast reporters to deliver live reports. The chapter offers some suggestions for handling the special pressures and responsibilities that reporting live places on broadcast journalists.

Reporting live from a mobile unit has always been routine for a radio reporter. Immediacy has been radio's big advantage. Since the early days of radio, Americans have been accustomed to getting the first news of an important story from that medium. Frequently, the news has come from a radio reporter at the scene.

Radio has lost some of its advantage as new technology has made it possible for television to put a live signal into homes almost as quickly and easily as radio does. But radio continues to be first in reaching a large portion of the listening audience—those traveling on the highways.

ORGANIZING THOUGHTS

Because they broadcast live so often, radio reporters have to learn early in their careers how to organize their thoughts quickly. They also have to develop the skill of ad-libbing. Radio reporters are often expected to report from the scene of a breaking story for much longer periods than their TV counterparts because normally radio is not under the same time limitations as television. It is much easier to interrupt a music format on radio with a breaking story, for example, than it is to interrupt a soap opera on television. Lost ad revenue is far less expensive for a radio station than for television and it is much easier for a radio station to make up lost commercials.

The best way to organize material for a live report is to use a reporter's notebook. It is particularly handy because it fits into a handbag or jacket pocket. Always take more than one pen or pencil. (In freezing weather or pouring rain, a pencil works a lot better than a pen.)

In anticipation of going live from the scene, broadcast reporters must keep notes on a variety of happenings. First, they must keep track of important comments that are made, whether during a news conference or a one-on-one interview. They must note exactly when the remarks were made so they can be located quickly on the videotape or audiotape. Some reporters take courses in speedwriting; others develop a system of their own. Experienced reporters learn that they cannot get so involved in taking notes that they lose control of the interview. They make entries only when comments are important enough to be used as a sound bite or in the narration that will surround it. TV reporters who have a camera with a time code recording system that shows the actual time of day each scene is recorded only have to note the time when they hear something important.

Reporting live presents different problems for radio and TV reporters. For starters, radio reporters work alone. TV reporters have at least one and sometimes two people with them in the microwave truck.

The production of the live report also is handled differently by the TV crew from the way a radio reporter goes about it. Sometimes the news conference or individual interview is microwaved back to the station while it is in progress. An associate producer or a writer at the station may monitor the feed and make notes. When the feed is over, producers can quickly confer with the reporter on which sound bites he or she wishes to use and then instruct the tape editor to cue them up. The reporter then does a live open from the scene, and the sound bites are played from the station. The reporter returns after the bites to do a live close.

It is also possible to do everything from the mobile unit. New technology allows TV crews to record and edit video in the truck, add the reporter's narration and actually play the story from the truck without using any of the support equipment at the station. This type of sophisticated equipment is usually found only in large markets.

WTVJ-TV Reporter Ed O'Dell and Cameraman Pedro Cancio rush to the scene of a story in Miami.
COURTESY OF WTVJ-TV, MIAMI

Another major difference between reporting live for radio and TV is obvious: the audience does not see the radio reporter. It *does* see the TV reporter, which adds some complications. The radio reporter can get comfortable in the front seat of the mobile unit, cue up his tape, spread his notes out and concentrate on delivering his narration without worrying about anyone seeing him. Meanwhile, his TV colleague may be applying makeup and memorizing her script so that she is not constantly looking down at her notebook during her time on camera.

Let's examine a typical live report filed by a radio reporter from the scene of a fire.

Two people are known dead in a fire that swept through an apartment house on Rose Avenue in the suburban West End community of Center City. Fire Chief John O'Hara says he doesn't know if everyone else in the building escaped.

(sound bite)

"We think everyone but the one couple got out of there but it's too early to tell. So far no one has reported anyone missing so we are hopeful."

(reporter)

The dead have been identified as Barbara Swift and her husband Robert. It's believed the fire started in their apartment shortly after midnight and spread to the rest of the building. So far, there's no information on what caused the fire, which was brought under control about an hour after it started. More than two dozen people were in the building. One woman who escaped, Val Hills, said she is happy to be alive:

(sound bite)

"There was so much smoke, that's what scared me the most. When I heard some shouting I got up and I knew there must be a fire. Fortunately, I was able to get to the stairs and get out."

(reporter)

Some 50 firefighters and 10 pieces of equipment are still at the scene. Some of the firefighters are still hosing down the building and others are going through the debris just to make sure no one else is in there.

Once again, two people are dead in this Rose Avenue fire in the West End. It's believed that everyone else escaped from the building. This is Frank Sneed. Back to you, Bill.

Meanwhile, a TV station was carrying this story from its reporter at the scene via microwave. The story opens up with the reporter on camera and the fire scene behind her:

O/C Heather

Two bodies have been removed from this burned-out apartment building on Rose Avenue and it's not yet known if there were any other fatalities.

The fire started around midnight in one of the apartments and spread quickly through the rest of the building. Earlier, we spoke with a couple who escaped from the burning building.

SOT

Font: Frank Lewis

SOT

"We were asleep when we heard shouting and jumped out of bed. I could smell smoke. I grabbed some trousers and my wife tossed on a robe and we got the hell out of there."

Font: Laura Lewis

"I was scared stiff. I'm just happy to be alive."

(Heather)

O/C two shot

With me now is Fire Chief John O'Hara. Chief, do you think every-one is out of there?

(Chief)

"Well, we're hopeful. So far no one has reported anyone missing so

that's a good sign. But you never
can be sure."

(Heather)

Do you know how the fire started?

(Chief)

"Well, we think it started in the
apartment of the couple who died
in the fire and then spread to the
other apartments, but so far we
aren't sure how it started."

(Heather)

Thank you, Chief.

OC/ tight shot of
Heather

The couple who died in the fire
have been identified as Barbara and
Robert Swift. There was no other
information available about them.

V/O

Shots of building
and firefighters
wetting it down

V/O

As you can see, this building is
completely gutted and if everyone
else got out alive it would be
amazing. Apparently some two dozen
other people were in the building.
About 50 firefighters have been
battling the blaze. They brought
it under control around one
o'clock — about an hour after it
began. Some of the firefighters
have been moving slowly through

Shots of smolder- ing building	parts of the burned-out building in an effort to determine if any- one could have been trapped in- side. Meanwhile, other fire- fighters continue to hose down the smoldering remains of the building.
O/C Heather	O/C Once again, two people dead and apparently everyone else escaped from this apartment complex on Rose Avenue in the West End sec- tion of the City. This is Heather Nelson, KTHU News.

After the radio and TV reporters finished their live reports they would, in all likelihood, be asked a number of questions by the anchors. Sometimes it is possible for the anchors and reporters to confer in advance on what questions the anchors will ask. Often, the reporters try to field whatever questions come their way without any advance preparation. That's when ad-libbing ability is important.

AD-LIBBING

There are methods that can help reporters improve their ad-libbing, or speaking without a script. One common method used by reporters to make sure they do not run out of things to say during a live remote is word association. Many reporters write down a list of key words or phrases in the order in which they want to cover their material. When they exhaust all the information dealing with a key word, they move on to the next one on the list until they have covered everything. All that good ad-libbing reporters need is that one word or phrase to keep them going, which is important because reporters frequently are forced into remote situations that require a considerable amount of ad-libbing.

ABC News Correspondent Barry Serafin says the best way to learn how to ad-lib is by doing it. He says he never thinks about reporting to an audience of 20 million people but concentrates on the idea that he is conversing with a single person in a "natural and human manner."

Serafin praises ABC News Anchor Peter Jennings' ad-libbing ability on what Serafin calls a "we're not sure what's going on here folks" kind of story. Serafin notes that Jennings is not afraid to say, "Well, we're not quite sure

ABC News Correspondent Peter Jennings anchors a broadcast of "World News Tonight."

CAPITAL CITIES/ABC, INC.

where we are going here but we'll let you know when we are, and in the meantime I'm going to do this."

"Jennings doesn't try to be a superman—he tries to be calm and composed," says Serafin. "He lets the audience know he's following the story with them—that he's human."

Serafin adds: "The main thing about ad-libbing is not to sound perfect. . . . Don't try to tell what you don't know. Don't speculate."

THE CHALLENGES OF ELECTRONIC NEWS GATHERING

Doing radio remotes is a great way to prepare for the world of *electronic news gathering* (ENG). It is easier for TV reporters to handle the challenges of live television if they have a radio background, but the number of reporters making the transition from radio to television is not as large now as it was at one time.

Most TV reporters now start their careers in television, and they have to learn how to do remotes from the start. During the transition from film to videotape and microwave in the mid-1970s, many TV reporters found it difficult to make the adjustment. They were accustomed to having 45 minutes or more to write their scripts while the film was being developed. The only time TV reporters went live was when the station or network bought a telephone line, and that was reserved for important occasions. Quite a few TV reporters were unable to handle the pressures of going live and changed jobs.

CBS News Correspondent Betsy Aaron made the transition but recalls the luxury of the film days when a reporter might have from 3 o'clock in the afternoon until airtime to write a script. "You had time to think," she said. "The time for reflection and making phone calls about your story has disappeared. The deadline is always immediate," she added, "and often the product suffers."

Serafin also recalls making the transition: "In the days of film you couldn't be changing, writing and producing the piece 10 seconds before it ran." Serafin remembered going live at the end of the Falklands War when an angry demonstration started outside the palace in Buenos Aires. "Because of technology," Serafin said, "I was really forced at the last minute to make some editorial decisions about what was going on. Was it just a little spasm of public opinion or was it the beginning of the end of the Government . . . or none of the above? I had to report to a network audience [without really knowing the answer] and it was difficult."

ABC News Correspondent Morton Dean agrees. He says it is "scary" when you have to go live and you are not quite sure what is going on. "I think that is the most difficult part of this business . . . covering a breaking story live," Dean says. "You are often out there 'naked' and you have to resist the pressure to give information that you're not certain of and to give your own personal thoughts as opposed to what's really going on." Dean says he's often asked to give his opinion about "what is going to happen" at the scene when he really does not know.

Dean recalled his reporting experience in the Gulf War when he was going live, and Iraqi Scud missiles were zooming overhead, and people were putting on their chemical outfits, and troops were running around with guns and taking their positions. "It's really very difficult to keep your wits about you," he said.

When asked if he was ever uncomfortable about his live reporting from the gulf, Dean said only to the extent that he developed a habit that may be considered bad in television: saying "I don't know" when he really doesn't know. "I think there's a terrible temptation to be glib," said Dean, "and just talk nonstop and maybe not say anything. You must have the courage to say 'I don't know,' and some people think that's a sin when you are on television."

Dean said there are times "when your mind is not working that quickly . . . and you have to feel secure enough to say 'I'm not sure about that . . . or I have to think about that.'" He also said there have been times when he refused to go live, telling his producer he really had nothing to say.

Aaron is concerned that some people in the field are so involved in the technology that they do not care about what reporters are saying. The result, she says, "is that you have people who will say 'only time will tell' in a hundred different ways. They say it very smoothly, but they don't know how to say anything else. They don't know what they're covering, or why, or the history or implication. . . . They just know it's a great picture and they make air. Sometimes," she says, "dead air is better than making air."

The same concerns about technology were expressed 12 years earlier by the late veteran newswoman Pauline Frederick of NBC. She noted that technology has "given our profession marvelous tools with which to work. But the question that should forever confront us is whether in our eagerness to use these instruments, the import of the message may become confused with the messenger who could be perceived as trying to make and shape the news."

CNN News Anchor and Correspondent Bernard Shaw also raises some questions about the new technology. "We can fire up, and fly in or roll in portable satellite earth stations, slap on a wireless mike, report live and not wait for tape at 11. We have digital this and digital that, telephones that connect to a satellite, fiber optics in the wings, and technology that will provide even smaller satellite dishes and antennas that will fit in an oversize briefcase. But," asks Shaw, "how are we using this stuff?"

Shaw goes on to suggest a number of situations that raise the question of whether broadcast news technology offers balanced and fair reporting:

"If in covering a nation at war, a correspondent shows pictures of devastation without pointing out that the host government is severely restricting the movement of reporters and showing only what that government wants shown, is the crucial element of perspective for the viewer or listener well-served?" asks Shaw.

"If there are no pictures to videotape and no sounds to record but only shreds of information gained from listening and observing, is expensive live capability that impressive?" he asks.

"If you are a reporter covering a protest around a nuclear power plant and you have the cameraperson shoot say 50 demonstrators tight so that it looks like 500 demonstrators, and if the reporter decides not to interview a plant spokesman because it's too close to satellite feed time, has that technology yielded better balance and a fair report?" asks Shaw.

All the correspondents agree that ENG has increased the risk of inaccuracy. As earlier chapters have stressed, nothing is more important for journalists than accuracy. Reporting live to a community, to the nation and often to the world carries with it a tremendous responsibility. There have been some notable cases of live reports that gave inaccurate accounts. For example, it was reported that presidential aide James Brady had been killed during the assassination attempt on President Reagan in 1981; in fact Brady survived his traumatic head wounds.

As with any story, but particularly when covering a story live, reporters

CNN Correspondent Bernard Shaw reports from the scene during the Gulf War.

must check and double-check their information and must rely heavily on attribution when there is the slightest possibility that the information may not be accurate.

KEEPING COOL   The Scud attacks during the Gulf War demanded a lot of "cool" on the part of network reporters. Some correspondents were reluctant to leave the roofs until they were ordered to do so by anchors and network officials. The matter-of-fact, low-keyed reporting of CNN correspondents Peter Arnett, John Holliman and Bernard Shaw from a hotel room in downtown Baghdad was certainly one of the highlights of the Gulf War reporting. The trio said that watching the air raids on Iraq from their hotel windows was a little like "watching a fireworks display." And to their credit, their calm and responsible reporting could have been compared to the way they might have handled an assignment at the Statue of Liberty during a Fourth of July celebration.

Peter Arnett, in particular, kept things in perspective, discouraging speculation about what was and was not going on when it was obvious that such speculation would have served no useful purpose.

The only time a correspondent seemed to lose composure was when some technical problem prevented the reporter from being heard or seen during the middle of a missile attack. Technical problems are frequently the cause of reporters losing their cool during less dramatic live reports.

All of us have seen a TV reporter in trouble during a live remote. The scene usually goes something like this: the reporter is standing in front of a camera getting ready to report live and something goes wrong with the earpiece system that allows the producer or cameraperson to speak with the reporter. The reporter ends up looking mystified because he does not know whether he is on the air. A cameraperson may be trying to signal what's going on, but sometimes this person is also in the dark. A worst-case scenario is when the reporter actually says, "Are we on?" when in fact he is. Sometimes these mishaps can be avoided if a TV monitor is available for the reporter. That way the reporter would be able to see that he is on the air without waiting for verbal instructions.

These situations are trying for reporters, who understandably do not like to appear foolish in the eyes of the audience, but the TV audience has become so sophisticated that it tends to ignore such mishaps or, at worst, to chuckle a little over the breakdown in communications. It's best for reporters to accept the fact that mistakes are going to happen and equipment is going to malfunction.

MEMORIZING AND DELIVERING LIVE REPORTS   Some reporters have an amazing ability to memorize scripts. But for most, memorizing one minute of copy presents a problem. Because all TV reporters are called on to do live reports, they must either develop the ability to memorize their material or use some tricks to help them. Most stations and networks have no problem with reporters glancing down at their notes during live reports, particularly during a breaking story. But it's less acceptable, especially in a routine live report outside a city-council meeting or the mayor's office, to see a reporter's head bobbing up and down every few seconds to read notes.

Former CBS News Correspondent Ben Silver says it sometimes helps "to just throw the script away." Silver recalls, "I was having trouble memorizing the close to a story and I must have done it 10 times when the cameraman finally said, 'Give me the script.' He took the clipboard from me and I did the close without any problem."

CHANGING LENS SHOTS

On particularly long taped standups, some reporters have the cameraperson change the shot during the delivery. The opening camera shot might be wide as the reporter delivers the first part of the standup. Then the reporter can pause while the cameraperson moves in for a tight shot. The reporter then delivers the second half of the script, and the audience is unaware that there was any break in the delivery. The two shots have to be drastically different to avoid a *jump cut*—the jerking of the head that would be seen if the camera shots were too much alike.

SUMMARY

The biggest challenge that most broadcast reporters face is reporting live. Radio reporters have always faced that challenge because they could be on the air from the scene of a breaking story in minutes with the use of a two-way radio. But TV reporters relied on film for their coverage until the 1970s, when two technologies were developed: small portable videotape cameras (minicams) and microwave. Reporters suddenly lost the luxury of preparing their reports while they were traveling back from the scene of a story and while the film was being developed. Suddenly, reporters found that with the introduction of microwave they were often asked to go on the air immediately, while their videotape was being rewound and edited or cued up within minutes of being shot. They discovered that most of their thinking time had disappeared.

These developments brought about not only new challenges but also new risks. When thinking time is reduced, the chance of inaccuracy is increased. So, TV reporters have two concerns: to collect information and sort it out quickly, and to make certain it is accurate. The immediacy of the new technology also requires that reporters learn to ad-lib, making their improvised speech look easy and comfortable.

REVIEW QUESTIONS

1. New technology permits broadcast news reporters to go live from almost any part of the globe with short notice. But these technological advances also place new burdens and responsibilities on journalists. Explain.

2. Before the arrival of microwave technology, TV reporters used to have more time to collect their thoughts. Why?

3. Good organization and note taking are important when a reporter covers a story live. How can these skills be developed?

4. Reporters who hope to be successful reporting from the scene of a breaking news story must develop certain skills. What are they?

5. How can reporters improve their ability to memorize and deliver live standup reports? Explain.

EXERCISES

1. Cover some event in the community, and then arrange for another student in the school's broadcast lab to videotape your standup report on the story you covered. After you have given your report, have the other student question you on tape. Return to the lab, and listen to the tape.

2. Cover a news conference with either an audiocassette player or video equipment. If you are using an audiocassette player, pick a sound bite and cue it up so that you can play it over the phone in the middle of a wraparound. If you are using a video camera, do an open and close at the scene without preparing a script. Return to the lab, and insert a sound bite between the open and close that you recorded at the scene.

3. Have another student read a lengthy story to you from a newspaper. Make notes as he or she reads the story. Study your notes for two minutes, and then record a report either on audiotape or on video. Play it back for other students and your professor, and ask for an evaluation.

CHAPTER 14

PUTTING THE TELEVISION STORY TOGETHER

hen reporters leave the newsroom on assignments, they never know how their stories will turn out. The producers and assignment editors may be looking for a package—a story that includes one or more sound bites, the reporter's narration and video. But sometimes they must settle for less because the story itself turns out to be less important than was originally thought or because the interviews are not strong or the video is weak. When that is the case, the story often becomes a voice-over to sound (VO/SOT), or is relegated to the simplest type of picture story, a voice-over (V/O).

There also are times when the assignment editor knows in advance that a story is not worthy of a package. A cameraperson may be sent on a story without a reporter just to shoot video and natural sound. The producer will be made aware of that and will plan on covering that story in the newscast as a VO/SOT or V/O. This chapter discusses these types of television stories.

THE PACKAGE

A TV newscast is mostly made up of packages. That's because, if they are done well, packages have all the elements that bring a story alive: good pictures, interesting sound bites and a well-written script. As was mentioned, if any of these elements is weak, the story may be downgraded or kept short. In other words, the quality of the video and the sound bites often determines the length of a package. But even great video and excellent sound bites do not always guarantee a long package. It depends on what else is going on in the news that day. Even on slow days, packages rarely run longer than a couple of minutes.

AT THE SCENE

Good organization is essential in putting together a successful package. Reporters try to decide quickly how they are going to produce the package. They may not have every detail pinned down, but they generally decide on some fundamentals, such as whether they are going to do the open, the close or a transition in the middle on camera. If there is a possibility that one of these on-camera options may be needed, it should be shot just in case.

TAKING NOTES

Good organization requires good notes. NBC News Correspondent Bob Dotson says he uses his notebook "like a pilot's checklist." He says he never finds the creative part of reporting to be a big problem. "I always find that the obvious is overlooked, like I forgot to get the wide shot or I forgot to ask the mayor whether he was going to run for another term."

Dotson notes that as soon as he knows he is going to do a story, he starts putting little boxes in his notebook with "thoughts, ideas, pictures, anything" he thinks he may need. "And then I scratch off what I don't need as I go along," he adds, stressing, however, "I do not leave a story until I have checked all the boxes that I do need so I don't overlook anything."

OPENING THE STORY

NBC Correspondent Roger O'Neil says, "If I can't get you with the first pictures and the first sentence, I've lost you. So, I spend several hours writing the first sentence, and the rest falls into place."

That luxury of time, however, is usually available only to network correspondents. Reporters at local stations would soon be looking for other jobs if they took two hours to pick their first shots and lead sentences. But O'Neil's comment does point out how important it is to get a good lead and strong video at the top of a story.

O'Neil notes that the first sentence is dictated by the first pictures, and the first pictures are dictated by the best pictures. "I can write a story 100 different ways," he says, "but I'm going to find the best pictures and find a sentence that fits those pictures."

GOOD PICTURES

The NBC correspondent takes issue with those who believe that words are more important than the pictures. He says those who believe that the script should be written first and the pictures added to support the words "should be in the newspaper business. We're in the business of pictures," he adds, "not the business of words."

He notes many reporters "fail to tell the story with pictures and then fill in the words" because they believe they don't have enough time to look at the pictures. "That's an excuse," O'Neil says. "I never write a script until I have looked at the pictures."

O'Neil's colleague NBC News Correspondent Bob Dotson also looks at his pictures before he writes. He described how he and his editor worked on the Carlsbad Cave rescue story in a recreation vehicle that was equipped with editing equipment: "We spun through the tapes as they came up, and I would make log notes . . . in the left-hand column of the script. What I start to do is tell the story visually in my mind—this is what happened, this is where it went and this is how I finish it. Once I've got that set in my mind I can sketch that out pretty quick."

Dotson said it then was relatively easy to go over to the right side of his script and write what viewers will not be able to see. "The problem with writing your script first and then trying to paste the pictures to it," he said, "is you end up with wallpaper and it doesn't flow. Suddenly you have a paragraph and no pictures to cover the paragraph."

The NBC correspondent said even when he worked as a local reporter and had to do a couple of stories a day, he still chose his pictures before writing his script. He said it's a "little like learning jujitsu. You learn the system and philosophy of how to approach a story and learn how to do it quickly and well. If you 'write your pictures' first, your story is going to stand out from all the others who don't."

"60 Minutes" Correspondent Ed Bradley believes TV news has been "driven too much by pictures and what's available in telling picture stories rather than information." "60 Minutes," because of its format, relies on a lot of "talking heads" and Bradley says "there's nothing wrong with a talking head . . . as long as it's shedding some light on something."

Most television reporters and producers find talking heads to be dull and replace the face with video relating to the story. When Bradley was reminded that "60 Minutes" is full of talking heads, he responded, "God bless talking heads."

GOOD WRITING

CBS News Correspondent Richard Threlkeld notes that all good reporters have something in common—they are good writers. "If you are a good writer," he adds, "you also must be a good reporter."

Threlkeld believes that to be successful as a TV reporter you "almost have to relearn what you have been taught in school when you had to do term papers and put all your thoughts down on the printed page for people to read." The CBS news correspondent notes that it may be obvious that television is a different medium from others but, unfortunately, "this doesn't sink into the brains of most broadcast journalists."

Threlkeld notes that everyone works differently; for example, CBS News Correspondent Bruce Morton gets "everything together in his head and then he'll sit around for a bit and then he will simply write a script about as fast as it takes me to tell it to you." Threlkeld says Charles Kuralt "agonizes more," while he himself is somewhere in between. "I get all the pictures together and all the printed material I need, and then I write fairly fast."

As for the debate on which is more important, the words or the pictures, Threlkeld says both are important. But, he adds, "I think what most reporters in TV fail to see—and never do see with some exceptions—is how important pictures are to writing."

Threlkeld says that while it's important to write well—in a conversational and colloquial style—the pictures, in most cases, must come first. "When you look at them, you must ask yourself 'how can these pictures tell the story?'"

The end result of all this, says Threlkeld, is that reporters end up "underwriting. And most of the best prose in both broadcasting and print is underwritten." And then, like so many others, Threlkeld reminds us that "one of the finest writers of this century, an old journalist named Hemingway, was a master at underwriting." He adds, "If you can underwrite and let the pictures tell the story, you are ahead of the game."

ABC News Correspondent Morton Dean says his approach depends on the story. His approach differs, for example, if he's working on a story and reporting from the scene or has a chance to come back to the studio to work on it. "My preference," he notes, "is to look at the footage and then write the script and make the pictures and sound work for me and interject myself only when necessary."

Dean says that when reporters work with a complicated story, they sometimes can't limit it just to the pictures they have. He notes, "You sometimes have to write material for graphics or include standups. You may have information that is essential to the story that you must get into your script one way or another."

Charles Kuralt says, "I believe in never writing a line without knowing exactly what picture I am writing to; so when the script is finished, the story is edited—at least in my head." Kuralt said that during his "On the Road" series, his cameraman Izzy Bleckman "knew never to shoot anything unless I was there taking notes, because we shipped the film unprocessed with the narration, and never even saw it until it was on the air." Kuralt said, "This worked fine, as long as I was there to imagine the shot as Izzy was making it, so I could be sure to work it in."

The following is the script Kuralt wrote in Strafford, Vt., and sent to his editor at CBS in New York. Along with the narration, he provided directions on the left side of the script and a separate *dopesheet* telling the editor what was on the film. Kuralt said all this detail makes the point that the "hardest part of every story is putting it together on paper."

```
pan village.                   This one day in Vermont, the town
Kuralt SOF
                               carpenter lays aside his tools . . .

                               the town doctor sees no patients

                               . . . the shopkeeper closes his

                               shop. Mothers tell their children

                               they'll have to warm up their own
```

. . . to Kuralt on camera SOF	dinner. This one day, people in Vermont look not to their own welfare, but to that of their town. It doesn't matter that it's been snowing since 4 o'clock this morning. They'll be here. This is town meeting day.
people walking up hill to town meeting	Strafford, Vermont, has grown to a population of 536 since it was chartered by King George the Third in 1761. Its first town meeting was held in the freedom days, March 1779. And every March for 175 years, the men and women of Strafford have trudged up
. . . and pan with one group up to town hall	this hill on the one day of the year which is a holiday for democracy. They walk past a sign that
people past sign	says, "The Old White Meeting House. Built in 1799 and consecrated as a place of public worship for all denominations, with no preference for one above another. Since 1801, it has also been in continuous use as a Town Hall."
snow outside, pull back from window to high, wide shot of hall	Here, every citizen may have his say on the question. The question is, will the town stop paying for outside health services. The

Brown voice under	speaker is a farmer, an elected selectman — David K. Brown, and Farmer Brown says "Yes."
Brown on camera . . .	BROWN SAYS: "I'll tell you the selectmen have had some, what I consider unsatisfactory service from them. Last year, we had an individual in town that was in a
faces of people listening	very deep depression and he did not have any immediate family in town and they called upon us to do something about it, and we went and he was trying or think-
Brown on camera again	ing about committing suicide. So we called the Orange County mental health, and this was I believe on a Friday night. They said they'd see him Tuesday afternoon. And if we had any problems, take him to Hanover and put him in the emergency room. Now I don't know if we should pay $582.50 for that kind of advice . . . "
others on feet, voice under	They talked about that for half an hour, asking themselves if this money would be well or poorly spent. This is not representative democracy. This is pure democracy, in which every citizen's voice is heard.

moderator	"ALL THOSE IN FAVOR, SIGNIFY BY SAYING 'AYE.'" "AYE." "ALL THAT ARE OPPOSED" "NAY" "I'M GOING TO ASK FOR A STANDING VOTE. ALL THOSE IN FAVOR, STAND PLEASE."
As they stand	It is an old Yankee expression, which originated here, in the town meeting, and has entered the language of free men: "Stand up and be counted."
moderator prepares to announce	And, when the judgment is made, and announced by James Condict, maker of rail fences and moderator of the meeting, the town will abide by the judgment.
he does	THERE ARE A HUNDRED VOTES CAST . . . 61 IN FAVOR AND 39 AGAINST. IT THEN BECOMES DELETED FROM THE TOWN BUDGET.
faces in meeting as somebody speaks voice under about street lights	This is the way the founders of this country imagined it would be, that citizens would meet in their own communities to decide directly most of the questions affecting their lives and fortunes. Vermont's small towns have kept it this way. Will or will not Strafford, Vermont, turn off its street lights to save money?

man in audience	PAPER BALLOT! PAPER BALLOT! ANY MEMBER HAS THE RIGHT TO DEMAND A PAPER BALLOT! IS THAT SECONDED? DOESN'T HAVE TO BE SECONDED! MODERATOR: "PREPARE AND CAST YOUR BALLOTS FOR THIS AMENDMENT."
line of people coming up . . .	If any citizen demands a secret ballot, a secret ballot it must
. . . handing paper ballots to deputy sheriff	be. Everybody who votes in Vermont has taken an old oath, to always vote his conscience without fear
CU's hands and ballots	or favor of any person. This is something old, something essential. You tear off a little piece
ballots being counted. We see "Yes" and "No."	of paper, and on it, you write "yes" or "no." Strafford voted to keep the street lights shining.
somebody takes a piece of pie	There is pie, baked by the ladies of the PTA. There are baked beans
woman dishing up beans (little woman standing beside line of taller people)	and brown bread, served at Town Meeting by Celia Lane as long as anybody can remember. Then, a little more wood is added to the stove, and a dozen more questions are debated and voted on in the long
wood into stove	afternoon. What is really on the menu
WS meeting	today is government of the people. Finally came the most routine of all motions, the motion to adjourn.

moderator and crowd	ALL THOSE IN FAVOR SIGNIFY BY SAYING "AYE" (LITTLE AYE) ALL THAT OPPOSE (BIG NAY) THEN WE DON'T AD-JOURN AND THE NAYS HAVE IT.
somebody else on feet talking, voice under people out of bldg into snow . . .	It is heady stuff, democracy. They wanted to go on enjoying it for a while in Strafford today. When finally they did adjourn, and walk out into the snow, it was with the feeling of having pre-
. . . down hill . . .	served something important, some-thing more important than their street lights — their liberty.
. . . and camera pans to village	Charles Kuralt, CBS News, On the Road to '76 in Vermont.

dopesheet

<u>SOF</u>
Roll 1 — Kuralt open, people arriving, about 200 feet.

ALL REMAINING SOF ROLLS ARE PUSH ONE STOP ASA 250

Roll 2 — 400 SOF — Registering to vote at Town Meeting, Strafford, Vermont . . . call to order by Moderator James Condict . . . pledge of allegiance . . . voting in booths, presidential primary . . . WS room over moderator's shoulder . . . faces . . . one of the selectmen, David K. Brown, farmer, reports on town budget . . . more faces.

Roll 3 — 400 SOF — crocheting red white and blue sweater . . . Selectman David Brown says Mental Health gives poor service . . . debate on $1179 for Community Health Services . . . etc.

Roll 4 — 400 SOF — Ayes and nays can't be distinguished . . . which leads to a standing vote . . . announcement of vote: 61-39 against spending the money . . . nice intercut of wandering child being snatched away from front of room by mother . . . debate on street lights, $1900 budget item. Farmer Jerry Smith (with beard) says one shines in his eyes at night . . . etc.

Roll 5 — 400 SOF — On street light question, call for a paper ballot on whether to cut street lighting in half. Details of balloting, hands CU, etc., then counting paper ballots and announcement of result, 59 yes, 82 no, so motion to reduce street lighting defeated . . . break for lunch, pies in foreground home cooked . . . baked beans and brown bread being dished out by Celia Lane, who has served baked beans at the Town Meetings since anybody can remember . . . high shot of room with eating going on . . . neighborly floor-level eating and chatter . . .

Roll 6 — 400 SOF — More chit-chat during luncheon break . . . janitor feeds more wood into the stove . . . high shot thru window of snow falling, pull back to meeting, repeat several times . . . counting ballots from above . . . faces in audience . . . Gile S. Kendall, farmer, selectman reelected . . . people coming forward to vote, faces in and out of frame.

Roll 7 — 400 SOF — Vote for second constable. Bob Nutting defeats Lois Smith and Gerald Smith . . . faces in crowd, rack focus young face to old face, etc. discussion of reappraisal of property values . . .

Roll 8 — 400 SOF — More reappraisal discussion. Girl, pull back to feeding fire. Jerry Smith makes a "You don't need government agencies in Vermont" speech . . . discussion of $750 appropriation to senior citizens center in neighboring town . . . and of radio for car of "civil defense" director . . . voting down adjournment! Sign: "The Old White Meeting House. Built in 1799 and consecrated as a place of public worship for all denominations, with no preference for one above another. Since 1801, it has also been in continuous use as a Town Hall." with people coming and going in front of sign. People leaving, pan down steeple. People down hill and pan to village. Empty town hall after they've all left.

Phil Scheffler, a senior producer for "60 Minutes," says Kuralt has a "particularly fine eye. He sees things others don't and sees them very clearly. That's also why he's such a good reporter." Scheffler says the thing that strikes you about Kuralt's writing is "how simple it is. It's unadorned. He's able to create a very clear picture in your mind as to what he's seen."

ORGANIZING THE STORY

One of the most frustrating orders for most reporters is "keep the story short." But NBC News Correspondent Roger O'Neil says he finds it is more of a challenge to do a short story than a long one.

O'Neil believes that the key to writing a tight script is *organization*. He says he is often accused of being "cold or mad at people, or the world," because he is quiet on the car trip back from a story. "I am quiet," O'Neil says, "because I'm thinking about the pictures I saw the photographer take—trying to arrange those pictures in my head. I am quiet because I am thinking about what I have to do when I get back to the station."

The NBC news correspondent says too many reporters do not take advantage of that trip back to the station. "They don't think about what they are going to do with the story until they sit down at the typewriter," he notes. "Then they complain they don't have enough time to tell the story because they haven't thought it out."

Reporters certainly should be using that time in the car to organize their thoughts, and it helps to have interviews on audiotape. Every broadcast reporter should carry an audiocassette recorder for this purpose. It is not necessary to have a good quality recording because the audiotape will not be used for broadcast, only to help the reporter select sound bites. It is a great timesaver.

NBC News Correspondent Bob Dotson says he uses the car ride both to and from the scene to get organized. "The minute I know that I am going to do a story," he notes, "I start thinking in terms of how I am going to develop it, what questions I would ask, where I would go from point A to B." Dotson adds that on the way back from the scene he listens to the audiotape and selects the sound bites long before he returns to the studio.

SELECTING SOUND

Dotson says that in addition to good sound bites he is always looking for good *natural sound*—what a novelist might call mood setters. "What you are really doing in TV is not showing or telling but trying to have people experience what it is like. Sound can help you experience it and sound can bring your audience back to the TV screen because so much of what we call news just washes over us all the time. But if you stop talking, and you hear a rooster crow, people are going to turn to see the rooster. They will put down the spoon, stop eating dinner, and come to the TV set."

As for sound bites, Dotson says, "I always use sound as an exclamation point. I do not use sound to explain. There just isn't enough time to let the subject explain. In a minute and a half, you have to use several voices to tell all sides of the story. So you, as a professional writer, give the basic information and use the sound bite for emphasis."

Dotson gives this example: "You have a sound bite from someone talking

A student at Northwestern University's Medill School of Journalism edits video for a story.
MEDILL NEWS SERVICE

about a picnic. The person says, 'We're going to have a picnic on Friday at one o'clock and we are going to have a band there and it's going to be a great time and we hope you all will come and it's sponsored by the Kiwanis Club.' You take the bite, which is really like an exclamation point—'We're going to have a great time'—and you, as a professional writer, fill in the information that leads up to the sound bite. And the sound bite proves what you just said."

WORKING WITH THE VIDEO EDITOR

Dotson compares video editing with rewriting. "It is like a catcher on a baseball team. That's the backstop, and all the other things you have done during the process of putting that story together can either be lost or saved in the editing room. Sometimes the fantasies you had as you were writing your story can be saved by the editor. That's where you are putting it all together—your sound and pictures and words—and editors have to be very hard on the process. They must say, "These symbols move the story forward, and these symbols you put in the basement and show your parents later on, because we don't have time for them."

Dotson adds, "I always look at a news story as a kind of good jazz ensemble. At some point there is a trumpeter, and at some point there is a drummer, and each person has his soul and it's important sometimes that they all play together. That's the same way with a story, and the editor helps reinforce that."

THE VOICE-OVER   In a voice-over (V/O), the newscaster or reporter reads copy as the video appears on the screen. Normally, voice-overs are not very long because they are usually used to break up a series of packages or to give the anchors some exposure. The following is the script for three short voice-overs used in a newscast produced by WBRZ-TV in Baton Rouge, La.:

| ```
Two shot O/C
Margaret and
Andrea
``` | ```
(Margaret)
Updating some of the other stories
making news across the nation . . .
authorities in Newport News, Virginia, are investigating an accident involving an Amtrak train.
``` |
| ```
Roll Sony V/O
Video of derailed
train
``` | ```
           (V/O)
A dump truck collided with this
train at a railroad crossing. The
force of the collision sent the en-
gine and all five passenger cars
off the tracks.
``` |
| ```
Video of injured
people
``` | ```
  The driver of the truck died in the
accident . . . about 50 people on the
train were hurt, but not seriously.
``` |
| ```
Wipe to Sony
Video of plane
wreckage

Font: Blevelt
Falls Lake Liles-
ville, N.C.

More video of
wreckage
``` | ```
         (Andrea V/O)
And divers in North Carolina are
searching for the bodies of nine
people who died when a military
transport plane crashed into this
lake in North Carolina.
  The victims were stationed at
Fort Polk. They were on a training
mission. So far, the cause of the
crash is unknown.
``` |

```
Wipe to Sony

Kennedy and wife           And a citizens group called Public
shaking hands
with people in             Citizen is demanding the National
Dallas
Kennedy motorcade          Archives release nearly 200 autopsy
in Dallas
                           photos and X-rays of President

                           Kennedy.


Video of people             A bill in Congress would require
on lawn as Ken-
nedy motorcade             the release of documents pertain-
goes by
                           ing to the assassination, but ex-

                           cludes the autopsy material to pro-

                           tect the Kennedy family's privacy.


ON CAMERA TAG                        (Andrea O/C)

                           A spokesman for this citizens

                           group says the materials should be

                           public record.
```

Most newscasts use voice-overs along with read stories to fill in the time around packages; voice-overs seldom run longer than 20 or 30 seconds. The first voice-over in the example ran 24 seconds; the second ran 16 seconds; and the third 27 seconds. They were separated by *wipes,* an electronic technique that slides one video picture off the screen as it replaces it with another, in this case with the opening video of the next story.

The use of the word Sony in the left column lets the director know that the video material is in the Sony tape decks. The director's copy of the script would indicate by number which deck plays which tape during the newscast.

THE VOICE-OVER–SOUND ON TAPE

As discussed earlier, when a voice-over is used to lead into a sound bite it is called a V-SOT or V/O-SOT. Here's an example of a V-SOT script:

```
                                      Newscaster

V/O

Video of police
officers at gradu-        Central City's fight against crime
ation
                          got a boost today with the gradua-
```

```
Video of female          tion of 45 new officers from the
graduates
                         police academy. Among the officers

                         eleven women. One of them is Ann

Video of Ann             Black, and she had her own cheering
Black and family
                         section — her mother and father, her

Video of Black           husband, and her three-year-daughter,
holding daughter
                         Sally. Black's father also is a

                         police officer.

SOT :05                          (SOT/ Sally Black)

                         "It's just a wonderful time . . .

                         to finally be on the force, like

                         my dad, and to have everyone I

                         love here to cheer me on . . .

                         it's just great."
```

At this point, the anchor could return on camera to do a *tag* to the story or go back to a *voice-over*, as is the case here:

```
                                        ANCHOR
V/O
Video of gradu-          The 45 new officers will not have
ates tossing hats
in air                   too much time to celebrate. They

                         report for duty in the morning.
```

V-SOT stories are usually used when a reporter was not assigned to do a package or the producer decided that the material was not strong enough, or of enough interest to the audience, to warrant the time necessary for a package.

REPORTER INVOLVEMENT

Some news directors want to see their reporters' faces often in their stories. They encourage reporters to appear on camera either at the end or in the middle of their stories. The theory is that the audience should think of the reporters and anchors as "family," and the more on-air exposure these family members get, the better management likes it.

NBC Correspondent Roger O'Neil says, "It's stupid for network and local stations to require standups just to get their reporters on the air." The always outspoken O'Neil adds, "It's ludicrous to take good pictures away just to put some ugly reporter's face on the air." ABC's Morton Dean and CBS's David

Culhane agree. Both say they like to stay out of their stories as much as possible, preferring to let the pictures and other people's words tell the story.

The best reason for a reporter to appear in a story is to help explain it. Some reporters would argue that should be the *only* time. On occasion, a reporter can help the viewer better understand the story by appearing on camera in the middle of it. Such a *stand-up bridge* is sometimes useful in tying together two parts of a complicated story, but it can also be disruptive when a reporter suddenly breaks up the flow of the story for no practical reason.

Some of the worst examples of reporter involvement occur when the reporters become a part of the story. Unfortunately, many news directors have no problem with reporters sliding down hills during a snowstorm or eating a hot dog at a street festival or lifting weights at the opening of a new health spa.

Charles Kuralt, in his book "A Life on the Road," writes this about reporter involvement: "With respect to my own appearances on camera, we have adopted the Tricycle Principle. We were somewhere in the Midwest, watching the local news on the TV set in the bus before going out to supper. There was a feature about a children's tricycle race, cute little toddlers pedaling away and bumping into one another, an appealing story pretty well-filmed and -edited.

"Izzy said, 'You know what? Before this is over, the reporter is going to ride a tricycle.'

" 'Oh, no!' I said. 'That would ruin the whole thing.'

"Sure enough, the reporter signed off in a close-up with a silly grin, the camera pulled back to show that he was perched on a tricycle, and he turned and pedaled clumsily away, making inane what had, until then, been charming. The anchorpeople came on laughing to sign off the show.

"The Tricycle Principle is simple: 'When doing a tricycle story, don't ride a tricycle.' The story is about children, dummy, not about you. Keep yourself out of it. Try to control your immodesty."

But some of the TV audience thinks such reporter involvement is cute, and that's enough for many news managers.

On the other hand, most news directors agree with Kuralt. They will tell you that they discourage such behavior and want reporters involved in their stories only when there is a legitimate reason. For example, it would not be inappropriate for a reporter to demonstrate how to use a new at-home device that measures blood pressure. Doing so could be the best way for the reporter to explain how the new device works.

SUMMARY

One of the things reporters find most exciting about their job is that they rarely know what's going to happen when they get to work or how the story they've been assigned to cover will turn out. The sound bites may be fascinating and the video colorful so that the story becomes a good package. But covering news also has its frustrations. An interview may be weak; some promised video opportunities may not materialize. The story then becomes a voice-over–sound on tape or a voice-over.

Good organization and notes improve the chances that a package will be a success. Reporters should not try to predict the outcome of the story they're working on, but they should know as much as possible about the subject and the players involved in their assignment when they leave the newsroom. And before they leave the scene, reporters should be certain that they have covered everything they need.

REVIEW QUESTIONS

1. Discuss the differences between read stories, voice-overs, voice-overs–sound on tape and packages.

2. Discuss some of the considerations that determine which of the described techniques in this chapter are used to tell certain stories.

3. What are the most popular ways of opening and closing a package? Discuss the merits of each technique.

4. What do most top broadcast news reporters say about the relative importance of pictures and words in packages?

5. Richard Threlkeld says all good reporters have something in common. What is it?

6. What factors determine how long a package runs?

EXERCISES

1. Pick a story out of the newspaper or from the wires, and write a 20-second voice-over. Record the voice-over at your school lab.

2. Pick another story that has some quotes, and script a 30-second V-SOT.

3. Prepare a package about a feature story. Limit it to one minute and 45 seconds and include two talking heads. If your school has the equipment, produce the package.

CHAPTER 15

THE INTERVIEW

ne of the basic methods used by reporters to gather information is the interview. Newspaper, radio and TV journalists use different techniques, but for the most part all try to achieve the same end: to find out as much news-making information as they can from the person they are interviewing. In broadcast jargon, the interviewee usually is referred to as the *talking head*, or simply the *head*.

Newspaper reporters have the luxury of going into depth in their interviews. Because radio and TV reporters have limited time on the air, they have less time to conduct their interviews. Therefore, they must be selective in their questioning and be well-prepared. This chapter discusses technique for conducting successful interviews.

PREPARING FOR THE INTERVIEW

Reporters should always research the subject and find out as much as possible about the person to be interviewed. Good places to start are the radio or TV newsrooms clip files and audiotape and videotape libraries. Some news organizations also have access to computer data-base services such as NEXIS, which indexes national and some regional newspapers, the wire services, and over 100 magazines and journals.

Reporters also must decide in advance of the interview what kind of information they want. Interviews are not always expected to produce news. Some are designed to solicit emotional responses, such as those conducted for a human-interest story. Others are attempts to find out more about the news maker or, perhaps, his or her family. Reporters might seek such information if, for example, the interviewee had been appointed to some public post or as head of the local hospital.

If a reporter is interviewing the winner of a congressional seat, she is going to be looking for information that is different from what she sought the day before when she interviewed the mother of quadruplets. The reporter will want to ask the congressman-elect about his priorities when he gets to Washington, why he thinks his campaign was a success and, perhaps, whether he believes his victory indicates some sort of national trend. When the reporter spoke to the mother of quadruplets, she asked questions about the problems of taking care of four babies, about whether the house is big enough to accommodate the family and so on.

PHRASING QUESTIONS CAREFULLY

Many people interviewed by reporters are shy by nature or intimidated by microphones and cameras. Many others just seem to measure their words carefully, so, to prevent one- and two-word responses, reporters must phrase their questions so they are impossible to answer with a "yes" or "no" or just a shake of the head.

If you ask a person, "Do you like farming?" you are bound to get a "yes" or "no" answer, but if you ask "What do you like about farming?" you should wind up with a sound bite. If you ask a witness to an auto accident "Did you see what happened?" you might, again, end up with a one-word response. If you ask "What did you see?" you'll most likely get a longer response. Children are particularly likely to give yes-or-no answers, so ask them open-ended questions and be patient.

AVOIDING LEADING QUESTIONS

Do not lead the interviewee toward giving a particular response. Some of the best reporters are sometimes guilty of this bad habit, one that is easy to fall into. During the Gulf War, a nationally known TV reporter asked a Bush administration official if he was "upset" after viewing pictures of an air raid that showed heavy destruction to a civilian target. The reporter herself clearly was upset by the pictures, and phrasing the question in that manner was a disservice for a couple of reasons: First, it probably influenced many viewers' feelings about the video, and second, it put the administration official in an uncomfortable situation. If he had said he was *not* upset, he would have appeared callous; if he had said he *was* upset, he might have sounded critical of the military, which may or may not have been fair or accurate. The reporter allowed her personal feelings about the air raid to influence the question. It was a leading question. She should have asked the administration official, "What did you think about those pictures?"

LISTENING CAREFULLY

Reporters should arrive at an interview with a list of questions that they intend to ask the news maker. But they also must develop a keen habit of listening carefully to the answers and asking follow-up questions. Many inexperienced reporters are so intent on asking their prepared questions that they fail to listen to the answers. Frequently, they do not realize that their previous question was not answered fully, or at all. Sometimes, to the embarrassment of all, the reporter asks a question that already has been answered. The astute news maker, often anticipating the reporter's next question, sometimes adds additional information to an earlier response. The rude awakening comes when the reporter asks another question on his or her list and the news maker says, "I just answered that."

To avoid falling into such traps, the reporter should put the list of questions to one side and refer to it only when necessary. CBS News Correspondent Ed Bradley says he always has a list of questions but does not get locked into it. He says if he's interviewing someone and the person moves to a subject farther down on his list, he goes with the interviewee because he can then go back and pick up where he was.

The "60 Minutes" correspondent notes there are people who "come in with an agenda, a list of questions, a predetermined mind-set as to where the interview is going to go; they don't hear what it is that people say." He believes listening is important because too many reporters have "a tendency to try to fill space . . . instead of listening to what it is that a person says." Bradley advises interviewers to allow some silence and let the person fill it instead of trying to fill it all by themselves.

Another effective technique is to establish direct eye contact with the person being interviewed. It's easier for reporters to concentrate on what people are saying if they look them right in the eye. This habit also establishes a good rapport. Maintaining eye contact with news makers lets them know that the reporter is listening and interested. If the reporter's eyes drift toward the list of questions, or to the cameraperson, the news maker might take that as a signal that he or she has said enough and wait for another question even though he or she might not have finished answering the question.

WARMING UP THE HEAD

Reporters differ on just how much they should disclose to the interviewee, the head, about the line of questioning before the interview starts. The advantage of *warming up* the head is that it gives the person time to collect his or her thoughts, usually ensuring a smoother interview. Without a warm-up, the interviewee might be caught by surprise. The person might say, "I had no idea you would ask that; I really do not know the answer," or try unsuccessfully to fake an answer. Warming up an interviewee also tends to put the person more at ease. A relaxed head usually provides a better interview.

Sometimes, however, reporters do not want the interviewee to know the questions in advance because they are looking for candid, unrehearsed answers. Sometimes the reporters plan to ask questions about a controversial topic designed to catch the person by surprise.

There is no rule against warming up the interviewee but some reporters are opposed to it. Almost all agree that it should be restricted to situations in which the reporter is looking for noncontroversial information. For example, a reporter would not warm up the head if the questions dealt with charges claiming the person misappropriated funds during an election campaign.

THE TOUGH QUESTIONS

Susan Morris, who teaches at the University of Pittsburgh and conducts workshops on interviewing techniques, believes "no one enjoys asking embarrassing questions. It's uncomfortable and difficult." But she adds, "I've learned that a certain toughness is required. While excessive pressure can destroy an interview, it's important to keep in mind that you are there to get answers, not to create a good impression. After the interview," she points out, "you have to write a news story, not a press release."

Morris also says it helps to blame the tough questions on other people. For example: "Today's newspaper reports that . . . What is your response?" or "Some of your critics say . . . Could you clarify the situation?" She says that "by attributing the charges to another source, you make it clear they are not coming from you personally."

THE SURPRISE QUESTIONS

CBS News Correspondent Mike Wallace is probably the reporter most identified with *surprise questions,* those that catch the interviewee off guard. Wallace's seemingly relaxed, easy-going style tends to disarm the individual he's questioning. His look of apparent bewilderment and confusion should, by now, serve as a warning that Wallace is ready to spring a trap, but the people he interviews keep taking the bait. The scene is familiar: There's a pause while the individual tries to figure out how Wallace knew enough about the person or the subject matter to ask the question that now must be answered.

Is such an interviewing approach fair? John Spain, station manager for WBRZ-TV in Baton Rouge, who has a distinguished record for investigative reporting, says, "I try to be honest and fair, but I'm not obligated to tell someone we are investigating everything we have come to talk about. If we did, he probably wouldn't do the interview."

Spain says that if the individual says he or she will only talk about certain subjects, then Spain has to decide if he still wants the interview. "But most

Mike Wallace reports for CBS's weekly news show "Sixty Minutes."
DM/GLOBE PHOTOS

people will talk to you," says Spain, "because they don't think they have done anything wrong and everything will be OK as long as they can tell their side of the story. They do, and that's when we ask them the tough questions that they didn't know we knew."

Spain said the long-standing rule followed by lawyers, "don't ask any questions unless you already know the answers," also applies to reporters. "We go as well prepared as we can," he says.

Spain adds that people "generally underestimate our knowledge, resources and ability to look into their actions. Why," he asks, "do people continue to talk to '60 Minutes'? It's because they totally underestimate what the media has been able to obtain in terms of research and background."

QUESTIONS TO ASK BEFORE THE INTERVIEW

In a noninvestigative situation, the main reason for interviewing people is to get information that is generally *not* known to the reporter and the public. Once the cameras and audio recorders are rolling, reporters shouldn't spend time asking people how long they have been employed, where they were educated or whether they are married or have children. If that sort of information is important for a story, it should be learned informally before the actual interview begins. You might want to include such information in the introductory sentence of your story, but there rarely would be a reason for you to waste valuable air time with video- or audiotaped responses on these subjects. The recorded questions and answers should be restricted to those that gather information about what the news maker knows or thinks about an idea or issue or, perhaps, to those that capture emotions.

KEEPING CONTROL OF THE INTERVIEW

Sometimes, reporters inadvertently allow news makers to take control of an interview. Politicians are particularly skilled at manipulating interviews. For example, some politicians take a couple of minutes to answer a question, while others ask reporters how long a response they want and then give an answer of exactly that length. Because politicians and others accustomed to working with broadcast journalists know that reporters think in terms of sound bites, they usually try to express their views in about 12 seconds to make sure their answers are not edited.

A problem arises when the news maker takes too long to respond. The choice then is either to interrupt or to allow the head to finish the answer and then reask the question, saying, "That was great, but could you cover that same ground again in about half the time?" Most often the individual will be happy to comply, which simplifies the editing process and results in a more natural-sounding response. Editing a sound bite down from a minute to 20 seconds sometimes alters the speaker's inflections.

Some news makers try to mislead reporters. They avoid answering some questions and skirt around others. Unless challenged, news makers often dominate interview situations. If the head doesn't answer the question or gives only a partial answer, the reporter should try to follow up. Frequently, the news maker then gives largely the same answer phrased differently. The reporter then needs to decide whether to ask the question a third time, or perhaps to say to the news maker, "I'm sorry, but you still have not answered my question." When the response is "That's all I'm going to say on the subject," that in itself makes a statement. The reporter might then note in the story, "When pressed to answer the question several times, so-and-so refused to elaborate on the original answer."

ASKING ENOUGH QUESTIONS

It takes time to develop the skill of knowing when you have asked enough questions during an interview. Reporters just entering the field tend to ask too many questions, usually because they are understandably insecure. But as reporters gain experience, they usually start developing a feel for when they have collected enough information.

Because time is precious to a broadcast reporter, asking too many questions means that the reporter spends more time than necessary at the scene or on the phone. That leaves less time for working on other stories and complicates the editing process.

Successful reporters who have researched the topic and the news maker know when they have just the right amount of material on tape. Because they have an idea of what information they hoped to hear, they know which sound bites they will probably end up using and they have a fairly accurate idea of how long those bites will run.

Experienced broadcast journalists often know immediately after the interview is over how they are going to put their stories together. With practice, reporters develop a habit of mentally processing information, sound bites and pictures in a way that allows them to organize their material quickly.

"DID I FORGET SOMETHING?"

The pressures of conducting interviews quickly can sometimes cause reporters to miss important information. It is often a good idea for the reporter to ask the interviewee if there is anything he or she would like to add or to ask candidly if there is anything important that the reporter might have missed. It is surprising how often the response is "Well, as a matter of fact, I probably should tell you . . . "

OFF THE RECORD

One of the frustrations of being a reporter is being told "I'll discuss that with you only if you promise not to use it." When the tape recorders are turned off, the news maker sometimes reveals what turns out to be the best part of the interview. That information, even if it is *off the record*, frequently is useful to reporters because it can put them on a trail that might lead to other people who will reveal the same information *for* the record.

It is essential that reporters honor any off-the-record agreement. A reporter who breaks that promise is guilty of a serious breach of ethics, a topic discussed in Chapter 18, "Ethics and the Law."

CURBING NODS AND SMILES   Television reporters must be concerned about their facial expressions and head movements during an interview, particularly in a studio situation when two or more cameras are being used. It also is important in field situations when listening shots of the reporter (called *reversals*) are being taken for editing purposes. It isn't inappropriate for reporters to smile or to nod their heads in agreement during an interview about a noncontroversial subject. However, when the issue *is* controversial and involves a subject with more than one point of view, a reporter cannot be shown expressing agreement or disagreement. A smile or frown or nod could send a wrong signal to an audience. The question of credibility and objectivity immediately comes into question. For example, to protest the Gulf War, some students managed to get onto the CBS "Evening News" set with Dan Rather. To Rather's credit, he ignored the whole incident and went on with the newscast. But at one affiliate station that replayed the incident, the anchor shook her head in obvious disgust as she came back on camera. She compromised her objectivity. Regardless of how she personally felt about the invasion of the CBS studio, she should have kept it to herself.

THE PHONE INTERVIEW   Radio reporters have the option of conducting many of their interviews on the phone. TV reporters use the phone only as a last resort because interviews without pictures are weak.

One of the disadvantages of the phone interview is that it's sometimes difficult to know when the news maker has finished giving an answer. Unless reporters listen carefully, they might interrupt the answer before it is complete, which sometimes makes editing the sound bites difficult. When you realize you might have missed something, apologize and ask the person to repeat the answer.

Phone interviews should only be used when it is impossible to interview the individual in person. It sounds unprofessional to do an interview on the phone with the mayor or someone else in your city or town when you could hop in a car and go to the person's office. Phone interviews are most effective when used to reach news makers in another part of the country or overseas. Such interviews demonstrate to the audience that the station is making a special effort to cover the news.

CHECKING FACTS   Some responses during an interview might not sound right. Whenever that happens, reporters should tell the news maker that something is puzzling them or that they do not quite understand the answer. If the answers still do not ring true or are still confusing, the reporters should check the information as soon as possible. Reporters could try contacting other sources who might have the same information or doing some research in the newsroom files, the library or computer data bases. If the information cannot be verified, reporters should explain that in the story. For example:

The head of the Newtown Power Company said there had never been an accident at the plant in the two years since it opened until today, when four people were seriously injured. We were unable to reach a union representative to verify the statement.

SOME OTHER TIPS   Susan Morris of the University of Pittsburgh has these other interview suggestions:

1. Develop a technique of asking short questions that get right to the point.
2. Phrase the questions without apologies and in a matter-of-fact manner. Avoid beginning a question with "I hate to ask you this, but. . . . "
3. Pause between questions even when dealing with less volatile subjects. You are likely to get more thoughtful answers.
4. If a person is hedging, take time to explain what the information is being used for. Explain that you do not have an editorial position.

SUMMARY   If you want to conduct a good interview, prepare for it. Do some research to find out as much as you can about the person you will be interviewing. Decide on the kind of information you want, and choose your questions accordingly.

Remember to listen carefully during an interview. Make sure your questions are answered to your satisfaction. If they aren't, say so, and follow up on your questions. Don't be used.

Try to maintain control of the interview. If you permit it, the interviewee will often take over. Keep to your objectives; don't let the head get off on tangents.

Finally, the most important thing to remember about interviews is that they are not necessarily a reliable source of accurate information because those being interviewed want to be perceived in the best light. Often interviewees are hiding something from you. Within reason, you should try to find out what they're hiding and be sure to check all facts they do disclose.

REVIEW QUESTIONS

1. Why must radio and TV reporters be more selective in choosing questions to ask in their interviews than their newspaper colleagues?
2. How should you prepare for an interview before you leave the station? Give some examples.
3. It's always a good idea to prepare a list of questions for an interview, but there also are dangers. Explain.
4. How should you phrase questions to make sure you get complete answers?
5. What kind of trouble can reporters fall into if they do not listen intently to the person they're interviewing?

6. Discuss the pros and cons of warming up the person you're interviewing.

7. Discuss tough and surprise questions.

8. What are the advantages and disadvantages of off-the-record comments?

9. Why must reporters be aware of their body language during an interview?

EXERCISES

1. Interview a faculty member in a department other than your own. But before doing so, find out as much as you can about the individual, and turn in those notes along with a story based on your interview.

2. Introduce yourself to a student whom you've never met, and conduct an interview. Write a story or produce a package about the person.

3. Read through your local newspaper, and pick someone in your community who is in the news. Interview the person, and then produce a wraparound report or package.

CHAPTER 16

COLLECTING INFORMATION
FROM DOCUMENTS

lthough the interview is the most common method of gathering information, it is not always the most reliable. Most spot news stories—fires, accidents, natural disasters, crime—usually can be covered with a few quick sound bites and video that supports the reporter's story. But if the story is more complex or interviews fail to provide all the answers, reporters must look to other sources of background information. This chapter explores the many documents available to reporters to provide such information.

PUBLIC RECORDS AND THE "SUNSHINE" LAWS

One of the great freedoms people in a democracy enjoy is the openness of society. Very little goes on in public life that is not recorded in one way or another. At times, however, those in public office attempt to cover up some of their activities. They can, and often do, complicate the reporter's efforts to uncover information. But persistent journalists are frequently able to circumvent such attempts at secrecy by examining public records. Reporters also have another strong weapon, the Freedom of Information Act (FOIA).

Congress passed the Freedom of Information Act in 1966, allowing the public access to records held by federal agencies of the executive branch. Since then, all 50 states have passed similar laws that permit the public to examine most records maintained by state and local governments. The freedom of information laws have been dubbed the "sunshine" laws because they are designed to shed light on the workings of government.

But that light hasn't always shined brightly. There have been numerous examples of government agencies refusing to disclose public records to private individuals or to journalists. The federal government, for example, has often claimed that revealing certain information would threaten national security. What was at issue most of the time was not the nation's security but information that would prove embarrassing to the agency or bureaucrat involved.

With that in mind, Congress amended the FOIA in 1974 and 1976, requiring federal agencies to release documents to the public unless the agencies could show some valid reason for not doing so. Nine exemptions were added to the FOIA, but the ones used most pertain to national security and foreign policy, advice and recommendations made within a federal agency, unwarranted invasion of privacy, files dealing with criminal cases that are current or pending, and trade secrets.

Because state "sunshine" laws vary, reporters seeking information from a state or local government office must examine that state's law before filing.

FILING AN FOIA REQUEST

The first thing a reporter must do when seeking government information is determine which federal agency has the information being sought. Sometimes, a telephone call to the agency will be enough to produce the information. If not, the reporter must then file an FOIA request in writing. The request should be written on the news organization's letterhead, and it should include the following:

1. An opening sentence making it clear that the letter deals with a Freedom of Information Act request.

2. An offer to pay reasonable fees for reproduction of records. (Some news organizations prefer to list an amount they are willing to pay, say $50, rather than use the term "reasonable amount.")

3. A request that the fees be waived because the information would benefit the public. (An optional statement indicating *how* the information would be beneficial increases the likelihood of the waiver being granted.)

4. A specific description of the documents being requested, including the actual titles of the documents if they are known.

5. A reminder that, by law, the agency has 10 days to provide the information requested or to explain why it is denying the request.

6. Some reporters like to inquire whether any other government agencies have requested the same information. This "fishing expedition" sometimes provides some unexpected information that's helpful.

It is a good idea to send the letter by certified mail and to request a return receipt. The envelope should indicate "FOIA Request" or "To the Attention of the FOIA Officer."

While the FOIA states that the agency has 10 days to respond to the request, it also allows the agency to take more time as long as it informs the reporter. Many agencies assign a number to the request, which should be used in any future contacts with the agency. A telephone call to the agency sometimes speeds up responses. If the agency does not reply within a reasonable time—two or three weeks—the reporter should send another letter, again reminding the agency of the time limits.

If an FOIA request is denied, the requester can file an appeal with the agency, which must be answered within 20 days. If that fails, the reporter can go to court to try to obtain the information, a costly and often lengthy endeavor. However, just the threat of a suit sometimes convinces an agency to release the information.

An FOIA request filed by producer Chris Szechenyi, who was with WRC-TV in Washington, D.C., at the time, is reproduced on page 253. The information obtained by Szechenyi made it possible for him to break a story involving the unreliability of defibrillators, high-tech medical equipment designed to shock a failed heart back to life. The producer discovered that during a six-year period, such equipment malfunctioned 512 times. He also discovered that the product made by one company, Physio Control Corporation, a subsidiary of Eli Lilly, accounted for 442 of those malfunctions. The company has about 80 percent of the defibrillator market. Szechenyi decided to find out all he could about Physio Control Corporation. He filed an FOIA request with the Food and Drug Administration. By law, medical-device manufacturers must report deaths to the FDA within 15 days if there is a reason to believe that they were caused by a medical device.

Szechenyi said he thought about doing a story about faulty medical equipment after Congress held hearings about problems with heart valves. "I was aware that there was a data base for all that information provided to the FDA on malfunctioning equipment by hospitals and manufacturers. But when I went to the government's National Technical Information Service (NTIS) to check on the information I found thousands of pages of reports. I knew there was no way to successfully gather all the information and come up with any intelligent evaluation. I realized I needed a computer to collate the information to find out which devices were causing the most problems."

Szechenyi then discovered that NTIS, for $350, would provide a computer tape that would give him the information that he needed. But he also realized he would need help to decipher the tape and joined forces with the Missouri Institute for Computer-Assisted Reporting (MICAR). The investigation took four months, and when it was over, Szechenyi and WRC-TV investigative reporter Lea Thompson produced a four-part series on medical-equipment problems. The probe was not limited to the Physio Control Corporation. Szechenyi said the defibrillator failures are "only a fraction of the [death] toll caused by a variety of defective medical devices." The investigative team discovered that there were 3,328 deaths and 52,000 injuries associated with medical devices during a six-year period. Szechenyi said, "We discovered that pacemakers, ventilators, heart valves and other devices designed to save lives are in fact losing lives."

Unfortunately, we could not get permission to reprint this award-winning script. Although we are not able to show you the actual script written by Szechenyi and Thompson, a synopsis of the video and sound bites that were used to tell the story follows. You can also examine the FOIA request filed by Szechenyi with the Food and Drug Administration. That is now a public document.

The report on equipment failures was divided into four segments. The first

August 20, 1990

FDA   FAX: 206-483-4996
PO Box 3012
Bothell, Washington
98041-3012

ATTENTION: ANITA ARMSTRONG, FOI OFFICE

To Whom It May Concern:

Under the Freedom of Information Act, I am requesting copies of the following records generated during 1980 to the present concerning Physio Control Corp.

1. Establishment inspection reports.
2. Any correspondence between the FDA district office and the company concerning its defibrillator/monitors.
3. Any and all regulatory actions by the FDA.
4. Minutes of any meetings between the district and the company concerning its defibrillator/monitors.
5. Any and all correspondence between the district and FDA headquarters concerning the company's defibrillator/monitors.
6. Any and all studies, surveys and scientific reports concerning the company's defibrillator/monitors.
7. Any proposals or recommendations by the district or headquarters concerning the company's defibrillator/monitors.

I am requesting that the FDA waive any copying costs associated with this request, as it will serve the public interest. However, if such a waiver would delay receipt of the documents for more than five days, then I would like to discuss the waiver request.

I would like to receive the documents as soon as possible, and look forward to your response within the 10 days required by the Act. Thank you for your assistance.

Sincerely,

Chris Szechenyi
WRC-TV Producer
202-885-4528

segment in the series was the most important one because it set the stage for the entire investigative report.

Lea Thompson opened the series with an on-camera statement about the number of people—a quarter of a million—who die each year of cardiac arrest. She noted that many survive such attacks because of the 911 emergency phone system and the medics who answer the calls for help. But, she noted, many others die needlessly because the life-saving equipment that the medics use frequently malfunctions.

After the on-camera open, Thompson went to a voice-over that showed medics treating a little girl who survived because the defibrillator *did* work that time.

At this point there was a sound bite from a medical services dispatcher who explained that quite often the story ends differently because the electric-shock equipment malfunctions for one reason or another.

In the next sound bite, a medical rescue worker described how, in his experience, the equipment never functioned in the field for more than a week without needing repair.

A montage of sound bites followed: a victim's sister said her sister would still be alive if the defibrillator had worked properly; the widow of another victim said the autopsy report had cited the failure of the machine, and, finally, a hospital spokesman blamed the FDA for not having any standard for the equipment.

Thompson then returned on camera to describe the extent of her and Szechenyi's investigation into the problem of malfunctioning medical equipment. She identified the company whose equipment was involved in most malfunctions; Physio Control Corporation, owned by Eli Lilly. She also criticized the FDA for not cracking down on the faulty equipment. She cited the statistics.

Next, in another sound bite, a member of an FDA task force said that the statistics concerning the number of reported deaths caused by faulty defibrillators were just the tip of the iceberg.

Now another medical worker blamed the faulty equipment for the death of a patient he had been trying to help. In the next bite, the woman who earlier had spoken of her husband's death described the scene in the ambulance when medics were trying to save his life after he collapsed while jogging. The bite was quickly followed by another one, this time of a medic who described how he had pushed the defibrillator equipment's buttons and how nothing had happened. The crew had replaced the batteries and tried again, he said, but the machine still had not worked. Then, he said, a second ambulance had arrived and provided a new set of batteries, still fresh in the box, and they too were dead. The patient had died.

Thompson returned on camera to talk about the man's autopsy report, which again blamed Physio Control's equipment.

In another sound bite, the medic involved in that incident blamed the manufacturer.

Two other quick bites followed, one by an engineer who spoke of poor design and the other by a medic who said that his patient would still be alive if the machine had worked.

Thompson returned on camera to note that the widow was suing Physio Control. Then, in an emotional sound bite, the widow recalled how much her family had suffered. She said that, because the death occurred just before her daughter's wedding, the daughter had to walk down the aisle without her father at her side.

This part of the series ended with Thompson, on camera, describing what would be covered in the next segment.

Szechenyi said that after his story was on the air, he realized that the FDA had not given him a key letter that it had sent to Physio Control Corporation concerning the company's defective equipment. He did a follow-up FOIA request and received the letter, but the series had already been aired. "If we had had that letter," the producer said, "it would have supported some points we made in the script and made it stronger." Szechenyi said the FDA's failure to provide the letter along with the other material raised suspicions in his mind that there was a "cozy relationship between the FDA and the manufacturer." He said it also showed that the FOIA is not "flawless."

But Szechenyi noted that the story, which won the National Headliner Award in 1991, could not have been done without the information produced by the FOIA. Almost as important to the investigation was computer technology. Since 1984, the FDA has put into its computers the investigation of more than 100,000 cases of medical-equipment failure. For each case, the computerized record contains the name and address of the manufacturer, the kind of medical device that was involved, a description of the problem, and a statement detailing whether the device merely malfunctioned or caused an injury or death. The record also states whether the FDA has finished its investigation and whether the device was determined to be at fault.

Szechenyi said that computer analysis "is only the first step in the reporting process. Once you have identified a product that is causing problems, . . . you have to find out if there were any recalls." Information about recalls can also be obtained from the FDA under the FOIA. The recall notices say what's wrong with devices, how many were distributed and what the company is doing to correct the problem.

Szechenyi, who has moved to Paris as a "60 Minutes" producer since working on this story, said FDA inspections of a company's plants also are available under the FOIA. He noted "it paid to be friendly" with the FOIA officer at the FDA field office in Seattle, who sent a stack of documents only three weeks after Szechenyi made the request. The producer said he got about 600 documents from the field office, and it waived all fees.

Szechenyi said that "behind the statistics and records are tragic human stories, and court records are the best source to find the victims." He also got results by contacting some top litigation lawyers. "I found one lawyer who handled a medical-equipment malfunction case," Szechenyi said, "and he told me about other attorneys who had similar cases, and that's how we got the human stories used in our reports."

A NEGLECTED TOOL

Szechenyi says that when he can avoid using the FOIA, he does so because filing a request is so much trouble. Perhaps that is why few journalists make use of the Freedom of Information Act. Only a handful of broadcast journalists have filed FOIA requests. Actually, prisoners and businesses have made more use of the FOIA than any other group. While some information obtained through FOIA requests can be found in other places, there are times, as Szechenyi admitted, when there is no way to do the story without the FOIA.

THE PRIVACY ACT

Some members of Congress were concerned that the FOIA would step on one of Americans' most treasured freedoms—privacy. So in 1974, Congress passed the Privacy Act in an attempt to protect individuals from unwarranted invasion of their privacy. The act forbids the government from disclosing information in its files pertaining to individuals. Many journalists, however, argue that the government uses the act to keep important information from the public.

GOVERNMENT REPORTS

Ironically, while the government often fails to disclose certain information from the public, it publishes volumes of manuals and directories that are important sources of information for journalists. Sometimes, the information found in these government publications is as embarrassing as the material an agency does not disclose.

Among the government publications found at public and university libraries that are particularly useful to journalists are the reports issued by the General Accounting Office (GAO)—a congressional agency. The GAO issues more than a thousand reports a year, and its recommendations to Congress often provide interesting and sometimes provocative story ideas for journalists. The now famous stories about the Pentagon paying 20 and 30 times what it should for hammers and other basic tools came from GAO reports.

Other government publications that are useful to reporters include the following:

The Code of Federal Regulations, which describes how laws and regulations are enforced.

The Congressional Record, which offers a daily report of congressional debate and other business. It also includes a list of most agencies and high-ranking government officials, including members of Congress, of its various committees, and of the judicial and executive branches.

The Federal Regional Directory, which lists federal offices that have records on local programs and activities involving the government.

The Federal Register, which gives a daily account of federal-agency activities and executive orders from the White House.

The Federal Regulatory Directory, which describes the 15 major regulatory agencies and lists the more than 60 lesser-known regulatory bodies. Also lists the names of top officials.

The U.S. Bureau of the Census publications, which provide statistical information on just about every aspect of life in America.

The U.S. Government Manual, which outlines the responsibilities and organization of the federal government. It includes all sorts of valuable information, including addresses, phone numbers and names of officials at various government branches.

The Washington Information Directory, which provides additional non-government sources not shown in the Government Manual.

All of these publications—and a great many more—are also housed in Government Depository Libraries located throughout the United States and on many university campuses.

BUSINESS PUBLICATIONS AND INDEXES

Reporters working on complex or investigative stories about business can find a variety of useful publications in the library, including Dun & Bradstreet's directory of companies worth a million dollars or more. Also extremely useful is Standard & Poor's Register of Corporations, which not only lists the corporations but also includes background information on major business leaders. Reporters looking for information on specific products find the Thomas Register of American Manufacturers series particularly helpful.

There are also magazines and newspapers that write about business and in-

Roger O'Neil, NBC news correspondent and bureau chief in Denver
COURTESY OF RAY FARMER/NBC NEWS

dustry. The most respected are the Wall Street Journal, Forbes, Fortune and Business Week.

TRADE PUBLICATIONS

The story of American industry is also told in hundreds of magazines and publications available in libraries. A great many of them are biased because they speak for the industry they represent. Nevertheless, reporters frequently find useful information in such publications. Quite often they provide leads for reporters seeking industry spokespeople. Trade publications are also an important source for information on what position various industries are taking on an issue.

DATA-BASE SERVICES

Computer data bases are invaluable tools for searching all sorts of subjects. Many libraries have computerized the catalogue of the information that's housed there, which makes locating the information much faster. Many libraries subscribe to data-base services such as NEXIS, InfoTrac and others that index hundreds of newspapers, magazines, academic and scientific journals, and trade publications.

Many radio and TV newsrooms that acquired computers for word processing, assignment lists, producer rundowns and various other news activities are also subscribing to data-base services, particularly NEXIS. These computerized information retrieval systems provide writers and reporters with a significant new research tool, the ability to find and scan thousands of publications and reports without leaving the newsroom.

OTHER PUBLIC FILES

Reporters have another useful method of locating information, particularly information about individuals—government files. Governments at all levels maintain files on scores of different activities that happen within their borders. When a baby is born, or when someone dies, or is married or divorced, or registers a car or opens a liquor store, or buys a piece of land or is arrested, or sues somebody or opens a restaurant, someone issues a document that is kept on permanent record. Anyone who wishes may look at and copy such documents.

POLICE RECORDS

The amount of information that reporters can obtain from police records varies from community to community. Reporters who establish a good rapport with a police desk sergeant often get the information they want with little trouble. Technically, any information on the police log or blotter should be available to reporters. But without a good rapport, it sometimes takes the threat of court action to get the information. The records include the name of the individual, the date of the arrest, the charges and the disposition of those charges. Once a person is behind bars, that information is normally available where the individual is being held.

COURT RECORDS

Information about the court cases most reporters deal with—criminal and civil cases—is available at a court clerk's office. In a civil case, anyone can obtain information about the complaint or petition brought by the plaintiff. The complaint usually describes what the defendant has allegedly done and why the plaintiff wants the court to award damages.

In criminal cases, reporters also have access to the charges brought against an individual. The records list the name of the complainant, most often a police officer, and the name of the defendant. The records cite the charge and describe what allegedly occurred that led to the arrest and court action.

Reporters soon learn that it's a lot easier, and quicker, to find these records if they are on a first-name basis with the court clerks.

BIRTH AND DEATH RECORDS

Knowing the facts of a person's birth often can be important to a reporter. A birth certificate shows the names of the parents, the date of birth, the name of the doctor who delivered the child and the name of the hospital. Death certificates also provide information that may be important to a story. They show the cause of death and the date and time it occurred. However, such records are not always public. If an individual left a will that involved real estate, reporters may also obtain a copy of the death certificate attached to mortgages and deeds found at the property tax office.

Being friendly and showing respect often make it easier to find some of these records or, perhaps, get a quick look at those that are not supposed to be open to the public.

ABC News Correspondent Morton Dean
STEVE FENN/CAPITAL CITIES, ABC NEWS

LICENSES

Almost every community issues licenses of many kinds, and sometimes knowing who received a license can be important to a newsperson. In a large city, there is little that goes on in business that does not require some sort of a license—even selling hot dogs on the street. Such licenses list the name and other personal information about the grantee. Such information would be valuable, for example, if a reporter was doing a story about a junkyard that was an environmental or safety hazard.

The licensing of guns has been an ongoing issue throughout the nation. Because there is no national gun-control law, the ability to check on people who may own guns depends on where the reporter is doing the checking. New York has strict gun laws; Virginia does not, a fact that bothers many people who live just across the border in the nation's capital, which has one of the worst crime and homicide records involving guns in the world.

Driver's license records and car registrations are also easily available in some states and can be obtained with a minimum amount of coaxing in most others if the reporter can provide a good reason for wanting the information.

Many professional people, such as doctors, architects and engineers, also must hold licenses. The state agencies or boards that issue those licenses have biographical information, including education and the applicants' specialty.

LAND RECORDS

The property tax office can provide a lot of information to an investigative reporter. It has records on who pays the taxes on property and, presumably, but not always, on the owner of the property. The records also reveal the former owners' names and the purchase price of the property, as well as who holds the mortgage on the property, if there is one. The names of the real-estate brokers and lawyers who were involved in the sale are also indicated. All of this might be important to know if, let's say, a reporter was checking on a city judge who seemed to be very lenient with drunk drivers and it was discovered in the property tax records that the judge was living in a million-dollar home in the suburbs.

FINANCIAL RECORDS

Checking a person's financial record is easy. In the eyes of many, except perhaps reporters looking for such information, it's too easy to find out about how Americans handle their finances. All reporters need to do is ask the business office where they work to call TRW or some other credit bureau, and the person's financial record will be on the reporter's desk in minutes. The record shows credit histories for 10 years or more, the names of those holding mortgages, where individuals shop and whether they pay their bills on time. The report also shows any bankruptcy declared during the past 10 years.

Anytime an individual moves and establishes credit of any kind, the new address is recorded, which can be useful to a reporter trying to find the person. There are also firms that provide a person's new address as long as the reporter supplies a Social Security number.

TAX RECORDS

Tax records are among the most difficult to obtain. Reporters do, from time to time, obtain information about a person's tax returns from the Internal Revenue Service, but it almost always is the result of a leak initiated by someone inside the agency. Some reporters manage to develop sources inside the IRS, but it is no easy task.

CITY DIRECTORIES   Professor Jill Olmsted of American University reminds reporters of the value of city directories, which list a person's name, address, spouse, children, employment and a variety of other useful pieces of information. Professor Olmsted says the directories are particularly helpful when a reporter is trying to talk to relatives of someone who is in the news. "For example," she says, "if you know only the name and state of a person taken hostage in Lebanon, you can check if they are local and find the family members to talk to."

Telephone books also are useful; they would be the first place to look when trying to locate someone if you know the town or city in which he or she lives. In some communities, the telephone company also prints telephone books that list people and companies by their addresses. They are extremely useful, for example, if a major fire breaks out on the 1500 block of Main Street. There are listings for all of the phones on Main Street that are not restricted, so all the reporter or assignment editor has to do is try to locate a phone near the 1500 block. A call to a phone listed at 1550 Main Street, for example, might find someone who can see the fire from an apartment window. It's then quite simple to put the person on the air while he or she describes the fire and answers a reporter's questions.

SUMMARY   Unfortunately, not very many radio or TV news organizations give their reporters enough time to make use of the various sources of information described in this chapter. Reporters spend most of their time working on breaking news stories. Investigative stories require a lot of research time and are expensive to produce. Most stations want at least one story a day from their reporters, which doesn't allow much time for checking court records or filing FOI requests.

If you do have an opportunity to work on stories that require in-depth research, the information in this chapter should be extremely helpful. The Freedom of Information Act is an important asset if you wish to examine the actions of government at any level, town , city, state or federal. The library at your college or university has scores of documents that will reveal more about the federal government, how it works, and what mistakes it makes. The report of the General Accounting Office, a congressional watchdog, and the Congressional Directory are particularly useful.

Also become familiar with the various business publications, indexes, journals and magazines in your library and learn about the ability of data bases such as NEXIS.

This chapter also describes how to use the various government files maintained by police and the courts, tax and land offices and bureaus that keep records on births, deaths, licenses and scores of other activities.

REVIEW QUESTIONS

1. What is the Freedom of Information Act?

2. Why is it so important to journalists?

3. Does the FOIA apply only to the dealings of the federal government?

4. List the different points that should be made in a letter requesting information under the FOIA.

5. Journalists can learn about the government and how it operates through various records and publications. List some of the most important ones, and explain how they are useful.

6. How can computer data bases be useful to reporters?

7. What kind of information can reporters obtain from police and court records?

EXERCISES

1. Suppose that you are filing an FOIA request with the Defense Department because you have a source that claims that when he worked for the Acme Tool and Dye Company in Centerville, a government contractor, as many as 60 percent of the products produced in the plant were rejected for various reasons. Prepare the FOIA request.

2. Pick three corporations among the Fortune 500 list, and find out the names of the top officials who run the companies. Also list any other companies that are owned by one of these parent companies, and find out the names of any corporations or individuals who own a substantial number of shares in a parent company.

3. Use a data-base service to find out how many articles were published in the last year about Dan Rather. List the names of the publications along with the titles of the articles and the dates they appeared.

4. Visit the local courthouse and find out the names of those who were convicted of driving while intoxicated during the past month.

CHAPTER 17

DEVELOPING SOURCES

 ust being on the air attracts some *sources*, people who provide information for news stories. As reporters and anchors become known and respected by their audience, they receive telephone calls and letters about a variety of subjects. Some are letters of praise, some are complaints. Also included among those calls and letters are some news *tips*. Some of the most important stories aired by radio and TV stations come from tipsters. Others come from sources cultivated at public agencies and insiders at corporations and other institutions. This chapter discusses developing relationships with such sources.

TIPS

Stations that establish reputations for doing investigative stories are more likely than others to get tips. Astute news directors encourage tipsters, often setting up private telephone lines just for that purpose. Most of the calls involve breaking news—fires, accidents, crime—but sometimes the caller has a nugget of information that leads to an investigative story.

Frequently tips are the result of stories that were reported earlier by the station. For example, a story about a politician using public funds for a personal trip to Las Vegas may attract calls from viewers who know about similar trips by other politicians. Who makes such calls, and why? Often, the calls and letters are from people who have been working closely with the wrongdoers. They may be annoyed because of the misuse of public funds or because they lost their jobs or because of jealousy or a long-standing grudge. That caller then becomes a source who might provide additional information on other stories or the names of additional sources. "I don't know all the details, but I can give you the name of someone who can, as long as you don't reveal my name," is the way the phone conversation might go. The phrase *don't reveal my name* is key to developing and keeping sources.

CONFIDENTIALITY

The fastest way to lose a source is to break a promise of *confidentiality*. Few sources give reporters sensitive information without a promise of secrecy. Once a reporter gives that promise, it must be respected, regardless of the consequences. A reporter's right to protect sources has often been tested in the courts, and reporters do not always win. On rare occasions, reporters have gone to jail or been fined for refusing to disclose a source.

Before entering into such an agreement with a source, reporters must analyze what they are agreeing to keep secret. Reporters disagree, for example, on whether it's a good idea to offer confidentiality to those who admit that they are actively involved in crime. Some reporters say they agree to such a pact if that's *the only way* to break the story. Others say they would never enter into such an agreement and warn those sources that if they disclose any information about criminal behavior on their part, the reporters will not guarantee secrecy. Washington Post columnist and investigative reporter Jack Anderson says, "We will give immunity to a very good source as long as the information he offers us is better than that which we've got on him."

If a reporter promises to keep a source secret and that promise is broken, it can be costly. The U.S. Supreme Court ruled in 1991 that news organizations cannot break promises of confidentiality to news sources. The landmark decision was the result of a suit brought by a public-relations consultant in Minnesota after two newspapers in that state broke their promise of confidentiality. The plaintiff, Dan Cohen, was working for gubernatorial candidate Wheelock Whitney when he agreed to give the Star Tribune of Minneapolis and the St. Paul Pioneer Press Dispatch information about a shoplifting conviction of Marlene Johnson, a candidate on the opposing ticket. Pioneer Press Dispatch reporter Bill Salisbury and Star Tribune reporter Lori Sturdevant had promised Cohen confidentiality. But their newspapers decided to withdraw the agreement and identified Cohen in the stories. He was fired from his job with a large advertising agency the next day.

The lawyers for the newspapers argued that the public had the right to know who had disclosed the derogatory information about the candidate and argued it was the newspapers' First Amendment right to publish Cohen's name. The Court voted 5 to 4 that Minnesota law requires "those making promises to keep them," and that the newspapers had no right to break their promise of confidentiality.

Salisbury said the Cohen case "may permanently change the relationship between reporters and anonymous sources. It should discourage editors from breaking reporters' promises, thus making sources feel more confident that their names will be protected." But Salisbury said the ruling also "chips away at the press's First Amendment protections, and it invites more lawsuits over broken promises." Cohen was awarded $200,000 for breach of contract.

ACCURACY OF SOURCES

A reporter should never use a source as a basis for a story until the information is checked for accuracy. Verifying a story is not always easy, especially when a reporter is working under deadlines. One of the best ways to make sure a story is accurate is to find several other sources who will disclose exactly the same information. This is known as *double-* or *triple-sourcing*. Some reporters insist on finding at least some sort of printed documentation before they broadcast a story. Quite often, if pushed, a source will provide such documentation or reveal where it can be found.

Most station managers have a policy that requires reporters to disclose their sources or documentation to at least one person in authority at the station before they are allowed to broadcast the investigative material. Failure to provide such safeguards invites disaster. The classic example cited in every textbook on reporting—and in every newsroom—is the Janet Cooke incident in which editors at The Washington Post failed to check a story about a child addicted to drugs. The well-written story won a Pulitzer Prize. Unfortunately, the profiled child was a composite of children the reporter had met, not an actual person, and the newspaper had to return the prize. Janet Cooke was fired, and The Washington Post changed its policy on checking its reporters' sources.

The late distinguished investigative reporter Clark Mollenhoff warned that "few informants are totally reliable, even though they may believe they are telling the reporter the full truth." He said the information taken from a confidential source should be used only as a lead to records, documents or other sources who are willing to be quoted by name.

In their book "Investigative Reporting," authors David Anderson and Peter Benjaminson write that it is sometimes a good idea for reporters to "talk to other reporters" about a source before investing a lot of time in documenting a story. The authors note that other reporters might already be familiar with the source, and the story he or she has to tell, and might have already "researched and debunked the information." They also say, "Nothing is quite as discouraging as working for days on a top-notch investigative piece only to discover that another reporter is typing out a final draft while you are still looking for the phone booth your source called from."

GAINING CONFIDENCE

Reporters who find good, reliable sources and prove to them that they will protect their confidentiality usually find that those sources will continue to provide information, sometimes for many years. Self-esteem is frequently one of the motives for tipsters, and feeling good about being involved in the breaking of a story often encourages them to find new items. Smart reporters tell their sources that they are providing a service to the community. This allows sources to see themselves as part of a team, and they will actively look for new information to provide to their colleague at the radio or TV station.

MAKING FRIENDS

Other good information comes from "friends" whom reporters cultivate in offices where records and documents are housed and, particularly for crime-beat reporters, at police desks.

Experienced reporters also suggest that "hanging out" at restaurants, coffee houses and bars where politicians and city and county employees gather is another good way to develop friendships and new sources. Such sources begin to accept you as one of them, and if they have any stories to tell or have heard some interesting rumors, they may share them with a friendly reporter.

LEAKS

Information from a source in the political or corporate world is known as a *leak*. As with sources who provide tips, government insiders, for one reason or another, reveal information of a sensitive nature to the press with the promise of confidentiality. Such insiders could be White House staff members, assistants to members of a state assembly, or someone in a mayor's office who wants the media to know something about an individual or about an action that is being planned or debated behind closed doors.

One of the most celebrated leaks in recent years complicated the nomination of Supreme Court Justice Clarence Thomas. Just before the Senate was to vote on Thomas' nomination, a story that Anita Hill, who once worked for Thomas, had told federal investigators that Thomas had sexually harassed her was leaked to the press. As a result, the vote was delayed as the Senate Judiciary Committee extended the hearings.

Two reporters, Nina Totenberg of National Public Radio and Timothy Phelps of Newsday, reported the information. The leak sparked a national debate within Congress and among Americans, who found themselves divided on the propriety of such information being leaked to the media. There were new calls for the plugging of such leaks and suggestions of penalties for those who were found guilty of perpetrating them.

Phelps and Totenberg were subpoenaed by a special Senate counsel, who attempted to discover the source of the leak. When both reporters refused to

Nina Totenberg, legal affairs correspondent for National Public Radio, testifies before a congressional committee during the Clarence Thomas confirmation hearings.

PHOTO BY MICHAEL GEISSINGER

identify their source, the counsel attempted to gain support for some action against them, such as a contempt citation, but he failed. Senators apparently were not anxious to test First Amendment rights by compelling the reporters to disclose their sources.

Totenberg said she "simply wasn't going to tell" who gave her the information and that she was "prepared to go to jail" rather than reveal who leaked the information to her. In an interview with Professor Emeritus Ben Silver of Arizona State University, Totenberg noted that she did not identify Anita Hill by name until Hill agreed to be interviewed. Otherwise, Totenberg said, "I would not have done it. I don't think you can trust an accusation as long as it remains anonymous."

When asked how she felt about reporting such allegations, Totenberg said, "It's more than just reporting an allegation, she [Hill] turned out to be a credible witness, although I can't vouch for the truth of the allegation."

Totenberg said her mail "is full of allegations," but unless she can verify them she doesn't broadcast them. "You can't fully corroborate all the time," said the NPR correspondent. She said that was true in the Anita Hill case but she eliminated the problem by speaking with a person she considered credible, Susan Hoerchner. She said Hoerchner, a judge on the California Workers' Compensation Appeals Board, told her that Hill had made the same sexual harassment allegation against Thomas eight years earlier during a conversation she had with Hill. Hoerchner said she and Hill had met when they were students at Yale University. Hoerchner later gave the same information to the Senate Judiciary Committee.

Leaks, of course, have been a way of life in Congress and probably in every administration since the creation of the U.S. government. The consensus among most Washington observers in and out of government is that it is impossible to stop leaks.

There is also a common point of view that leaks, for the most part, probably provide a service to the American people. A leak from a source believed to be in the Nixon administration, the so-called Deep Throat, led to the Watergate scandal that resulted in the downfall of President Richard Nixon.

As for the leak involving Clarence Thomas, CBS News Correspondent Richard Threlkeld said he may be "getting jaded" as he gets older. He noted that "one man's leak is another man's essential release of timely information. The Republicans were mad because a Democrat apparently leaked info about Anita Hill. But," Threlkeld pointed out, "some years ago during Abe Fortas' contentious removal from the Court, Senator Strom Thurmond's office leaked info about him, and his misdoing, to the press, and that made him leave the Court." Threlkeld asked, "What's wrong with that? Senator Thurmond, I am sure, would call that timely release of essential info, so I'm not that concerned about leaks."

The CBS newsman concluded, "There always have been leaks and there always will be. . . . There are no gaskets in the faucet of public information that would stop them."

*Anita Hill is sworn in at the Clarence
Thomas confirmation hearings.*
AP/WIDE WORLD PHOTOS

*Supreme Court Justice Clarence Thomas during his confirmation
hearings.*
REUTERS/BETTMANN

TRIAL BALLOONS

A different type of leak is the *trial balloon*. In this case, the leak has the endorsement of the White House, the mayor or some other government official or agency. The trial balloon tips off one or more people in the media about some controversial action the department or official is thinking of taking. The purpose of the trial balloon is to measure reaction in advance not only from the people but also from the media, lobbying groups and others. If the trial balloon is greeted with strong opposition, then the official or agency could quietly forget the action it had contemplated. On the other hand, if there is no loud protest, or the planned action is received with enthusiasm, the action probably would proceed as planned.

OFF-THE-RECORD STATEMENTS

Another source of information frequently used by the media is the *off-the-record statement*. As in the case of confidential sources, if a reporter consents to the off-the-record agreement, it must be honored.

The advantage of accepting information that cannot be broadcast is that it often leads the reporter to another source for the same information. Once a new source is developed, the reporter is free to quote the second source. Without that off-the-record material to begin with, the reporter may not have known about the subject at all or known where to start looking for the details.

AUTHORITATIVE OR INFORMED SOURCES

When sources of information cannot be substantiated by ordinary means, reporters often attribute the information to a spokesperson, or authoritative or informed sources. There are times, for example, when correspondents at the White House, State Department and Pentagon obtain information from government officials that may only be used with the understanding that the source is not to be named. So reporters who wish to use the information must say, "a spokesman at the Pentagon" or "a source at the State Department revealed today." Reporters who do not wish to use such vague attribution would be unable to use the information.

Most people in the radio and TV audience take such attributions for granted, assuming that if the reporter is quoting a spokesperson the story is probably true. Most often it is, but there's no guarantee.

BACKGROUND BRIEFINGS

Government officials frequently will give information to reporters but insist that neither the officials nor the agencies they represent be identified. These meetings are called background briefings. If reporters wish to use the information revealed at such briefings, they must attribute it by using phrases such as "official sources" or "well-informed sources."

SUMMARY

Developing good sources and keeping them confidential make up the backbone of effective reporting. Much of this chapter discusses the importance of maintaining relationships with sources. Most reporters honor confidentiality agreements, and some have even gone to jail rather than disclose their sources. They knew if they had revealed their sources, they would have lost their credibility and effectiveness as journalists.

It is equally important to know that sources are reliable. It is essential to check and double-check the information they provide; never use information from only one source as the basis for a story. At the same time, don't dismiss information without thoroughly checking to see if it could be true.

If you agree to keep information off the record, make sure you do, otherwise it will be the last time that person will give you *any* information. Also remember that when you do agree to keep something off the record, start looking for sources you can quote for the record.

REVIEW QUESTIONS

1. What motivates people to give a radio or TV station tips?

2. Explain why you would or would not broadcast information provided by a tipster.

3. Discuss some ways to develop sources.

4. What is a leak? Give an example.

5. What is a trial balloon?

6. What does *off the record* mean?

EXERCISES

1. Suppose that you are a TV assignment editor and you receive a call from an individual who claims she saw the mayor meeting with a well-known mobster. Describe in detail how you would handle the situation.

2. Suppose you are a news director for a radio station. You get a call from a student at the local university who says he has been dealing in narcotics but wants to quit. He says he will tell you the whole story about drugs on campus, but you have to keep his identity secret. Do you agree and put a reporter on the story? Explain your decision.

3. An individual has been leaking information to you for several years and has always been reliable. But she now tells you a story about corruption that could bring down the city administration if true. Do you tell anyone else at the station what you have been told? Do you disclose your source? Explain in detail.

CHAPTER 18

ETHICS AND THE LAW

his chapter and the next focus on the important and complex issues of ethical and legal concerns—issues difficult to separate. All journalists must be concerned about ethics, and the law is there to remind journalists of their responsibilities, if necessary.

GRATUITIES

Reporters are frequently tempted with *gratuities,* or gifts. There is not much to say about the subject except that it is impossible for reporters to maintain their credibility if they accept any kind of gift from people or organizations they cover. Many offers come from public-relations people. Some gifts may come at Christmas, while others may arrive at the door of a reporter or producer following the broadcast of a story about a product or service. The gifts should be returned.

Some news directors pass out such gifts to non-news staff, but doing so sends the wrong message to the donor. If the gifts are not returned, the senders have no way of knowing that they were not appreciated and might assume that they can expect some favor the next time they're promoting something.

One news director says that when Christmas gifts arrive, he does give them to the people in the mailroom but does not say who sent them. He says he also calls the donor and lets him or her know that he can't accept gifts and has passed them along to the mailroom staff. "That's easier than packing the stuff up and sending it back," he says. "It also lets the PR people know that I can't be bought, and it makes the people in the mailroom a little bit happier."

CONFLICT OF INTEREST

Sometimes, the issue of what is an acceptable practice is not so clearly defined. Is it wrong for a theater or film reviewer to receive free tickets from the show's producers? Some newspapers pay for their reviewers' tickets, but the vast majority of reviewers *do* accept free tickets, and there is no reason to believe that it influences what they write about a film or play.

Some news organizations, however, get nervous when more is at stake, fearing a *conflict of interest.* For example, hotel owners sometimes offer newspeople a free plane ride and accommodations to promote a new hotel. Is it possible for the reporter to maintain objectivity when the host has provided him or her with a thousand dollars or more for travel and entertainment? Some journalists claim it would take more than that to corrupt them. Some of them may even write negative stories about the trip, but the temptation to be favorable toward the host is great. To avoid such potential conflicts of interest, many news directors forbid these trips and any such offers.

ACCURACY AND RESPONSIBILITY

The need for accuracy in journalism has been stressed throughout this book. The subject also appears in this chapter because accuracy is an essential part of the discussion of ethics.

Some inaccuracy will always creep into news writing and reporting; people make mistakes. The ethical thing to do if errors occur is to correct the mistakes immediately.

Accuracy becomes an ethical problem when the facts in a story are wrong not because of carelessness but because of bias, preconceived conclusions, a failure to give all sides of the story or for any other reason that the information seen and heard by the audience is distorted or untrue.

NBC News Correspondent Roger O'Neil says, "I'm very concerned about

An anti-abortion demonstration in Baton Rouge. Reporters must always present both sides of a controversial subject.
PHOTO BY JAMES TERRY

getting the facts straight. I double-check what I say because I know how powerful and frightening my words can be. I can ruin people's lives, and I have. I can ruin businesses, and I have. But fortunately, my facts were right."

Being accurate also means taking responsibility—the responsibility to write and report the truth in a manner that is as objective and fair as possible. Taking responsibility means looking at *all* the issues, not just the easy or popular ones. It means examining controversies and producing special reports throughout the year, not just during the sweeps rating periods. Taking responsibility means covering important stories that don't always offer good pictures. Responsibility means writing and reporting with care, understanding and compassion. It means dealing with people in a professional and civil manner.

LIBEL

Although it should not be the motivating factor for insisting on accuracy, there is always the threat of *libel* facing those journalists who through carelessness, ignorance or malice make inaccurate statements in their scripts and reports that reflect on the character or reputation of an individual or group. Libel laws differ from state to state, but essentially writers or reporters can be sued for libel if anything they write or report exposes an individual or group to public scorn, hatred, ridicule or contempt; causes harm to someone in their occupation or profession; or causes someone to be shunned or avoided.

Reporters must also remember that it is not necessary to have actually used a person's name to be sued for libel. If the audience knows to whom a reporter is referring, even without the name, the reporter could be sued for libel if the comments harm the person's reputation.

Although *libel* traditionally refers to printed material and *slander* to spoken words, the distinction between the two terms has little meaning for broadcast reporters. Recognizing that broadcast material is usually scripted, many state laws regard any defamatory statements on radio and television as subject to libel laws.

Attorney and former reporter Bruce Sanford says there are certain words that writers and editors should be wary of using. Here is a partial list of what Sanford refers to as "red flag" words:

adultery	deadbeat	illegitimate
atheist	double-crosser	incompetent
bankrupt	drug addict	infidelity
bigamist	drunkard	intimate
blackmail	ex-convict	liar
bribery	fascist	mental disease
cheat	fool	perjurer
corruption	fraud	shyster
coward	gangster	unethical
crook	hypocrite	unprofessional

Remember also that using the word *alleged* before a potentially libelous word does not make it any less libelous.

DEFENSES

Courts usually recognize only three defenses against libel: truth, privilege and fair comment.

The *truth* is the best defense, but in some states the courts have ruled that truth is only a defense if the comments were not malicious.

Privilege covers areas such as legislative and judicial hearings and debates and documents that are in the public domain. If a reporter quotes a potentially libelous comment made by a senator during a debate, the reporter could not be sued for libel.

Fair comment also is used as a defense against libel. Public officials, performers, sports figures and others who attract public attention must expect to come under more criticism and scrutiny than most people. So if a sports commentator, for example, says that college football coach Joe Brown is a "lousy coach and the team would be better off if this inept, incompetent jerk moved on to a high-school coaching job, which he might just possibly be able to handle," he might get a sock on the nose if he ran into the coach but he would not end up in court for libel.

However, there are limits to what reporters can say even about public figures; the facts must be true. If the sports commentator had included the comment that Brown's "real problem is that he is smoking too many joints at night," then Brown would indeed have a libel case unless the sports commentator could prove that Coach Brown actually spends his nights smoking pot.

FALSE LIGHT

A complaint similar to libel, called *false light,* involves the improper juxtaposition of video and audio that creates a false impression of someone. This invasion-of-privacy issue has actually brought on more suits against TV news organizations than libel has, and it is more difficult to defend.

Karen Frankola, an instructor at the University of Missouri, described a case involving a reporter working on a story about genital herpes. The reporter was having difficulty figuring out how to cover the story, so she relied on some walking-down-the-street file video. Frankola said that in the package used on the 6 o'clock news, none of the passers-by was identifiable. But the story was edited differently for the 11 o'clock news, and the audience saw a close-up of a young woman while the anchor was saying, "For the 20 million Americans who have herpes, it's not a cure." The woman in the close-up won damages from the TV station.

Frankola said that false light "may get past a journalist more easily because it's not as obvious that false information is being given." She noted that the reporter in the herpes story did not say "the woman has herpes," which would have been a red flag to the editor. But, Frankola said, "the combination of words and pictures implied that the woman had the disease."

The Reporters Committee for Freedom of the Press issued a report showing that 47 percent of subpoenas issued to TV stations deal with such invasion-of-privacy actions. The group's executive director, Jane Kirtley, believes the number of suits is growing because "people are developing a much greater sense of privacy, a desire to be let alone."

For most Americans, privacy is a cornerstone of their existence. They expect it to be respected. Journalists should invade that privacy with trepidation, particularly at times of grief, as was discussed in the chapters on reporting.

BOUNDARIES

How far should reporters go to get a story? If reporters have a strong suspicion that someone in government is a crook, don't they have the right to do whatever it takes to report the story to the public? Some journalists say they do. Other newspeople believe if they bend the rules too much, they become suspect and may be viewed as no different than the people they are investigating. Each reporter must decide the ethical merits involved in certain investigative practices.

CONTROVERSIAL TECHNIQUES

Among the controversial information-gathering techniques employed by investigative reporters are impersonation, misrepresentation and infiltration. Should journalists use such techniques to get a story? Is it right, for example, for a reporter to pretend to be a nurse so that she can get inside a nursing home to investigate charges that residents are being mistreated? Is it proper for a journalist to tell a college football coach that he wants to do a story about training when he's really checking on reports of drug abuse and gambling? Is it permissible for a reporter to pose as a pregnant woman thinking about having an abortion in order to find out what kind of material a right-to-life organization is providing at its information center? All of these incidents actually occurred, and they represent only a few examples of the controversial methods used on a routine basis. Are they ethical?

Investigative reporter Jim Polk, who moved over to CNN after spending many years with NBC, says he never misrepresents himself, impersonates others or uses any other techniques that he feels are unethical. "Our business is the truth," he says, "and I do not think you get the truth by practicing deception."

About the reporter who posed as a nurse to get into a nursing home, Polk admits that there are times when an argument for using such tactics is "honest," but he adds, "All too often the argument is simply an excuse for those who prefer a short cut rather than long-term hard work and drudgery to nail down the facts."

Polk says there is one role that he will play—that of citizen. He says he may go into a courthouse and ask for a document without signing in as a reporter because any citizen is entitled to the same information. "If I am going to put somebody on the air, gather information about an individual, I believe in disclosing who I am."

John Spain, the general manager of WBRZ-TV in Baton Rouge, who has

Station Manager John Spain of WBRZ-TV, Baton Rouge, looks over Reporter John Pastorek's script before a newscast.
PHOTO BY JAMES TERRY

won many awards for investigative reporting, says that while he has been working in the public's interest, he has "never taken that as a license to break the law or be immoral or do things that are justified under the *glorious heading* of the First Amendment." Spain says, "I don't think we have any special rights, and I think we have to be very careful when we start thinking we do in terms of being dishonest or breaking the law."

Spain says he has had great success being "up-front with people and telling them who we are and why we've come to talk to them. I don't think I, or anyone on my staff, has ever misrepresented themselves." He adds, "I think we've done some very serious investigations over the years and have been able to practice our craft without misrepresenting ourselves."

CBS News Correspondent Robert McKeown admits that he has misrepresented himself at times in order to get the "truth." He believes you can't always accomplish that goal if you admit you are a journalist. He recalled that during the Gulf War, he and a camera crew stole some fatigues, flak jackets and helmets in order to work their way through road blocks. "I am not sure we would have been successful getting our story—a story that we should have got—unless we misrepresented ourselves."

McKeown says everyone has a "gut feeling about what is right and wrong" when it comes to ethics. He says reporters also have to bring a sense of mission to what they do and, by definition, have to bring "a kind of antiestablishment attitude" to the job. "You have to be prepared to piss off people and realize that in some stories if you don't, the stories are not going to be successful."

HIDDEN CAMERAS AND MICROPHONES

Reporters sometimes use hidden cameras and microphones when they're doing an investigative story in an effort to record incriminating material. They also use wireless microphones to eavesdrop on conversations. Such devices are routinely used by teams working for "60 Minutes," "20/20" and other investigative TV news programs.

There seem to be no laws against videotaping with a hidden camera something that is going on in public. But reporters must know state and federal laws if they plan to make use of hidden microphones. Federal law forbids the use of them unless one person involved in the conversation knows of the recording. If a reporter places a hidden microphone in a hotel room to record a conversation between two or more people, that would be a violation of federal law. If a reporter is carrying a hidden microphone, there is no federal violation, but some states do forbid the practice. It's also a violation of federal law, and some state laws, to use so-called wires, microphones that transmit a conversation to another location.

CNN's Jim Polk admits that he has used hidden cameras from the back of a truck with one-way glass, but he says it is really "espionage, spying—a dirty little technique." But, he says, "We have used it on the mob." Polk says that as long as the video that's shot with a hidden camera is of people doing illegal things in public view, he has no problem using the technique. But he says that using hidden microphones is "playing with fire. It's a dangerous technique that is easily mishandled, and it should be used with caution and only under certain circumstances."

John Spain of WBRZ-TV agrees, for the most part, but he says he has used hidden cameras on some stories when he felt the video was essential. He recalled using a concealed camera in a story about some alcohol beverage control officers who were getting drunk while they were on duty. "They were supposed to be enforcing the alcohol laws," Spain says, "and we needed the video to show what they actually were doing."

But Spain believes hidden cameras shouldn't be used unless necessary. He cited two examples, back-to-back stories on "Prime Time Live." The first story was about a meat-inspection facility. The plant had been exempted from having federal inspectors because it was doing its own inspection. "Prime Time Live" had help from someone at the plant and got a camera inside. What they taped and played on the air was video of carcasses being dragged along the floor and intestines being ruptured on top of meat that had been stamped "U.S. Inspected."

Spain said, "I bought into that story big time, because it was providing a public service. Most people eat meat, and they have a right to know how it is processed. The story also brought about change. The day after it was aired," he said, "the secretary of agriculture sent inspectors into the plant."

But the veteran journalist said he had a lot of trouble with the story done by "Prime Time Live" the following week. Hidden cameras were used again; this time to "expose" a man who had skipped to another state to avoid paying child support.

Spain said it bothered him that the network picked on one man out of millions to point up a problem that admittedly was a serious one. "The network crossed the country with the man's wife and daughters and then walked into a place of business and cornered the father with a hidden camera." Spain said that what the man had done was wrong, but that he now had a new wife and children and that, in Spain's opinion, the network was not justified in embarrassing the individual to illustrate the problem.

Spain added that the audience never did hear the man's story because after the ambush interview he refused to speak with the reporter. Spain said, "I don't know what the public interest was in the life of a father who didn't pay child support."

AMBUSH INTERVIEWS

The type of interview described by Spain, an *ambush interview,* is frequently used by TV reporters, though the technique has come under much criticism. As the name implies, reporters who are unable to schedule an interview with an individual frequently stake out the person's home or office until they are able to ambush the person as he or she comes into or goes out of the building. We have all seen such interviews. The reporter and cameraperson force themselves on the individual, trying to shoot video and ask questions as the person tries to escape. Is this appropriate?

ABC News Correspondent Barry Serafin says an ambush interview is only justified when there's "a genuine public accountability involved. Sometimes you cannot allow a person in public office to refuse to talk to you; you really have to get to the person and make him accountable." Serafin recalled that during Watergate journalists "would do an ambush or whatever else it took to get some information."

John Spain says he does not like the ambush interview unless, as Serafin notes, it involves the public interest. "If we have made every effort to interview an individual and have been denied access," says Spain, "we would do an ambush. If you raise your hand and take an oath," he adds, "you have an obligation to answer to the public."

RE-ENACTMENTS   Considerable debate has been generated over the use of *re-enactments* of events to tell a news story. Most news directors frown on the technique, but some see nothing wrong with re-enactments as long as they are clearly designated as such with a supertitle plainly stating "This is a re-enactment."

The most important ethical consideration in the use of re-enactments is that they should not confuse the audience about what they are looking at. Viewers should be able to determine quickly which scenes are actual and which are re-enacted.

Some news directors believe re-enactments have no place in news. As one news director puts it, "Let the 'Hard Copy' people do the re-enactment."

STAGING   A concern more serious—and more common—than re-enactment is *staging,* the faking of a shot, sound or other aspect of a story. In most newsrooms, staging can and should be a cause for dismissal. Ironically, some reporters see little harm in staging if the staging is accurate. "What's wrong," one asks, "if you round up protestors at an abortion clinic who may be out to lunch and get them shouting again? That's what they would be doing after lunch, anyway."

It is *not* the same, and reporters who think that way pose a serious threat to their news organizations. There are many other kinds of staging that go on too frequently. All of them are unethical. Here are a few examples:

> A reporter misses a news conference, so he asks the news maker to repeat a few of the remarks he made and pretends the sound bites actually came from the news conference.

> A news crew goes to a park to shoot some children playing on swings and seesaws, but there are none there. A cameraperson is sent to find some children.

> A reporter doing a story on drugs on campus needs some video to support the story, so he asks a student he knows to "set up" a group smoking pot in a dorm room.

> A documentary unit doing a story on crime asks a police car with its sirens blasting to make a few passes by the camera "to save time."

Harmless deceptions? Perhaps. But where does staging end? If reporters are willing to set up a pot party, is there *anything* that they would feel uncomfortable about staging?

Some news directors insist that staging is never acceptable. Others are more flexible. For example, if a reporter arrives to do a feature story about a pizza parlor that claims to make the largest pizzas in the city and discovers no one in the restaurant has ordered the large size, it would be permissible to have a pie made to show on camera. However, the reporter also should note in the story that while she was in the restaurant, no one actually ordered one of the big pies.

Few news directors would object to a reporter asking a clerk in the IRS office to accompany him to the racks displaying various tax forms so that the cameraperson would have an appropriate background for the interview. This activity is not really considered staging but *setting up* a shot, and it is viewed as acceptable. The same would be true, of course, if the crew moved the furniture in the office of someone to be interviewed on camera so that the cameraperson could get a better shot.

"UNNATURAL" SOUND

Natural sound is one of the most effective tools used by broadcast journalists. No one wants to see children riding down a hill on sleds without hearing their shouts, and video of a marching band would not be very interesting without the music. But what does a reporter do when the audio recorder or camera does not pick up the sound? Should the reporter add *"unnatural sound,"* that is, sound effects? There are sound-effect tapes and records to match just about any activity. Certainly the sound of laughing children is available. The reporter might not be able to match exactly the music the band in the parade was playing, but how many people would know the difference?

The answers to these questions is that such use of sound effects would be unethical. The same goes for dubbing in any natural sound that the recorder might have missed at the scene of a story. If the sound of fire engines was lost at the scene, that's unfortunate; the answer is not to substitute sound effects. It would be better for the reporter or anchor to admit to the audience that there were sound problems on the story.

VIDEO DECEPTION   Most TV stations maintain a videotape library that includes footage of events going back years. Most stations pull some of that video, known as *generic footage,* when they need shots of a general nature to cover portions of the script. Some stations routinely superimpose the words *file footage* over such video, but other stations run the video without any such admission unless it's obvious that the video is dated.

Most journalists have no problem with using file footage of people walking down the street or shots of cars and trucks rolling down the highway if it works with the script. But pulling old video from the morgue about disturbances in the Little Haiti section of Miami for a story about a new outbreak of violence in that neighborhood would be deceptive unless the audience knew the difference between the old and new footage they were watching. Instead of the font *file footage,* many news directors insist that the file footage have the original date superimposed over the old video.

For the most part, TV stations do not plan to deceive the audience when they use old footage; they are just careless. But there have been examples of deliberate deception over the years—instances when old war footage was used, for example, to cover new fighting. In some cases, stations have used footage of a completely different war to go along with a story on fighting in another country. Such deception, if discovered, could mean the loss of a station's TV license.

IMPROPER EDITING   One of the reasons video and audio recordings are rarely accepted in court cases is that they can be doctored very easily. As one audio engineer puts it, "With enough time, I can make people say anything I want."

Most of the time, the distortion of people's comments on radio and television is not intentional; the tape is just poorly edited. There have been many cases in which people who have been interviewed by radio and TV reporters complained that the editing changed the meaning of their comments. By clipping a statement, they charged, the editing distorted the point they were trying to make. It certainly is true that a reporter or producer intent on showing someone in a certain light can accomplish that goal rather easily. The error of omission is a serious concern. To pick up one part of a person's statement and ignore an equally important part of it could certainly distort the individual's remarks.

When tape must be edited for time purposes—which is almost always the case—it is the responsibility of the reporter or producer to make sure the sound bite is representative of what the person said. If it is not, it is essential that in narration following the bite the reporter accurately sum up the part of the sound bite that was eliminated.

AVOIDING JUMP CUTS

Some of the tricks employed in the editing process also raise some ethical questions. In order to avoid *jump cuts*—the jerking of the head that occurs when video cuts are juxtaposed—film editors (it started long before the advent of video) came up with cutaways, reversals and reverse questions.

All of these techniques are designed to cover up video edits. Editors, producers and everyone else in the newsroom defend the use of most of these techniques because they make the finished product much smoother to watch. "Who wants to watch a head jumping across the screen?" is the answer editors give for using a cutaway, a reversal or a reverse question. It is hard to argue with that response. What bothers some people is that such techniques are not quite honest because the audience, for the most part, does not realize what the editors are doing. In an effort to avoid jump cuts, editors also distract the audience's attention from what the editors are doing by inserting other video between the edited material.

In a *cutaway*, it appears that the cameraperson just decided in the middle of an interview or speech to show the TV audience that the room was crowded with spectators and reporters. This cutaway shot may show another cameraperson shooting the scene or a reporter scribbling in a notepad or just a row of the audience. What that shot does is make it possible for the editor to take part of the video comment and marry it to any other video comment made by an individual while he or she was speaking. The first part might have been at the beginning of the speech, while the second comment might have been made 10 or 20 minutes later.

"So what, there's nothing dishonest about that" is the response from many editors, and for the most part, there probably isn't anything dishonest about it if one accepts that it is not necessary for the audience to know that the tape was edited. The real harm comes when the video is badly edited and does not accurately represent what the individual said during the interview or speech and the audience has no way of knowing this.

Another editing technique used to avoid jump cuts is the *reversal,* also referred to as a *reverse shot* or *listening shot.* After completing an interview, the reporter pretends to be listening to the interviewee while the cameraperson takes some shots of the reporter. The worst examples show the reporters smiling and nodding their heads in agreement. These shots then are sandwiched in between two bites of the interview, and again the audience, for the most part, believes that the cameraperson simply decided to take a picture of the reporter at that point in the interview or believes there were two cameras in the room.

One of the key scenes in the popular Hollywood film "Broadcast News" deals with the unethical use of the reverse shot. In the film, an ethically minded TV news producer jilts an anchor-reporter because he used a reverse shot of himself crying in the middle of an interview when he actually had not cried during the interview itself. That was outright deception. Fortunately, such examples are not typical of the reverse shots that appear in TV news stories. Most of the objections to the reverse shot are not about deception but about concern over the audience's inability to know that the video has been edited.

The most dangerous of these techniques, which does not appear to be as popular as it once was, is the *reverse question*. A reverse question is one the reporter asks a second time after the interview has been completed. The camera is facing the reporter this time. The technique allows the editor to avoid a jump cut by inserting video of the reporter asking the question. The problem occurs when the reporter does not ask the question exactly the same way the second time. News makers themselves have sometimes complained about reverse questions when they realized that the questions they heard on their televisions were not exactly the same as those they had been asked when they were in front of the camera. Any change at all in the second version of the question raises serious ethical questions.

Producers and news directors who routinely allow the use of such techniques sometimes draw the line when the president or some other top official is making an important policy statement. In such cases, many producers allow the jump cut—particularly if it is not jarring—so that the audience knows that the remarks by the chief executive or other official have been edited. Instead of using a jump cut, some producers prefer to *wipe* between bites.

INFLATING THE NEWS

Reporters must attempt to keep a news story in perspective. Otherwise, it is easy to give the audience the wrong impression about what is actually happening. It was mentioned earlier that a reporter should never stage video by rounding up demonstrators who were on a lunch break. But let's assume that when the reporter showed up, the protest was in full swing. Did the presence of the camera have an effect on the demonstration? Did the shouting suddenly get louder? If the camera did have an effect on the crowd, which would not be unusual, the audience might get the wrong impression. In such a case, it might be appropriate for the reporter to mention this:

> Actually, the turnout for the demonstration was smaller than was predicted . . . and our camera seemed to encourage some in the crowd to whip it up just a little bit more than when we first arrived.

It is also important for the cameraperson to show accurately what was going on at the scene. If there were only a half-dozen demonstrators, the audience might, again, get the wrong impression if the camera shot used was a close-up. A wide shot would have revealed that the group was small.

WILL THE REAL REPORTER PLEASE STAND

There always has been a certain amount of glorification of the anchors in broadcasting, and there's a growing tendency to give anchors more of the credit and those who actually do the work less. It's common practice for producers and writers to write copy for anchors. Everyone knows about this practice, and there's no ethical issue involved even though a portion of the audience probably thinks anchors write their own copy. Many do write part of it. However, some journalists are concerned about the growing practice of using writers and producers to prepare packages that make use of the anchor's voice; packages that, some would argue, would best be prepared by reporters. Part of the problem, of course, is that many stations are cutting back on their reporting staffs and are compensating for the loss by having writers and producers handle some of the work reporters once did, without leaving the newsroom. Is this deception?

Bill Small, former senior vice president of CBS and now a professor of communications at Fordham University, says it's "always improper if you leave the impression that you covered a story when you didn't."

However, Small notes that at CBS and other networks it isn't "uncommon" for producers to do most of the work on some stories. It's routine for producers to conduct an interview in advance of a correspondent's arrival on the scene to "tie it all together."

Small is also concerned about the proliferation of material available to broadcast stations via satellite and the increasing use of the same syndication video by all the networks. "I'm a firm believer that there shouldn't be one story for all the networks," he says. "Each one should do its own."

Small is even more annoyed by video news releases, which he calls "handout journalism." He says that if any of this material is picked up, its source should be properly identified.

Professor Robert Mulholland, former president of NBC and now chair of the Medill School of Journalism at Northwestern University, shares some of Small's concerns, particularly on the question of anchors and reporters voicing-over syndicated video. Mulholland asks, "How do you know that the video was honestly gathered or edited?"

"Things get up on a satellite," he says, "and everybody brings it down. The days when you only broadcast news that your own employees gathered is pretty much gone. The cutbacks in staff have been in news gathering. . . . The gathering of news has become a pool process, and that disturbs me."

Rob Sunde, news director of the ABC Information Network, also is concerned about these issues. On the question of writers and producers doing packages that the audience thinks are the product of anchors, Sunde says, "Everyone involved is cheated, those involved in the production and those at home receiving it." He adds, "When we see reporters at the scene, we expect that they covered the story, giving us what they saw, heard, felt, smelled. That's reporting. When someone else takes credit for that or pretends that he or she did the work, that's unethical."

Sunde says one of the worst examples of unethical conduct occurred during the William Kennedy Smith trial when a radio reporter for a network used two different names so that he could report for another news group.

SUMMARY

The title of this chapter, "Ethics and the Law," indicates that the two are sometimes difficult to separate. Accuracy is an ethical journalistic concern, but when information in a story is inaccurate because of bias or carelessness, it can also become a legal issue, libel.

Likewise the use of certain undercover devices by reporters, such as hidden microphones and cameras, raises ethical questions that must be resolved by each newsperson or news manager, but their use also has legal implications because in some states their use is forbidden. Certainly, the argument used by many journalists that you "do what you have to do" to catch someone breaking the law seems reasonable on the surface. However, many reporters believe that they must stay within the law or they are not acting much better than those they are investigating.

Many reporters admit that they "bend" the rules. For example, CBS News Correspondent Robert McKeown misrepresented himself in order to get at what he called the "truth" during the Gulf War. A strong argument could be made that the American people had a right to know what was going on during the conflict when the military was less than honest in dealing with the media. Was it wrong for McKeown to circumvent military rules to get his story on the air?

Perhaps McKeown expresses it best when he says, "Everyone has a gut feeling about what is right and wrong" when it comes to ethics.

REVIEW QUESTIONS

1. Should reporters ever accept gifts? Discuss.

2. When does accuracy become an ethical issue?

3. What are the defenses against libel? Do they always work?

4. Explain the term *false light.*

5. Name some of the controversial techniques employed by investigative reporters.

6. All ethical journalists are opposed to staging the news. Give some examples of such unethical behavior.

7. For what purpose are reversals used by most TV stations? Is there anything unethical about them?

EXERCISES

1. Ask two or more reporters from radio and TV stations to take part in a discussion of controversial techniques used by some investigative reporters. It might be a good idea to record the session so that it can be played for other classes to get their reactions.

2. Which of the following statements do you think could be considered libelous, and why? Would the defense have any arguments acceptable to the courts? Explain.

The governor drinks so much it's a wonder that he gets any work done.

Part of the governor's problem is that his wife is a drunk.

The governor is a lazy, good-for-nothing fake.

If the governor would stay at home more instead of running around with women he wouldn't be in such hot water with the voters.

3. Suppose you are a TV reporter assigned to a demonstration. When the assignment editor sent you out, the demonstrators were shouting and waving fists. But when you arrived, they had stopped for lunch, except for one person who continued to picket.

How would you and your cameraperson handle the situation?

CHAPTER 19

MORE LEGAL AND ETHICAL ISSUES

CAMERAS IN THE COURTROOM

The introduction of cameras in courtrooms has raised new, serious questions about journalistic ethics and the responsibility of the broadcast media, particularly television. The issue of whether to allow camera coverage of trials has been a continuing debate, with the TV news representatives, for the most part, arguing that cameras should be allowed in courtrooms. Those opposed to the idea argue that the cameras compromise the rights and privacy of all those involved in a trial.

Even in states where cameras are allowed to record the proceedings, the cameras are operated on a pool basis to minimize the intrusion. The jury is not shown.

In early 1993, only Indiana, Mississippi, Missouri, New York and the District of Columbia still barred cameras completely from courtrooms. But there are a variety of restrictions in most of the states where cameras are allowed. In some states, the judge decides. In others, everyone involved in the case must agree to allow the cameras. In still other states, the decision depends on the nature of the case. And in some states, cameras are permitted only in certain courts or on an experimental basis. Sound confusing? It is. There is absolutely no consensus on the role of cameras in courtrooms, but those advocating their presence have made significant progress in the past few years.

One of the most liberal states when it comes to permitting cameras in court is Florida, which does not require consent of the parties involved. Therefore, cameras gave the world a front-row view of one of the most sensational trials in recent history—the trial of William Kennedy Smith, accused of raping a woman at the Kennedy compound in West Palm Beach.

The issues about whether cameras should be allowed in courtrooms were perhaps defined better during the trial than they had ever been before. If the defendant had not been a nephew of Senator Edward Kennedy, the networks would have had little interest in the story. CNN carried it gavel to gavel.

Smith was acquitted of the charge of rape, but serious questions remain. Were his rights violated? Millions of Americans heard and watched Smith in the courtroom while the prosecution graphically described the incident and the charges. Will the fact that Smith was acquitted wipe out the pictures and words

William Kennedy Smith speaks to
reporters during his trial for rape.
REUTERS/BETTMANN

that TV audiences around the nation and world heard and saw? It's a good question. Was it more important for TV audiences to see and hear that trial than it was to protect Smith's rights? Was it right to obscure the accuser's face when she was testifying to prevent her identification? Should her identity have been protected?

RESPONSIBLE REPORTING

Each evening during the Smith trial Americans were subjected to the most vivid description of the alleged rape. The live broadcast coverage of the Smith trial raises serious questions about the responsibility of broadcast journalists when cameras are in the courtroom. Was it responsible, for example, to use a tight shot of the defendant while the audience heard explicit details of the alleged rape? Is it responsible, during the prime-time, so-called family TV viewing period, to broadcast a discussion on whether William Smith was or was not able to maintain an erection while he was allegedly raping the woman?

After shocking many viewers with sound bites that gave the details of the alleged rape, Dan Rather of CBS News issued a warning the following night, saying that some viewers might find the material offensive. ABC Executive Producer Paul Friedman said he tried to avoid using the explicit material as long as possible but "finally had to." He did not say so, but it seems possible that the use of explicit material by Rather the night before was a factor. Friedman said he had no idea how far such reporting would go, but he said ABC had decided to draw the line on the final day of the trial. "If the verdict had not come in," he said, "we decided that we would not use the prosecutor's closing remarks in which she referred to semen in panties."

"I do not know the answer to the problem," Friedman said, "but once you decide to cover something like this, such [graphic] details are the heart of the story." He said he felt that advance warnings to the audience about explicit material are important, and ABC added them during coverage of the Smith trial after receiving a complaint from an affiliate news director.

NBC Executive Producer Steve Friedman said he never was committed to carrying the graphic sound bites during the Smith trial. He said the decision by ABC and CBS to use the material did not influence him; NBC did not use any of the graphic material. However, the network was criticized by the competition because it chose to identify the alleged rape victim.

CBS News Correspondent Bruce Morton, who reported on the Smith trial from West Palm Beach, said, "We made sure everyone in New York knew before we went down there that it was going to be a very graphic trial. They were monitoring the trial, and we submitted scripts in advance . . . so there were no surprises."

"NO HOLDS BARRED"

Morton said that with a camera in a courtroom it would be "pointless and silly to omit key elements in the testimony even if they were very graphic, and it would be wrong to try to paraphrase them in some way that was less explicit." He added, "If you are going to cover these things, you ought to cover them the way they are."

Morton also noted that when he was covering demonstrations outside the White House in the 1970s during the Vietnam War, he was in favor of broadcasting the anti-war cry, "One, two, three, four, we don't want your fucking war." But, he says, "I was overruled."

Morton agreed with the opinion that the Senate hearings on the Clarence Thomas nomination to the Supreme Court "focused the attention of the country on the Kennedy Smith trial to a degree that might not have happened otherwise because it brought the issues of sexual harassment, date rape, etc., more strongly to people's attention."

Morton also argues for cameras in courtrooms. He says he would hope that there would be enough "diversity among the media that all would not do the same thing. As long as there are a lot of outlets, there will be some tabloid and nontabloid channels."

General Manager John Spain of WBRZ-TV in Baton Rouge says cameras should be given the same First Amendment right in a courtroom as a newspaper person's pencil and pad. But he says that while "there's a strong need to tell people what's going on, it must be balanced with some responsibility."

GOOD TASTE

Spain adds, "We have to know what is good taste and what is titillating. I think we could tell the rape trial story without using that kind of language. I think the public expects more from us."

A TV cameraman records the proceedings of a court hearing.
AP/WIDE WORLD PHOTOS

Spain adds, "We have always rejected some sound bites for one reason or another over the years, and I do not think people's attitudes or standards have changed that much. I think we are talking about *news,* and people expect us to be responsible. Journalists shouldn't be in the role of providing an electronic funnel—we do have some editorial responsibility and we should exercise it."

Spain, a former president of the Radio and Television News Directors Association, says affiliates are "caught in the middle" when it comes to carrying material that may be offensive to the audience. "Obviously we can't edit the material, even if we wanted to, because we are taking it live. All we can do is take the complaints from viewers and call the network and say 'we think you made a bad decision.' "

Will Wright, the news director and vice president of the Fox station KRIV-TV in Houston, did not use the graphic material from the Smith trial. He said his editorial staff, which is 80 percent female, was sensitive to how they approached the story. "A good manager listens to, and takes advice from the staff," Wright said, "and we decided not to use the material that could be considered tabloid. We took a very responsible approach."

Writing in the Wall Street Journal, Robert Goldberg said the Smith trial raises several questions about the TV coverage, "beginning with whether there should even be a camera in the courtroom." He added, "What I kept wondering is how are they able to put all this lurid detail on daytime TV? How can they carry this talk about the terrible violence of rape, about tearing clothing and inserting body parts, all in the most sexually explicit language, in an era when networks won't even broadcast condom ads, ads that could actually save a few lives."

TITILLATING NEWS

National Public Radio Correspondent Susan Stamberg found the rape trial coverage to be a "titillating distraction from the issues that are so deeply important in this society that journalism is too lazy to pay attention to and the public doesn't want to hear."

She said cable television has had such an impact on news, particularly at the network level, that "everyone is desperate. They're scrambling and as a result the level of public debate and decency is utterly debased. Life and death issues have become spectator sports, undermining the role of journalism. Tragedy, life, reality becomes an entertaining thing to turn on when you are eating dinner. That's where these electronic possibilities have brought us."

Stamberg added, "it's almost that all we talk about is sex because it grabs the public's attention."

When News Director Bill Vance of WBNS-TV in Columbus, Ga., was asked about "good taste," he laughed, saying he was unaware any still existed in broadcasting. Vance acknowledged that he used some sound bites from the Smith trial that he would not have used on the air 10 years ago, but he noted that "standards are changing and they will continue to change, especially as cable becomes more pervasive and as more events are covered live."

Vance recalled that at one time it was considered improper to show uncovered dead bodies on TV news. But then, he said, "Algerian terrorists started shooting people in Paris, and the networks started showing uncovered bodies, and our policies changed."

Vance pointed out that reporters today have much broader standards that mirror a different set of values than in the past. "These values," Vance said, "reflect the attitudes of many in the audience, and I can't afford to maintain a newscast that has values of 30 years ago in today's society because it wouldn't succeed."

Vance said it has been his experience that news organizations can put just about anything on the air at noon or eleven at night, but they "run into trouble at dinner time. It's not that you shock the kids who are listening or that you shock the parents," he said. "The adults become very uncomfortable when they are sitting in the same room as their children when that sort of thing comes on the air."

The late NBC Correspondent Pauline Frederick was concerned about these things in 1980 when she told a Radio and Television News Directors Association awards banquet that it seemed to her that "the standard for broadcasting should be what Walter Lippmann prescribed for statesmanship. Lippmann said, 'Statesmanship consists in giving the people not what they want but what they will learn to want.' "

Frederick asked if broadcasting was "exercising such statesmanship by offering details of rape, pillage, destruction, drugs, incest, life beyond the pill, teenage suicide, child molesting, battered parents, the degradation of people in pieces and how to beat the system." Frederick said these subjects "sound like some of the titles for X-rated movies around Times Square. As a matter of fact, they were the subject matter of recent local and national news programs designed to snare listeners and viewers from the competition."

TABLOID JOURNALISM

WBNS-TV News Director Bill Vance places some of the responsibility for changing standards on the popularity of tabloid programs such as "Hard Copy," "Current Affair" and "Inside Story." Vance says the fact that these programs regularly follow local and network newscasts in many markets is "blurring" the real meaning of news for many viewers.

CBS News Correspondent Betsy Aaron takes the analogy a step further. She says some of the things on network news are "worse than 'Hard Copy.' We're pretending we're 'Hard Copy' people, but we want to keep our clothes on, so we're born-again virgins every night." She says the theory is "We'll do the 'Hard Copy' stories but we'll do them the right way." Aaron cites the Kennedy Smith rape trial as an example.

"Although it's legitimate news," she says, "it's also legitimate to cover the love-affair phenomenon that the United States has with the Kennedy family." She says that instead of doing stories like that, we heard reports about body parts. "The scripts were so well done that they didn't sound like 'Hard Copy,'" she says, "but they *were* 'Hard Copy.'"

The CBS news correspondent continues, "If we're going to go the 'Hard Copy' route, then I want us to be the best of 'Hard Copy,' not the worst. Don't tell people that you are still doing what you used to do because buying video from people and narrating over other people's footage is *not* what we used to do, but that's what we're doing now."

Aaron says she is not too concerned about the networks' graphic coverage of the William Kennedy Smith trial because broadcasters "put violence on the air . . . and show dead bodies in Los Angeles or overseas, and that's OK." She adds, "We have a double standard on these things." She recalls that a sound bite was once eliminated because the person used the word *crotch* and notes "you can't show a nude statue if it is shot provocatively."

News Director Will Wright of KRIV-TV in Houston says there is an "appetite" for tabloid TV. "As stations try to survive the ratings war, they will try anything—they will tinker with formats and try new ideas to grab attention. There is an overwhelming pressure to make sure their jobs are secure." But ultimately, Wright says, "we do have to stay the course and do journalism the way it was meant to be done, with honesty, integrity, veracity and a sense of fairness."

WBRZ-TV Station Manager John Spain agrees. He says that when a station is trying to find itself, it looks at all sorts of opinions and may go for a "quick flash." But he says the audience will ultimately reject that approach because it knows better.

PROFANITY

Profanity should never be used in a script. Live interview situations sometimes present problems. On occasion, people being interviewed will use foul language or make some other sort of unacceptable statement. Some radio stations have a delay mechanism that actually tapes all live interviews and broadcasts them a few seconds later. This gives an alert engineer or interviewer time to eliminate the offensive material. Without this protection, about the best the interviewer can do is apologize for the offending remarks and cut the individual off the air.

Sometimes, politicians and other well-known people will make "off-color" statements that require special consideration. President Harry Truman shocked his 1950s listeners when he used "S-O-B" to describe a music critic who unfavorably reviewed a singing performance by the president's daughter. Most stations did not use the president's remark, but such words are not considered so offensive today. There is little doubt that most stations would now use Truman's remark, but stronger language still is forbidden. The point could be made, however, with phrases such as "the Senator's language was too strong for us to repeat here" or "the Senator's angry statement included a number of expletives."

TABOO SUBJECTS?

In the 1940s and 1950s, the word *rape* was not used on the air. The euphemism *criminal assault* was commonly used instead. Now, of course, rape is a frequent subject of discussion on talk shows and newscasts. In those earlier days of broadcasting, it would have been equally repugnant to refer to condoms on the air. But now the broadcast debate on whether condoms should be distributed in schools is commonplace.

Even as late as the early 1960s, a radio talk-show host broke off an interview with an advocate of euthanasia because he was getting threats from listeners who warned that they were going to complain to the FCC if he continued the discussion.

It is difficult to think of a subject that might be considered taboo for broadcast in the 1990s. The decisions on good taste normally reflect the policies of station management. Some stations are more conservative than others. If management feels that certain language or subjects are not acceptable for broadcast, those feelings normally work their way down to the news department.

THE FAIRNESS DOCTRINE

Like many of the issues addressed in this chapter and the previous one, *fairness* is both a legal and an ethical consideration. Until now, we have concentrated on the ethical importance of fairness. Now, let's consider the legal aspects of fairness. Do broadcast stations have a legal responsibility to be fair? Broadcast managers, the Federal Communications Commission, Congress and scores of special interest groups have been fighting over that issues for decades.

In 1949, the FCC established the Fairness Doctrine, which said, in part, that broadcasters had an obligation to serve the public interest by "not refusing to broadcast opposing views where a demand is made of the station for broadcast time." It also said that licensees have a duty "to encourage and implement the broadcast of all sides of controversial issues. . . ."

Over the following years, the broadcast industry and the Radio and Television News Directors Association applied extreme pressure on the FCC to eliminate the doctrine, arguing that because newspapers are not forced to present all sides of an issue, broadcasters should not be required to do so either.

According to supporters of the Fairness Doctrine, the major distinction between newspapers and broadcasters is that the government, in selecting only one licensee for a frequency, is in effect limiting access to the airwaves, which have traditionally been considered the property of the public.

The Fairness Doctrine was challenged on occasion but was upheld in the courts. In 1964, in a landmark case known as Red Lion (which is described in detail in the next section), the Supreme Court upheld the doctrine. However, over the intervening years even the FCC itself questioned the Fairness Doctrine.

In 1984, twenty years after the Supreme Court ruling, the FCC, while finding that a TV station in Syracuse, N.Y., had violated the Fairness Doctrine, also acknowledged that the doctrine was not serving the public and was probably unconstitutional. The TV station, WTVH, and its owner, Meredith Broadcasting, used the FCC statement to challenge the Fairness Doctrine in the U.S. Court of Appeals. But the court refused to decide in the case, saying that the FCC had the power to eliminate the doctrine if it didn't like it. That's exactly what the FCC did.

But that was not the end of the issue. There had always been strong support for the doctrine in Congress, which in 1987 passed a bill making the Fairness Doctrine law. The bill was vetoed by President Reagan.

President Bush also opposed the doctrine, but its supporters will no doubt attempt to pass new legislation under President Clinton. Although the president has not spoken out publicly about the issue, Vice President Gore voted in favor of the bill when he was in the Senate.

THE RED LION DECISION

The constitutionality of the Fairness Doctrine was tested in 1964 in the landmark Red Lion case involving a New York writer, Fred Cook, and the Red Lion Broadcasting Company, which owned radio station WGGB in Red Lion, Pa.

In a broadcast aired by WGGB, the Reverend Billy James Hargis accused Cook of writing for a magazine that championed communist causes and of writing a book that was intended to destroy Senator Barry Goldwater. Cook demanded that the radio station give him air time to reply. When the station refused, Cook asked the FCC to intervene. It did, ordering the station to give Cook free time. When WGGB management still refused to grant the time to Cook, the case ended up in the courts. It eventually reached the U.S. Supreme Court, which ruled that Cook had a right to the free time. The Court said that if anyone's "honesty, character or integrity . . . is challenged on the air the station must notify those attacked . . . and offer air time for reply." The Court ruling said the station must notify the individual or organization that was attacked even if the subject of the attack was unaware of it. The ruling requires stations to send a script or tape of what was said about the individual or group within seven days of the broadcast and to provide air time for a reply.

SUMMARY

This chapter discusses the responsibilities that accompany the new technology available to broadcast journalists. Radio and television stations, for example, are broadcasting trials from all but a handful of states. Some of these states have restrictions. Judges seem divided on the propriety of having cameras in the courtroom, particularly when they are used to report on so-called sensitive issues.

Among journalists, there is no such division. Almost to a person, broadcasters support cameras in the courtroom, maintaining that they have a First Amendment right to bring their gear into court because it is just a much heavier version of a print journalist's pen and pencil.

But even if you accept that cameras have a right to feed trials, regardless of their nature, into living rooms, the question of responsibility remains, and that is very much an ethical issue in the minds of many newspeople. Does a network have a responsibility to feed out "everything" from a courtroom? If they do not carry everything, some executives claim, they would be censoring the news. Others argue that journalists always have censored news to eliminate bad taste.

The other major ethical issue this chapter discusses is tabloid journalism. The opinion seems to be unanimous that local stations, and networks to a lesser degree, are moving in the direction of tabloid journalism, where sensational stories and re-enactments are the norm. Most of this trend is blamed on money and ratings. As one journalist puts it, "When you are hurting in the ratings and the advertising revenue keeps dropping, you will try anything." One can only hope that this is a short-lived phenomenon.

REVIEW QUESTIONS

1. How many states still have a ban on cameras in courtrooms?

2. What kinds of restrictions do some states have on cameras?

3. What is the media's argument for having cameras in courtrooms?

4. What is the Fairness Doctrine?

5. What was the Red Lion decision?

EXERCISES

1. If cameras are allowed in courtrooms in your state, attend a trial where cameras are being used, and discuss how they were used and whether you believe it was beneficial for the public or detrimental to those involved in the trial. If cameras are still forbidden in your state, interview a judge about the issue.

2. Collect a group of journalists, lawyers, professors and other appropriate people for a discussion of all aspects of journalistic ethics. Record the panel discussion for use in other classes.

3. Host a similar debate with news directors on the issue of tabloid journalism.

4. Watch each of the TV stations in your market, and report on their selection of stories and how they presented those stories.

CHAPTER 20

SPECIALTY REPORTING

here are increasing opportunities for journalists who can offer specialized knowledge along with their writing and reporting skills. Additional expertise makes a reporter more valuable to a radio or TV news organization, and that translates into higher salaries and jobs in larger markets. This chapter explores some of the specialties that are particularly attractive to radio and TV news directors.

ENVIRONMENTAL REPORTING

The growing concern over the environment in the past decade has encouraged broadcast news managers to allocate more news time to the subject. In many newsrooms, the environment is still covered by general-assignment reporters, but more and more news managers are hiring broadcast journalists who have become familiar with environmental problems. Knowledge of the subject can be acquired in college but reporters often gain their expertise simply by taking the time to learn about the complex issues.

There are scores of periodicals dealing with every aspect of the environment, and reporters intent on learning about environmental issues should expect to spend many hours in the library or should subscribe to the publications. A wide variety of environmental seminars also are offered throughout the country by private and government groups. The Environmental Health Center issues a newsletter. "Greenwire" is a news service offering stories about the environment, and the Society of Environmental Journalists provides help and resources for journalists trying to improve their knowledge of environmental issues. The Radio and Television News Directors Association frequently discusses the environment at national and regional meetings. There also are helpful computer data bases, such as the Toxic Release Inventory, which stores information on 366 toxic chemicals.

CNN Correspondent Debra Potter, who covers the environment, believes no beat is more important. She says broadcasters owe it to their audiences to cover the subject because it "touches viewers and listeners where they live."

Potter says communities throughout the nation are wrestling with environmental issues such as waste disposal and water quality. She notes polls show that Americans believe that the environment is one of the five most important issues facing the nation.

The CNN correspondent stresses that environmental reporters who know and understand the issues—who know where to look and which questions to ask—get a jump ahead on environmental stories. She also notes that environmental issues are difficult to explain and that environmental reporters must act responsibly "by not raising false hopes or unfounded fears."

Bob Engleman of Scripps-Howard newspapers says that covering the environment is like covering any other complicated issue of importance. He advises following these steps:

1. Learn the issue.
2. Maintain skepticism.
3. Seek out all viewpoints.
4. Ask probing questions.
5. Report the story as accurately and as fairly as possible.

ABC News Correspondent Jeff Greenfield says that unless reporters covering the environment completely understand the various aspects of the story, they would be "better off not doing it at all." He believes that if reporters misinform people about politicians, they do not cause too much damage. But, he adds, "if you falsely report to the community that children are at risk because of something in the schools or the land or water you have done much harm." At the same time, Greenfield notes that reporters who fail to inform the public about a real risk do even greater harm.

The editor of Freedom Forum Journal, Craig Le May, says environmental reporters must "look at what local industries are doing—how they make and transport products, how they do business." He also warns reporters that much of the environmental information available is from press releases, which are not reliable.

Le May says it is up to reporters to search through all the public relations and make sense of the issues. He notes that the rule for cultivating sources is the same as for other types of assignments: "Get the best people and find out what they have at stake in what you are reporting." He warns, for example, that researchers at universities are often funded by organizations with a fixed point of view, so reporters have to be skeptical of their findings.

Le May also urges reporters to beware of trade groups that "masquerade as environmental organizations." He notes that the National Wetlands Coalition sounds like an environmental group, but it actually is a lobby group for the largest oil, gas and utility companies.

Robert Logan, the director of the Science Journalism Center at the University of Missouri, also urges reporters to be "skeptical of everybody. Everyone is selling something," he warns, "even if they are not into making money." Logan says reporters should remember that the investigative rule "Follow the money to get to the bottom of something" is bad advice for environmental reporting. He suggests instead, "Follow the best scientific evidence first, and then look for the money."

Here's a report from environmental reporter Don Wall of WFAA-TV in Dallas on the possible dangers of electromagnetic fields:

```
on cam/2-shot                         ((CHIP))
                                >>> ARE ELECTROMAGNETIC FIELDS

                                PRODUCED BY POWER LINES . . . DAN-

                                GEROUS TO YOUR HEALTH?


                                      ((TRACY))
                                >> THE PUBLIC UTILITY COMMISSION

                                OF TEXAS HAS RELEASED THE RESULTS

                                OF A 3-YEAR STUDY THAT SAYS PEOPLE

                                WHO LIVE NEAR POWER LINES HAVE

                                NOTHING TO WORRY ABOUT.

turn to box: a                      ((tracy turn box))
current danger                   BUT EVEN T-U ELECTRIC SAYS MORE

                                RESEARCH NEEDS TO BE DONE.

                                 CHANNEL 8'S ENVIRONMENTAL REPORTER

                                DON WALL EXPLAINS IN THE FIRST OF HIS

                                TWO-PART SERIES, "A CURRENT DANGER."

                                (———)

sot
supers on tape

runs: 4:14




SCENE FROM                       >>> (THUNDER AND LIGHTNING . . .
FRANKENSTEIN
                                POWER EXPLODING AS THE CURRENT

                                PASSES INTO THE MONSTER.)

                                 IT WAS THE POWER OF ELECTRICITY

                                THAT GAVE LIFE TO FRANKENSTEIN'S

                                MONSTER.

                                 (it's alive, it's alive . . .)
```

(WIDE WITH CHIL-
DREN WALKING IN
FRONT OF POWER
LINES . . . GRAPH-
ICALLY FIELD EMA-
NATES FROM POWER
LINES)

IN A LESS SPECTACULAR, BUT NO
LESS DRAMATIC WAY, ELECTRICITY
GIVES POWER TO OUR DAILY LIVES.

AND EVERYTHING THAT CARRIES ELEC-
TRICITY EMITS AN ELECTROMAGNETIC
FIELD — AN EMF — WHICH OUR BODIES
ABSORB.

S: DON WALL, WFAA-
TV, FORT WORTH
(AT NIGHT, HOLD-
ING TWO FLUORES-
CENT BULBS)

"THIS IS WHAT WE MEAN BY AN ELEC-
TROMAGNETIC FIELD.

I'M STANDING UNDER A TYPICAL
138,000-VOLT POWER LINE, LIKE
THOSE THAT RUN THROUGH MANY NEIGH-
BORHOODS, AND THE EMF IS STRONG
ENOUGH TO ILLUMINATE THESE FLUORES-
CENT LIGHTS.

THERE ARE NO PLUGS, AND NO CORDS.
THE POWER TO LIGHT THESE BULBS IS
IN THE AIR."

AND THERE ARE STUDIES WHICH CLAIM
THAT EMF EXPOSURE IS DANGEROUS.

SOME STUDIES LINK PROXIMITY TO
POWER LINES WITH CHILDHOOD LEUKEMIA.

ANOTHER STUDY SAYS EMF'S MAY
CAUSE BRAIN CANCER.

THE FINDINGS ARE CONTROVERSIAL
AND SCIENTIFICALLY SOMEWHAT
UNCERTAIN. MANY RESEARCHERS
BELIEVE POWER LINES ARE PERFECTLY
SAFE.

BUT THERE IS NO DOUBT THAT PEOPLE
WHO LIVE NEAR POWER LINES ARE EX-
POSED TO GREATER EMF LEVELS THAN
PEOPLE WHO DON'T.

S: PLANO

THESE THREE WOMEN — WALKING ALONG
THE BLUEBONNET TRAIL — THINK EMF'S
FROM POWER LINES MAY HAVE CAUSED
THEIR SONS' BRAIN TUMORS.

("OBVIOUSLY, BY BUILDING THIS
PATH UNDER THE POWER LINE,
SOMEBODY'S ASSUMING THAT IT'S PER-
FECTLY SAFE?")

"I'M NOT SURE THAT ANYONE TOOK IT
INTO CONSIDERATION, FRANKLY."

9 CHILDREN WITH BRAIN TUMORS HAVE
BEEN DIAGNOSED IN THE HIGHPOINT AREA
OF PLANO, A CLUSTER OF DISEASE
THESE MOTHERS HOPE WILL BE STUDIED.

KRIS ALBERTA'S FAMILY LIVED IN A
TOWN HOUSE RIGHT NEXT TO THESE
POWER LINES.

(YOU WERE OUT HERE ALL THE TIME?)
QUITE A BIT. I USED TO WALK THE
DOG OUT HERE. MY SON WOULD COME
OUT HERE AND HE RODE HIS BIKE,
JOGGED."

HER 16-YEAR-OLD-SON, DUSTIN, WAS
HEALTHY, UNTIL THEY MOVED HERE.
A YEAR AGO, HE WAS DIAGNOSED WITH
BRAIN TUMORS; HE DIED IN MARCH.

S: KRIS ALBERTA

"BEING HERE FOR TWO YEARS IT'S A
POSSIBILITY THAT IT COULD HAVE CON-
TRIBUTED OR CAUSED HIS BRAIN
TUMOR, AND NO, I DON'T FEEL SAFE
WALKING UNDER HERE, OR ANOTHER.
WHEN I SEE PREGNANT WOMEN OR YOUNG
CHILDREN UNDER HERE, I DON'T THINK
THEY ARE SAFE."

THAT'S HOW SUE FARROW FEELS TOO.
SHE AND HER SON PLAYED IN THIS
PARK SEVERAL TIMES A WEEK WHEN HE
WAS SMALL.

9-YEAR-OLD DUSTY HAS HAD 6 OPERA-
TIONS RELATED TO HIS BRAIN TUMOR.
FOR NOW, HE'S DOING WELL.

BUT HIS MOTHER SEARCHES FOR AN-
SWERS.

S: SUE FARROW

"HE'S A YOUNG KID. HE'S EATING
GOOD FOOD, HE'S NOT OUT POISONING
HIS BODY IN OTHER WAYS. THERE HAS
TO BE SOME TYPE OF AN OUTSIDE IN-
FLUENCE THAT COULD TRIGGER, OR PRO-
MOTE OR SET OFF A TUMOR." (AND YOU
THINK IT COULD BE POWER LINES?)
"POSSIBLY YES."

THESE WOMEN BELIEVE SIGNS SHOULD
BE POSTED, WARNING PEOPLE OF
POTENTIAL EMF DANGERS FROM POWER
LINES.

KRIS

"I DON'T WANT ANY OTHER CHILD, OR ANY OTHER PARENT TO GO THROUGH WHAT WE DID, IF IT CAN BE AVOIDED. AND THIS IS SOMETHING THAT COULD BE AVOIDED."

DR. JOEL GOLDSTEEN AGREES. HE'S AN URBAN PLANNER AT THE UNIVERSITY OF TEXAS AT ARLINGTON.

(SEE AERIAL OF POWER LINE NEIGHBORHOODS IN TARRANT COUNTY)

HE'S DONE A STUDY OF TARRANT COUNTY THAT SAYS ROUGHLY 70,000 PEOPLE ARE POTENTIALLY AT RISK FROM OVERHEAD POWER LINES.

GOLDSTEEN SAYS UNTIL THE RESEARCH ABOUT POTENTIAL DANGERS IS CONCLUSIVE, CITIES SHOULD NOT BUILD JOGGING PATHS OR SCHOOLS AND CHILDREN SHOULD NOT BE ALLOWED TO PLAY UNDER OR NEAR POWER LINES.

S: DR. JOEL GOLDSTEEN UNIV. OF TEXAS ARLINGTON

"YOU CAN'T DO THAT. YOU CAN'T CONTINUE BUSINESS AS USUAL. CITIES THAT ARE DOING THAT ARE DOING A DISSERVICE TO THEIR RESIDENTS AND THEY ARE ACTING UNETHICAL AND UNPRINCIPLED."

AND, FOR NOW IT REMAINS AN EMOTIONAL ISSUE — PERHAPS EVEN MORE THAN A SCIENTIFIC ONE.

SUE FARROW

"YOU TALK ABOUT EMOTIONAL MOMS. WE MAY BE EMOTIONAL. MAYBE THAT'S WHAT IT'S GOING TO TAKE TO GET

```
PEOPLE AWARE TO COME OUT AND SPEAK

ABOUT IT."

T.U. ELECTRIC DOES NOT BELIEVE

POWER LINES ARE HARMFUL, BUT THEY

AGREE THAT MORE RESEARCH NEEDS TO

BE DONE.

  AND THEY SAY THERE ARE THINGS YOU

CAN DO TO MINIMIZE YOUR EXPOSURE

TO ELECTROMAGNETIC FIELDS.

MORE ON THAT TOMORROW.
```

BUSINESS REPORTING

Many radio and TV news organizations regularly program business news. Some even offer daily business programs. Others that do not often set aside time for business segments in regular news programs or have someone on the staff who covers business news.

Business specialists need to understand the complex issues of business and finance. These issues include mergers and takeovers, the savings-and-loan scandal, the ups-and-downs on Wall Street, and interest rates and trade deficits.

Students thinking about a career as a business reporter should load up on courses in economics, marketing and other business-related subjects and, perhaps, consider graduate work in business. An MBA degree carries a lot of weight with many news managers.

As always, research is a necessity. Broadcasters specializing in business reporting should read periodicals such as Barron's, Business Week, The Economist, Forbes and Fortune. The Wall Street Journal is the bible for the business world, and The New York Times, The Washington Post and their counterparts in other large cities have excellent business columns and reports that business specialists should follow.

There are also many good trade publications devoted to business and industry. While many of these publications have biases that the reporter must consider, they should by no means be discounted. They are full of information that helps reporters learn about industries and new systems, techniques and products.

The business reporter uses the same basic techniques as a general-assignment reporter—developing good sources and cross-checking information for reliability. Covering business is a little like covering politics. There's a lot of speculation, and a good reporter soon learns to be skeptical about any predictions concerning the economy, interest rates and the stock market.

Those thinking about specializing in business news should remember that the opportunities are not as great as in some other specialties, such as environmental and medical reporting. That's because radio and TV stations do not normally spend as much air time on business subjects as on these other issues, partly because many news directors think that except for the Dow Jones averages, most business news is either too dull or too complicated to explain to the public. At the same time, many stations that do have business reporters say they get good feedback from the public on business news.

HEALTH AND MEDICAL REPORTING

Health and medical subjects rank high in interest among radio and TV audiences for obvious reasons. We all want to remain healthy. Reporters with a knowledge of health and medical issues are an asset to news managers. Most large news staffs have someone assigned to a medical and health beat.

Many broadcast news producers regularly include health and medical stories in newscasts. Reporters do not have much trouble selling producers on a good medical story; and finding good stories is usually not difficult, depending on the size of the market.

Health providers are public-relations conscious, so hospitals and research centers often bring stories involving their facilities or research to the attention of radio and TV newsrooms. Listeners and viewers also provide tips on medical-related stories, usually when someone close to them has been involved in something good or bad at a medical facility. Many tips concern malpractice, but some involve lifesaving techniques and appealing human-interest stories about children waiting for organ transplants and the generosity of people who contribute hundreds of thousands of dollars to make the surgery possible.

CNN Medical Correspondent Dan Rutz

Objectivity is always an essential part of all reporting, but sometimes medical reporters must be particularly sensitive about their reports because providers often appear to be in the wrong. Doctors are accused of charging too much and of refusing to accept Medicaid patients. Hospitals are criticized for turning away some patients and gouging others. Many of these stories are true, but reporters must examine both sides of any issue. Reporters sometimes discover that hospitals are on the verge of financial collapse because of rising costs and heavy investment in equipment. They find that the government is slow in paying Medicare patients' bills and is often unrealistic when it comes to the amount it allows doctors to charge.

Good medical reporters look for positive stories about doctors and hospitals to balance the negative ones. If and when reporters find they are beginning to dislike the medical profession as a whole, it's probably time for them to start looking for another beat. But health and medical reporters also cannot allow themselves to be duped. They must constantly ask tough questions about the medical establishment and whether it is meeting the needs of the American people.

Science and health-related courses in college help journalism students prepare for medical reporting. These students also should read the many health and medical magazines that are available. Teaching-hospital libraries also have stacks of journals from major research centers. Although these resources are there primarily for medical students, persuasive reporters usually have no difficulty gaining access to the journals once the staff is convinced the reporters are not malpractice attorneys.

CNN's medical reporter is Dan Rutz. Here's an anchor lead-in and Rutz's story about chronic fatigue syndrome.

O/C	Anchor
	The Centers for Disease Control has completed a study of chronic fatigue syndrome. As Dan Rutz tells us, this mysterious ailment apparently is more common than experts had believed.
Rutz V/O Doctor is examining patient	V/O People with chronic fatigue syndrome fight an illness with no known cause. Many shuffle from

doctor to doctor in search of care
and understanding.

SOT   SOT
Font: Dr. Richard
Prokesch   "For many years it was thought

that these people were crazy and

that this really is not a dis-

ease . . . and now I think a lot

of people are believing that

there is something, probably

more than one thing, that is

causing it."

V/O   V/O
Gunn at computer
                                                Walter Gunn and others from the

Centers for Disease Control sam-

pled patients' records and inter-

viewed people diagnosed with

Computer screen   chronic fatigue syndrome. The re-

searchers disqualified everyone

Over shoulder   with a history of any other disor-
shot of Gunn at
computer   der, such as depression, that

might have caused or contributed

to their symptoms.

SOT   SOT

                                                "We were quite surprised that

about 26 percent of fatigued peo-

ple referred to us did in fact

Font: Walter Gunn   meet the case definition. We
Centers for
Disease Control   didn't expect to find it to be

more than five percent originally."

V/O	V/O
Full Screen Fonts	To be counted, patients had to have sustained at least six months of fatigue severe enough to have cut their activities at least
*Severe Prolonged Fatigue *Other Diseases Ruled Out *Chronic Flulike Symptoms Ruled Out	by half. All other possible causes had to be ruled out by test or examination and patients had to have had the flulike symptoms associated with the disorder.
O/C Standup	O/C
	The survey in Atlanta and three other cities reveals far fewer cases of chronic fatigue syndrome than activists claim. The CDC admits that the estimate is low but nevertheless considers it valuable in proving to skeptics that the disease is for real.
V/O	V/O
Mary Niebling talking on phone	Mary Niebling runs a chronic fatigue support group when she feels strong enough to attend. Numbers are
Niebling sitting at sink while she washes dishes	important to Niebling, who pushes for more research into a cause and cure for her chronic mystery.
SOT	SOT
Font: Mary Niebling	"I have lost everything that means anything to me, my mar-

	riage, my children, my home, my
	career, my finances, my intel-
	lect."
V/O	V/O
Niebling entering	Since there is no test for
doctor's office	chronic fatigue syndrome, public
	health officials say it is hard to
	come up with an accurate count.
Doctor examining	Doctors are seeing more people
Niebling	like Mary Niebling and the CDC
Nat sound	receives from one thousand to
	three thousand calls a month from
	people who think they have it too.
	Dan Rutz, CNN Medical News, At-
	lanta.

**CONSUMER
REPORTING**

Pollsters tell us that most Americans are more concerned about their economic situation than they are about their health. People without jobs often do not worry about their health until they find they have no money to pay the medical bills. So, news stories that affect a consumer's pocketbook are popular with audiences and news directors.

Consumer reporters have fertile fields to till: shady business operators, inferior products, overpriced services, undelivered goods and services, and many more. They do not have to look far to find their stories. They hear from listeners and viewers by the hundreds, many who have been victimized or swindled in one way or another.

Quite often the consumer reporter has the chore of trying to correct the problem. Those reports are often tacky. We see a reporter talking to a person who has not been able to get a rug ordered 90 days ago. The dealer keeps promising that it will arrive any day and keeps breaking the promise. Then the "action reporter" takes over, and the next thing you know the person gets the rug (and a cameraperson is probably there), and the dealer promises it will never happen again.

Consumer reporting works best when the reporter investigates serious problems and scams that affect a lot of people. Reporters provide a real service when they alert the audience to beware of a company that guarantees consumers

*Consumer Reporter Jack Atherton of
WTVJ-TV, Miami*
COURTESY OF CHANNEL 4, WTVJ-TV,
MIAMI–FORT LAUDERDALE

credit cards for a fee and then doesn't produce; a home-siding company that's tricking retired couples into paying double what they should to repair their homes; a garage that charges customers for unnecessary repairs.

But consumer reporters provide other services to the public. They frequently report on new products that may be of use to the physically disabled or about a new low-cost prescription service for senior citizens or about the best way to discover low-cost airfares. They also are at their best when exposing serious "ripoffs," as in this report from consumer reporter Jack Atherton of WTVJ-TV in Miami:

KEL/EXCLUSIVE	WHEN YOU BUY A NEW CAR . . . JUST HOW NEW IS IT?
	TROUBLESHOOTER JACK ATHERTON HAS
TWO BOX	(2BOX) EXCLUSIVE NEW DETAILS . . . AND ADVICE ON HOW TO BEWARE!
TAKE JACK LIVE . . .	(— TAKE JACK LIVE)
	KELLY, THE INITIAL COMPLAINT WE GOT WAS ABOUT A FORD TAURUS . . . BUT NOW WE'RE HEARING THAT LOTS OF NEW CARS MAY BE OLDER THAN YOU THINK.
TAKE ENG INSERT . . .	(— TAKE ENG INSERT —)

CG/EXCLUSIVE	THIS HIALEAH DOCTOR SPENT A WHOLE YEAR HUNTING FOR A NEW CAR . . . UNTIL HE SAW A MAGAZINE AD FOR THE '91 TAURUS SHO.
CG/DR. WILLIAM WAGNER FORD CUSTOMER	DR. WILLIAM WAGNER, A FORD CUSTO-MER, SAYS: (1 AT 2:28) "WHAT FINALLY MADE ME DECIDE WAS THAT THEY HAD IMPROVED THEIR 5 SPEED MANUAL TRANSMISSION. "THEY ADVERTISED THAT." "YES."
CG/HOLLYWOOD CG/LAST WEEK	ACCORDING TO DR. WAGNER'S DEALER — HOLLYWOOD FORD — THAT IMPROVEMENT WAS A NEW WAY OF CONNECTING THE STICK SHIFT TO THE TRANSMISSION; WITH STURDY METAL RODS INSTEAD OF AN OLD-FASHIONED CABLE. ONLY TROUBLE WAS . . . DR. WAGNER — AND AN UNTOLD NUMBER OF OTHER FORD CUSTOMERS — DID NOT GET THE RODS.
CG/RICK REICHANAD-TER HOLLYWOOD FORD	RICK REICHANADTER, HOLLYWOOD FORD, SAYS: (1 AT 17:37) "WERE CUSTOMERS TO YOUR KNOWLEDGE NOTIFIED OF THE FACT THAT SOME OF THE CARS HAD OLD-STYLE SHIFTERS?" "NO. UH. UH." "WOULDN'T YOU WANT TO BE TOLD?"

"IF I BOUGHT A CAR?"

"WOULDN'T YOU WANT TO BE TOLD?"

"SURE."

BUT HOLLYWOOD FORD SAYS EVEN DEAL-
ERS DIDN'T KNOW. WELL, THE HELPCEN-
TER VOLUNTEERS HELPED GET DR.
WAGNER A NEW CAR — WITH RODS. BUT
NOW THE STATE ATTORNEY GENERAL'S
OFFICE IS ALSO INVESTIGATING.

CG/MARK BARNETT
ASSISTANT ATTOR-
NEY GENERAL

MARK BARNETT, ASSISTANT STATE AT-
TORNEY GENERAL, SAYS:
(5 AT 2:39) "WHEN THEY MAKE AN EX-
PRESS CLAIM THAT A CERTAIN IMPROVE-
MENT HAS BEEN MADE AND IN FACT IT
HASN'T BEEN MADE IN ALL THEIR
CARS, THEN THAT'S AN UNFAIR AND DE-
CEPTIVE TRADE PRACTICE. BUT MORE
IMPORTANTLY, I THINK AS A GENERAL
RULE THERE'S AN IMPLIED STATEMENT
MADE THAT WHEN YOU HAVE A 1991 CAR
YOU'RE GETTING THE 1991 PARTS."

BUT THIS A-S-E MASTER MECHANIC
TOLD US THAT MANY CAR MANUFACTUR-
ERS PUT OUT-MODED PARTS IN WHAT
ARE SUPPOSED TO BE NEW CARS.

TRACY HOPPE, MASTER MECHANIC, SAYS:
(TAPE 3 AT 3:51) "UNTIL THEY RUN
OUT OF THOSE PARTS THEY USE THEM
UP."

```
                                    "YOU'VE SEEN THIS?"

                                    "YES. I'VE SEEN THIS MANY TIMES."

          TAKE LIVE TAG . . .        ( — TAKE LIVE TAG — )

                                      JUST HAD A COUPLE OF STRANGE CON-

                                    VERSATIONS WITH A FORD SPOKESMAN.

                                    AT FIRST HE SAID THOSE METAL RODS

                                    DON'T EXIST YET. WELL, YOU JUST

                                    SAW THEM! THEN HE SAID, WELL

                                    YOU'RE RIGHT ABOUT THAT. BUT ANY-

                                    WAY, THE CABLE SHIFTERS FORD IN-

                                    STALLED IN SOME '91 MODELS ARE

                                    VASTLY BETTER THAN OLDER ONES . . .

                                      BUT THAT'S NOT WHAT THE HOLLYWOOD

                                    DEALER SAYS.

                                      ANYWAY, HERE'S SOME ADVICE IF

                                    YOU'RE BUYING A NEW CAR . . . OPEN

                                    THE FRONT DOOR ON THE DRIVER'S

                                    SIDE AND SEE WHEN THE CAR WAS

                                    MADE. IF YOU GET ONE EARLY IN THE

                                    PRODUCTION RUN — SAY IN THE SUMMER

                                    OR FALL MONTHS — THE CHANCES ARE

                                    GREATER THAT IT'S GOING TO HAVE

                                    OLD PARTS.
```

SPORTS   Many people are attracted to broadcast sports reporting because of their interest in sports and because they think it's more fun than covering city council meetings. The problem is that so many beginners have the same idea that there are not enough opportunities to provide jobs for them all. TV stations that may have six or more general-assignment reporters usually have only one full-time sports reporter-anchor.

Sports reporting also requires some additional skills that general reporting does not. Personality has become important; knowing sports inside out is not

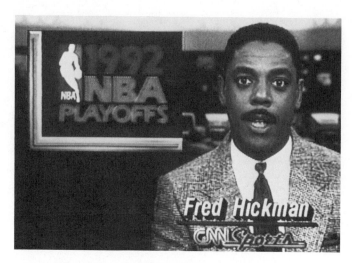

Fred Hickman is one of CNN's top sportscasters.

enough anymore. Most news managers look for sports people who can attract an audience with their style of delivery.

Good organizational skills also are important. Sports reporters, particularly in small markets, are expected to cover local games and also to be able to cut a lot of video quickly from a variety of sports contests that are being recorded throughout the evening. Sports seasons tend to overlap, which means that college and pro football and basketball games are often held at the same times as pro hockey matches and a variety of other sports. Many stations also cover high school sports. Collecting all this information and cutting video of all these activities is demanding.

How does a journalism student prepare for a sports reporting job? The best way is probably through an internship. Sports reporters look for sharp college students who know sports and know how to edit videotape. Quick learners may find that they soon cover high school games and even anchor on the weekends. Because most sports anchors, like news anchors, are looking for opportunities in larger markets, there are sometimes frequent turnovers at the sports desk. The weekend sports person who learns the job well sometimes gets the sports anchoring job during the week.

Sports anchors with a lot of talent and personality can demand good salaries in large markets. But like other anchors, they often are subject to the ratings and the whims of management. Job security is less certain for sports anchors than it is for most beat and general-assignment reporters.

WEATHER   Good weathercasters are also well-rewarded. In large markets, the weathercasters are often paid almost as much as the news anchors and sometimes even more. In medium-sized markets, weathercasters usually do not earn quite as much as the anchors but often earn more than sportscasters. The competition for jobs is not as keen as it is in sports because most people entering the field consider weather reporting rather dull, which means there are many opportunities for those who pick weather reporting as a career. And it's not always as dull as it may seem. Most stations expect weathercasters to report from the oceanside when a hurricane is on its way or to be knee-deep in flood-filled streets while predicting when the rain is going to stop.

The weather people most in demand are those with degrees in meteorology. Unfortunately, those delivering the weather in most markets are not trained meteorologists. Some stations still hire people right out of school and expect them to deliver professional weather reports. Many viewers do not notice the difference in the weather person's background, particularly when sophisticated-looking radar maps and graphics are employed. But students who are serious about anchoring the weather should study meteorology; the money invested in earning a degree will probably pay dividends.

If weather reporting is your goal, you also have to learn about computer and chroma-key (special effects) technology. Jerry Brown, a meteorologist for KUTV in Salt Lake City, says, "The discomfort level in front of the chroma board too often is readily apparent. It's not that the weathercaster doesn't know what to say. The problem is how to visually integrate a storyline and chroma-key graphics into a cohesive 'show-and-tell' presentation."

Brown says the weathercaster must "maintain continuous eye contact with one of three monitors, ad-lib and synchronize hand and body movement, all the while pirouetting across the screen. Done right," he says, "it looks effortless." But it's not easy.

Anchor-Reporter Paul Gates of WAFB-TV, Baton Rouge, works on a script.
PHOTO BY CHRISTOPHER J. ROGERS

Brown says that when weather interns ask for help setting up a weathercast audition tape, he tries his best to help, but he warns, "While a novice news anchor may on rare occasion master a teleprompter, I have never seen anyone approach professional level on their first try at chroma-key." But Brown says that "marked improvement does come with practice." He suggests seeking a good professional coach. Coach Jeff Puffer, who is with Frank N. Magid Associates, works with people at the company's offices in Marion, Iowa, but he says he also likes "to work with meteorologists at their own chroma board where they are familiar with the aspect ratio of key wall and graphics." He notes, "You can't be talking about Dallas and looking at Omaha."

Weathercaster Brown makes another important point. "A personable weathercaster is the single most important aspect of a weather presentation." He says, "It constantly dismays me how little attention the average viewer pays to the weather maps I create."

Station managers look for personality along with a knowledge of maps, computers and chroma-key technology. The auditions for weather anchors are considerably different from auditions for beat reporters. While the news director looks for good writing and reporting skills, the general manager looks for a great smile and a quick wit.

Sometimes the weather is more than just looking at the day's highs and lows and the five-day forecast. Sometimes the weather is the lead story. Here's an example from reporter Paul Gates of WAFB-TV in Baton Rouge.

```
SLUG: COLD WEATHER
DATE: Mon NOV. 4,
      1991
REPORTER: PAUL
          GATES
NEWSCAST: SIX P.M.
```

OUTDOOR CONSTRUC- TION WORKER WITH BOARDS OVER SHOUL- DER TALKS TO CAM- ERA AS HE WALKS AND PUFFS WHITE BREATH.	08/51/53/02 NAT SOT :03 "IT'S ICE COLD OUT THERE THIS MORN- ING, MAN . . . 28 DEGREES THIS MORNING WHEN I CAME OUT MAN, BUT I GOTTA DO IT THOUGH."
VO-CONSTRUCTION GUYS STANDING AROUND FIRE CLAP- PING HANDS AND STOMPING FEET.	B— IS LIKE A LOT OF OTHER FOLKS . . . CAUGHT A LITTLE OFF GUARD BY THIS FIRST EARLY FREEZE OF THE SEA- SON.

HEATING MAN C—— WALKS UP TO DOOR OF HOME AND DOOR IS OPENED BY HOME-OWNER.	BATON ROUGE IS ONE OF FOUR CITIES IN LOUISIANA SETTING A RECORD LOW OF 27 DEGREES. THE OLD RECORD WAS 29 DEGREES, SET BACK IN 1899.

HEATING CONTRACTORS WERE DOING A BOOMING BUSINESS TODAY . . .

02/37/17 NAT SOT :02

MAN IN DOORWAY TALKING NAT SOT TO C—— THE HEAT-ING MAN. C—— THEN WALKS INTO HOME OUT OF FRAME

"WELL, THE HEATER WON'T COME ON."

"OK, LET'S TAKE A LOOK AT IT."

C—— THE HEATING MAN SOUND BITE.

11/19/18 SOT :11

"THIS IS THE MOST CALLS I'VE EVER TAKEN IN ONE DAY, EVEN DURING THE SUMMER, SO WE'RE REALLY BUSY AND WE'RE TRYING TO GET TO EVERYONE AS QUICK AS WE CAN, BUT UNFORTUNATELY WE'RE GONNA HAVE SOME OF THEM SPILL OVER INTO TOMORROW."

VO-TITE SHOT OF C—— 'S HANDS IN-SIDE HEATING UNIT . . . WE SEE C—— IN THE ATTIC WORKING ON UNIT, VARIOUS SHOTS.

C—— SAYS 65 PERCENT OF HIS CALLS ARE TO LIGHT PILOT LIGHTS . . . AND IF YOU DON'T KNOW TOO MUCH ABOUT ALL THAT STUFF IN THE ATTIC, IT'S BEST TO CALL A HEATING EXPERT.

11/06/01 SOT :05

C—— THE HEATING MAN SOUND BITE.

"WHEN WE LIGHT A PILOT LIGHT WE ALWAYS CHECK AND SERVICE THE FUR-NACE FOR THE WINTER. IT'S ALWAYS A

	GOOD IDEA TO HAVE A PROFESSIONAL DO IT."
FILE VIDEO AND NAT SOT OF HOUSE BURNING.	FLAMES UP . . . NAT SOT (FROM FILE) HOLD FOR :02 SECONDS
VO-CONTINUE FILE VIDEO OF FIRE.	THERE IS DANGER IN THIS COLD WEATHER. TOO MANY PEOPLE MUST RELY ON SPACE HEATERS AND TOO OFTEN THAT CAN BE FATAL.
SOT OF FIRE DEPARTMENT'S PUB-LIC INFORMATION OFFICER.	01/55/28 SOT :11
	"YOU'LL HEAR OF A STORY BEFORE THE WINTER'S OUT THAT SOME ELDERLY COU-PLE OR SOMEONE HAS PLACED THEIR SPACE HEATER TOO CLOSE TO THE BED WHILE THEY'RE SLEEPING AND IT STARTS A FIRE AND THEY LOSE THEIR LIFE."
GRAPHICS PRODUCTION.	KEEP SPACE HEATERS CLEAR OF FLAM-MABLE OBJECTS.
1. KEEP SPACE HEATERS . . . 2. GIVE SPACE HEATERS A . . .	AND GIVE SPACE HEATERS A SOURCE OF OXYGEN.
GRAPHICS OVER BACK-GROUND OF FLAMES. REPORTER STAND-UP SOT	GATES BRIDGE STD, UP 03/15/22 :06 "ONE GOOD THING ABOUT THIS COLD SNAP FOR AREA MERCHANTS . . . SLUGGISH WINTER CLOTHING SALES . . . WELL, THAT'S REALLY PICKED UP."

VO-SHOTS OF CLOTHING SHOPPERS . . . TITE SHOT OF SHOP-PING CART WHEELS ROLLING DOWN AISLE.	FOR WEEKS WINTER CLOTHING HAS HUNG LISTLESSLY ON THE RACKS . . . BUT NOW, THE WHEELS OF WINTRY COM-MERCE ARE TURNING AND THE STUFF IS MOVING OUT.
REPORTER WALKS IN AND CHATS NAT SOT WITH A SMALL CLUS-TER OF LADY SHOP-PERS.	01/33/17 NAT SOT :09 "WHAT ARE YOU LADIES SHOPPING FOR? INSULATED THERMAL UNDERWARE. KINDA GOT CAUGHT BY SURPRISE UH? YEAH . . . UMMMMM, IT'S SO COLD."
VO-C — THE HEAT-ING MAN WITH A NOTE PAD AND PHONE JAMMED TO EAR RAPIDLY SCRATCHING DOWN NAMES AND NUMBER^{S} . . .	MEANWHILE, BACK WITH C— OF B.'S HEATING . . .
CUT TO TITE SHOT OF C—'S NOTE PAD FULL OF NAMES . . .	00/43/29 NAT SOT :03 "YEAH, I GOT A BIG PIECE OF PAPER . . . GO WITH THEM."
VO — WIDE SHOT OF C— THE HEATING MAN TAKING THE INFO OVER THE PHONE.	HE'S STILL MAKING APPOINTMENTS, AND THE ONLY WAY TO GET SERVICE IS TO GET IN LINE. PAUL GATES, WAFB NEWS.

SUMMARY

As with just about every other position in this technological era, the better pre-pared you are, the better chance you have of getting a reporting job. If you have a minor in environmental studies, health studies, economics or business, for example, you could be more attractive to news directors than people who have only general knowledge. Specialty or beat reporting is among the most interest-ing jobs in broadcast news because it provides an opportunity to spend more time developing and working on stories. Many beat reporters also find the work more rewarding because they can develop an expertise that provides an added dimension to their stories. But one disadvantage is that there are not as many jobs available for specialty reporters. There may be ten general-assignment reporters at a large radio or TV station and only a couple of specialty reporters.

From a practical point of view, however, whatever extra knowledge you have when you apply for work is going to be to your advantage. Even if you do not get a job as, say, an environmental reporter, the news director may be impressed that you took several courses in the subject. If you get a general-assignment job, you will probably find that when an environmental story shows up, you'll be assigned to it. And if your work is particularly good, you may wind up with a beat.

REVIEW QUESTIONS

1. Many radio and TV stations are hiring environmental reporters. What's the best way to prepare for such a career?

2. Why do radio and TV stations devote a lot of time to stories about health and medicine?

3. How can students prepare themselves for work as health and medical reporters?

4. One of the most popular specialties is consumer reporting. Why are consumer reporters so popular with audiences?

5. Many people want to be sports reporters, but they face stiff competition. Why is that so?

6. Do you believe that there are opportunities in weathercasting? Discuss.

EXERCISES

1. Arrange to accompany a radio or TV reporter who is covering an environmental story. Try to understand the issues involved, and check to see if the reporter covered them fairly. Turn in a report.

2. Ask friends and fellow students if there are any consumer issues that annoy them. Select one that you think has particular merit. After researching it, do some interviews and put together a wraparound or package.

3. If a radio or TV station in your community assigns a reporter to a health and medicine beat, ask the reporter how she gets most of her story ideas. If there are no medical reporters, ask the news directors how they cover that beat and whether they are happy with the results.

4. Ask a TV sportscaster if you can spend an afternoon or evening with him to see if you think you would like the job. Later, do the same thing with a weathercaster.

CHAPTER 21

USING THE HARDWARE

lthough this book emphasizes the need for journalists to develop writing and reporting skills, students also need to acquire some basic technical and production skills, such as how to use video cameras, tape recorders and editing machines. Such skills are necessary in the increasingly competitive world of broadcast journalism.

There have always been small stations that require reporters to shoot their own stories, interviews and even stand-up reports and then bring that material back to the station where they edit it for that evening's newscast. At some of these small stations, the reporters often even anchor the news and introduce the packages they have shot and edited. Many other stations are cutting back on their news staffs, which means that beginners who have *all* these skills will have a definite advantage. This chapter introduces you to some of the technological tools used in broadcast news and the skills you need to operate them.

CHECKING THE EQUIPMENT

Camera equipment keeps getting better and easier to operate. Most people with even minimal technical skills can learn how to work a camera with a few lessons. This chapter does not attempt to provide those lessons, but it does offer some advice on how to shoot the kind of video necessary to put together a good package. Before discussing shooting techniques, let's look at some basic procedures that reporters must follow when using video equipment.

Make sure all the equipment is operating properly before leaving on a story. Shoot some video and play it back to make certain that the camera and recorder are functioning. Also test the microphone and the lights. Don't wait until you arrive at the scene to discover that something is not working.

BATTERIES AND A POWER CORD

Be sure to have plenty of *battery power,* and carry an *extension cord* and an AC adaptor. Some new batteries will power equipment for four hours. One good battery and a backup should be all you need to complete your story. If you are working indoors and doing interviews, using an AC power source helps you conserve your batteries for shooting outdoors. It's also a good idea to carry a

Microwave dishes outside CNN headquarters in Atlanta

three-to-two prong adaptor because many older buildings do not have three-prong outlets. A four- or six-outlet power strip also comes in handy. If a backup microphone and light are available, it is wise to take them along in case a problem develops.

After returning from a shoot, always remember to put the batteries back on charge. It's essential that the batteries be fully charged before they are used again. If not, they could lose part of their memory. For example, if you get into the habit of running a battery for five minutes and then charging it up, the battery eventually will last only five minutes. One way to avoid the problem is to use the battery to its maximum every two weeks or so to prevent loss of memory. This can also be done by leaving the battery in the camera while the camera is turned on. When the battery is completely dead, then it should be charged to its maximum. News photographer Lennie Tierney warns against rigging a light to a camera battery to drain it quickly, however. He says this would drain the battery too rapidly, causing heat, a battery's worst enemy.

TRIPODS

Most camerapeople who have been in the business for a while have little trouble shooting video with the camera on their shoulders. But even the pros will use a *tripod* for an interview if they have the time to set it up. For those just beginning, it is best to use a tripod as much as possible, particularly for interviews, because weaving heads are not acceptable. But try shooting some of your cover footage (discussed later in this chapter) without a tripod when the video is not critical, so that you can start to feel comfortable with the camera on your shoulder. Unfortunately, many of the cameras used in colleges are difficult to use on the shoulder because they are lightweight models. It is easier to shoot from the shoulder with the heavier, more expensive cameras used in newsrooms because the weight adds stability.

EARPHONES

If you are responsible for recording good sound, wear *earphones* during the interview. You cannot depend on the camera's sound-meter reading because it just tells you that sound is being picked up. It does not guarantee that the sound is being recorded or tell you anything about the quality. The only way to pick up static or other disturbances is to listen to the sound through earphones.

CASSETTES

A *cassette* will not record unless it has a record tab or button. If someone has pulled the tab or button out to make sure the material on the tape will not be erased, another one must be used if the tape is being recycled. However, if you discover the tab or button is gone and you don't have another one, place a piece of masking tape or a piece of the cassette label over the hole. That will work just as well.

FILTERS

Every camera has a built-in *filter system* to accommodate different lighting situations. If you are shooting inside with artificial light, you must use a different filter than you would outdoors in natural light. If you use the wrong filters, the colors on the tape will be badly distorted. News photographer Lennie Tierney says there are two essential numbers to remember when thinking about filters: 3,200 degrees Kelvin (K) and 5,600 degrees. Indoor light or artificial light is 3,200 K light, and outdoor or sunlight is 5,600 K light. Cameras may also have additional filters for shooting outdoors in very bright situations, such as after a snowfall or on the beach. The initials *ND* that appear on some 5,600 K filters stand for "neutral density." These filters produce the same colored video as the 5,600 K filter but cut down the amount of light entering the camera.

WHITE BALANCING

Along with filters, a *white balancing system* is also built into video cameras to provide accurate color. Tierney explains how the system works: "Anyone who has ever looked at a sunset knows that sunlight varies quite a bit in color. Indoor lighting also varies quite a bit. But our eyes naturally adjust to different lights to make things look normal. To a video camera, fluorescent lights look green, incandescent lights look red and sunlight looks blue. If you don't use the right filter and white balance your camera, the video will be off color."

A WAFB-TV microwave truck prepares to send a live signal to the station's tower, seen in the distance.
PHOTO BY JAMES TERRY

To white balance the camera, you must aim it at something white—such as a white wall or piece of white paper—while you push the white balance switch or button on the camera. You must repeat this process each time you shoot at a different location.

All modern ENG video cameras have preset and automatic white balance settings. In the preset mode, the video will look good if the color temperature of the light in which you're shooting is near 3,200 K indoors or 5,600 K outdoors. Many photographers use the preset white balance for most of their shooting.

The automatic white balance setting is for use when the light in which you're shooting is not near 3,200 K or 5,600 K. Fluorescent lights, for example, are not close to 3,200, so to make the video look right, flip the white balance selector to automatic, fill the screen of your viewfinder with a white object and then hit the white balance switch on the camera. Doing this prevents the video from having a sickly green fluorescent look.

MIXED LIGHT

Light entering a room through a window can often cause problems for news photographers. The best thing is to avoid shooting near windows. Even a window with the blinds closed can create a distracting blue highlight if it is in the background of an interview shot. For a beginner, it is best to shoot the interview either with all artificial light or outside with natural light. If there is enough light coming through a window, the interview can be shot nicely with the natural sunlight if the outdoor filter is used. As you gain experience, you'll learn the various filter and white balancing combinations to use in *mixed lighting.* Meanwhile, here are a few tips from Lennie Tierney that will help you avoid mistakes:

1. Always check your filter first. It must be on 3,200 K for artificial light or 5,600 K for sunlight.
2. When in doubt about lighting color (temperature), check that you are using the appropriate filter, switch to automatic setting and white balance your camera on a white object.
3. When in a hurry, use the preset setting and the appropriate filter.

FOCUSING

Poor *focus* can destroy a story. Cameraman Tierney advises beginning photographers to focus every shot. "I zoom in to every subject, focus on it and then pull out to set the composition I want. When shooting a large subject such as a stadium," Tierney says, "I'd zoom in to the farthest part of the subject, like the backfield fence, focus on it and then pull out to reveal the entire subject."

Tierney says shooting moving subjects is more difficult, especially in low-light situations such as at a basketball game. "It is second nature to an experienced photographer to roll the focus barrel on the camera lens in the right direction in order to keep the subject in focus as it gets closer or farther away," says Tierney. He suggests that beginning photographers practice this technique by shooting people as they walk around the newsroom.

When you are shooting a head, zoom in and focus on the eye or nose—the same way you would if you were using a 35-millimeter camera.

TIME CODING

Most video recorders purchased today record not only pictures and sound but a numbered index called a *time code.* This time code can be set for *running time* or *time of day.* When the running-time code is set, the time code on the tape advances by hours, minutes, seconds and frames. For the time-of-day code, the recorder is set to the correct time of day, and whenever the tape records, the correct time of day appears on the tape. This is often used when shooting sports highlights. The photographer is often on the sidelines shooting with the time-of-day code while the reporter is in the press box. When some exciting play is made, the reporter simply notes the time. During the editing process, the editor then finds the time of day given to him or her by the reporter, and the exciting play is easily isolated for broadcast.

LOCKING UP THE CAMERA

You must allow time for your recording equipment to *lock up* (produce a stable picture) each time you start and stop the camera. Each piece of equipment is different. Some recorders require more time than others to achieve a stable picture, so roll off at least 10 seconds before you ask the first question or try to take a shot. Not only does the recorder need time to lock up; the editing equipment needs some good stable video to make a good edit.

**SHOOTING
TECHNIQUES**

Let's look now at a few fundamental shooting techniques that beginners should learn immediately.

First, avoid zooms and pans. There should always be a purpose for every camera movement, and unless there is some important reason to zoom in or pan on something, avoid those movements. It is better to cut from one shot to another.

Consider composition carefully. Shoot heads slightly off center, not right in the middle. Shoot the head over the reporter's shoulder or at a slight angle. Profiles do not work well because they lose the viewer's attention. The head should be looking at the reporter and, as a result, at the audience at home if the camera is positioned correctly just behind or slightly to the side of the reporter. It is sometimes effective to shoot the head tightly at a slight angle. The head should be in the corner with little or no open space. These shots are common on "Sunday Morning," "60 Minutes" and other investigative and magazine programs. Some of the best photographers in the business are assigned to these programs, so students should routinely watch these shows for both their editorial content and their camera work.

Keep in mind, however, that these programs normally do not font heads. Camerapeople working for a regular newscast must get some medium shots that will leave enough room for fonts. Some news directors discourage tight head shots because most sound bites are short and it is difficult to font them. But tight shots are sometimes effective if the interview is dramatic or emotional or the head is interesting because of age, beauty or some other reason.

Some camerapeople like to get a variety of head shots, but it is important to remember not to change shots while someone is speaking unless there is a good reason. If, for example, the person on camera begins to cry, you would probably want to zoom in for a close-up. However, that movement should be done *slowly*.

Remember that the reporter will not appear on camera most of the time, so all of the shots should concentrate on the head. The reporter is brought into the picture after the interview is completed, when the cameraperson shoots the cutaways and reversals that are used as a part of the editing process to avoid jump cuts. As was discussed earlier, editing interviews presents a problem because sound bites cannot be juxtaposed without creating a jump cut. Without something in between the two sound bites, the head appears to jerk when the sound bites are edited together.

Although there are details in Chapter 18 on the ethical aspects of using reversals, illustrations of how to shoot this popular method of avoiding the jump cut are included here because reporters and camerapeople are routinely expected to shoot them.

In the first picture on the facing page, the cameraperson is shooting the news maker. In the second picture, the camera is reversed, and the reporter is being photographed as though she were listening to the news maker. The reverse shot works best when part of the interviewee's shoulder and cheek is in the picture. But it is important to remember that the camera must shoot over the correct shoulder. One way is to imagine that a line is running between the reporter and the news maker. The cameraperson should not cross that line

Cameraman John Connelly shoots an interview over the shoulder of Reporter Cynthia Nickerson of WBRZ-TV, Baton Rouge.
PHOTO BY JAMES TERRY

Cameraman Connelly gets reversal shots for use in editing the Nickerson interview.
PHOTO BY JAMES TERRY

when shooting the reversal or the reporter will appear to be looking in the wrong direction.

COVER FOOTAGE

The best way to avoid jump cuts is to use appropriate *cover footage*, video illustrating what the news maker is discussing. Good pictures usually are more interesting than heads, anyway, and cover footage allows editors to connect as many sound bites as they like without jump cuts.

ESTABLISHING SHOTS

Some of the first pictures a cameraperson takes at the scene are *establishing shots.* These are wide shots of the activity at the scene of a fire or an accident, of floodwaters pounding against seawalls or of baseball fans lined up outside the stadium before a World Series game. Establishing shots set the stage for what is to follow, and they often provide the opening video for the story.

SHOOTING ENOUGH FOOTAGE

Reporters, especially inexperienced ones, frequently wonder whether they've asked enough questions. Camerapeople often feel the same way. With experience, they learn when they've shot enough pictures, but initially they all tend to overshoot, fearing like reporters that they might miss something. Eventually, a cameraperson and a reporter who work together come to know when they have enough video. Until that time, shooting too much video is better than returning to the newsroom with too little.

RECORDING NATURAL SOUND

The importance of natural sound has been discussed earlier. But we end this section on the use of hardware with a reminder about the importance of good natural sound. Good pictures are essential for good television, but pictures are not nearly as effective without the natural sound that goes with them. As for radio, natural sound is crucial because the sound provides many of the "pictures" for the radio audience.

The control room at WBRZ-TV, Baton Rouge
PHOTO BY JAMES TERRY

CHAPTER 22

THE JOB SEARCH
IN A CHANGING INDUSTRY

I t is difficult to predict where broadcast news is heading, but most experts believe it will continue to change over the next decade and will probably be quite different from what we now see and hear. It's not clear how the changes will affect new people entering the field. This chapter discusses some of the changes and offers suggestions for finding a job in this evolving field.

THE FUTURE OF BROADCAST NEWS

There seems to be a serious question about whether the networks will continue to provide the kind of news that we have come to expect in the past. Their most serious problem is money. All of the networks, except CNN, have cut back their news staffs drastically. The days when CBS, ABC and NBC had almost unlimited funds for covering the news are over because of shrinking advertising dollars.

The explosion of entertainment cable stations has hurt the networks more than anything else. Advertisers now have more places to spend their money, and they are spending much of it on cable channels that allow them to reach specific audiences. The catch-all approach to reaching consumers—which is what the networks offered for so many years—has become less attractive.

Does this mean that the Rathers, Jenningses and Brokaws will disappear? Not necessarily, but what they will be anchoring may be quite different. The financial resources the networks have to work with will no doubt continue to be limited. The networks already have closed down some of their national and international bureaus, and the extensive cutbacks in news personnel that have been going on for several years may not be over.

There also seems to be no doubt that the increasing influence in broadcasting of profit-minded and conservative corporations such as General Electric (which owns NBC) will mean that network news will be expected to do more to pay its own way than it has in the past. The move of NBC's newsfeed service to Charlotte, N.C., to save money is a good example.

CBS News Correspondent Ed Bradley and former CBS "Evening News" anchor Walter Cronkite criticize the personnel cuts at the networks. Cronkite ac-

NBC News Anchor Tom Brokaw
COURTESY OF NBC NEWS

knowledges that the networks have economic problems but claims that they have "cut more than the fat of the [news] budget, they've cut right down to the bone, to the point of amputation." Bradley uses a similar analogy, saying the personnel cuts took not only the fat but "the muscle, bone and the sinew of the news organizations. . . . We lost a lot of good people." Bradley adds, "There's more concern about news being profitable . . . and justifying expenditures, and I think it's going to dictate the kind of news we see on the air."

The CBS news correspondent says, "The 'Evening News' is an expensive operation to tell people in 22 minutes what happened in their world today, but it's important for our network to fund it."

Cronkite notes that because of all the news on satellites and on CNN, "somebody is always taking the bloom off the [networks'] breaking news story." As a result, he says, the networks probably have to consider "more interpretive type stories. I just hope," he says, "they stick with serious interpretive stories and don't go too soft."

Cronkite is quick to add that he doesn't think the networks are "dinosaurs by any means." He says, "They still are the best and easiest means of marketing that broadcasting has."

Peter Herford, a veteran journalist and former CBS News vice president, believes the three New York-based networks "are trying to maintain an image of national and international coverage while simultaneously making the transition to a different kind of network evening news." He says stories that report on lifestyles and trends and background reports on the news are "becoming a staple of the network diet . . . because it is easier to control the costs of stories planned in advance than for the kind of crash-and-burn coverage which characterized network news as little as five years ago." For example, in early 1992 CBS "Evening News" ran a week-long series devoted to preparing income taxes, a story that traditionally would be on a local newscast. The network promoted the series several days before it started, something it would have found difficult to do in the past because of its concentration on breaking news.

THE NEW PLAYERS

Herford notes that people depend less on the three networks' evening newscasts than they once did because of National Public Radio, "World News Monitor," "The MacNeil/Lehrer Report," C-Span and, of course, CNN. He says the network influence also has diminished because of the increasing attention that many local stations have begun to pay to reporting national and international news. The success of independent news-gathering organizations such as Conus, a cooperative of local stations, has also decreased station dependence on the networks.

Although many jobs are disappearing along with the networks' viewers, Herford is optimistic. "From the standpoint of broadcast journalism as a craft," he says, "there is a great deal of hope. Instead of only three broadcast networks, there will be dozens of nationally distributed sources of information. Before long," he says, "CNN will have competition for the all-news cable audience."

So far, no one has challenged CNN in the around-the-clock dissemination of news nationwide, but there are at least five all-news local TV stations. In 1991, ALLNEWSCO, owned by Allbritton Communications, began providing news full time to the Washington, D.C., area, and Time Warner introduced its New York One News to New York City. In Boston, Hearst Communications and Continental Cablevision joined forces to create New England Cable News, which offers regional newscasts throughout the day. They joined News 12 Long Island, which began operation in 1986, and California's Orange County News channel, which began in 1990.

CNN investigative reporter Jim Polk, who spent several decades with NBC News before making the move to CNN, says, "It is going to become more and more difficult for the other networks [ABC, NBC and CBS] to compete with CNN, which hasn't even peaked yet. The three networks have."

Polk notes that CNN may not have as many experienced people as the networks, but the organization has "more people in more places and that gives them an advantage." He adds, however, "As the networks cut back on expenses, they are cutting back on experienced people."

What bearing does all this have on the future of people who hope for careers in broadcasting? Actually, not too much because the entry-level jobs available to college graduates are rarely found at the networks, with the exception of CNN. Because of its non-union status, CNN still offers opportunities for newcomers, though not as many as it did in the 1980s when the network was just getting started. Many of the people who started out in Atlanta in entry-level *video journalist* (VJ) jobs have moved on to become writers, reporters, editors and producers. There may be opportunities for achievers at some of the new emerging cable news operations, but most of the positions for people entering the field are still likely to be at local stations.

**GETTING
STARTED**

Before you send out résumés and audition tapes, ask yourself some questions. First, do you want to stay in your home town? If you're willing to move, do you want to head for a big city, a small town or anyplace there's an opening?

The best answer to all your questions should probably be "I'll go anyplace I can find a job and I'll do whatever they want me to as long as it's in broadcasting." If that is your answer, you have the best shot at finding work. A lot of people will not go to Alaska, for example, so finding work there is much easier than in California, New York or Florida.

If you decide that you *must* stay in your home town, then the best approach is to do an internship at the local station while still in college. If the news director gets to know you and likes your work, there may be a job waiting for you when you graduate. News directors like to hire people who want to stay around for a while because there is usually a lot of turnover at local stations. So if you let the boss know you plan to stay in the area, it could be a plus for you.

For those who want to go to large-market stations right away, it usually means starting as a researcher or desk assistant. Large metropolitan-area radio and TV stations do hire college graduates without experience for entry-level positions that sometimes lead to writer, reporter and producer jobs; but there is no guarantee they will, and it sometimes takes a year or more to climb out of those entry-level situations.

Which is the best approach, the large or small market? Most people would probably say the small market because you have an opportunity to learn how to do everything. CBS News Correspondent Betsy Aaron says the small-station route is the way to go because "you get a chance to do things, to make mistakes. Starting at the networks leaves a big hole in your education and experience."

Aaron started out as a secretary-researcher for a network radio commentator, Edward P. Morgan, in 1959. "In those days," she says, "very few women were being hired as reporters." She adds, "I'm probably the oldest woman still

Professor Mike Kabel works with broadcast students at Southern University in Baton Rouge.

PHOTO BY JAMES TERRY

doing hard news on TV. Barbara Walters is a bit older, but she isn't doing hard news."

Aaron recalls that while she was working in Washington for Morgan, she got a call from ABC. "It had a fancy job title," she says, "but it was basically another secretary job." She stayed at that job for two years and finally decided to send out a résumé tape to some 80 stations. She was hired by WFIL-TV (now WPVI-TV) in Philadelphia. "I was hired as a token," she acknowledges, "but I ended up being the first woman to cover city hall after I warned them that I would not do very well on the cooking and social beat. I'm sure that's what they hired me for." But she quickly adds that it was a great place to learn because "they let you do everything, even edit your own film."

WOMEN'S PROGRESS WAS SLOW

Aaron says that when she started with CBS in 1976 the only women she can recall being in TV news at the time were Lisa Howard at ABC and Pauline Frederick at NBC. Aaron says, somewhat bitterly, "For a time, I thought I was 'one of the boys' and was being treated equally. It wasn't until much later that I realized that I had never been treated equally."

Aaron says that what saddens her the most is that "the young men who are making the decisions about which women go on the air today are making those decisions the same way the older men used to make them. Women in their fifties don't fit anyplace. I'm an exception, but I'm paying the price for the lines on my face."

Speaking at the Radio and Television News Directors Association annual banquet in 1980 when she received the Paul White Award, Pauline Frederick said she never knew Paul White but "it probably was just as well because he probably would not have hired me." Frederick said she had what was considered taboo at the time, a woman's voice.

Things did get somewhat better for women in broadcasting over the next 40 years, but not good enough for Nan Siemer, a news editor for WTOP-Radio in Washington, D.C. Siemer says that when she started out in the 1970s, she probably got her first job because she has a deep voice. "At the time, many news directors *still* didn't like women's voices on the air."

"THE CORN FIELDS"

Like Betsy Aaron, Siemer thinks people entering the broadcast field should start in small markets or, as Siemer puts it, "the corn fields." She began at a radio station in Danville, Ill., after graduating from Lindenwood College, a small school in St. Louis.

She worked for a number of other small stations over a seven-year period, getting fired a couple of times when new owners took over the stations. She took some time out and got her master's degree. Then she returned to work and lost that job in another ownership change. At that point, she says, "I decided to set my sights on Washington, D.C. I spent six months interviewing with every station in the city."

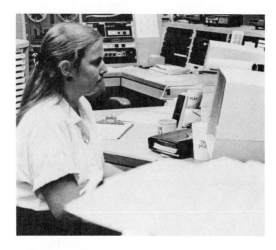

WTOP-Radio News Editor Nan Siemer checks an anchor's script on a computer.
COURTESY OF WTOP-RADIO

When she was about to give up, Siemer heard of an opening at WTOP-Radio. "Because I had made some good contacts at RTNDA meetings," she says, "I got the job." She admits, "Sometimes it's not what you know but who you know." Her advice to college students: "Get involved in RTNDA as soon as you can."

Rob Sunde, news director of the ABC Information Network and past chairperson of RTNDA, agrees that the place to start a career is at smaller stations. "Work long hours, do as much as you can and perfect your skills as much as possible," is Sunde's advice to those starting out in broadcast journalism.

Sunde started out in the 1950s at age 15, working weekends for a station in his home town in Connecticut. He worked at five different radio stations over a three-year period, and after a break for military service, he spent another six years with local stations before ending up at CBS and later at ABC. Was it a good way to get started? "It was at the time," Sunde said, "but times have changed."

EDUCATION IS ESSENTIAL

Sunde says that today the most important thing for young people is a college education. He dropped out of Brown University when he found juggling his studies and full-time employment at radio stations a bit too much to handle. "In those days," he says, "things were still experimental, and there was a lot of 'flying by the seat of your pants,' but things are different now and young people must be better educated today."

Walter Cronkite, who also did not finish his college education, agrees with Sunde that people didn't need a degree to break into journalism in those days. Now, he notes, a college degree is necessary to get a good newspaper or broadcast news job, and many successful people in journalism have advanced degrees in specialty areas, such as economics.

THE JOB SEARCH   Begin your job search by reading the help-wanted advertisements in Broadcasting magazine and in flyers available from RTNDA and other broadcast associations. As you look for such leads, prepare a good résumé and résumé tape so they will be ready to send if you find any interesting openings. Undoubtedly, the most important factor in landing a reporting job is a *résumé tape.* If you want a job in television, the tape should include an assortment of your very best packages and, if possible, a sample of some anchoring. If you want to work in radio, put together a sample of some good wraparounds and any anchoring you may have done.

The most important thing to remember in preparing a résumé tape is that you will not have much time to sell yourself. News directors get scores of tapes every week; they do not have the time or desire to look at tapes for long unless they are hooked immediately. Most news directors admit that they rarely watch or listen to a tape for more than 20 seconds unless they hear or see something that impresses them. If something does, the chances are great that they will continue to watch or listen to the rest of the tape. So, put your best package or wraparound up front; use strong video and sound at the top; and make sure the story itself is a grabber.

Don't make compromises. News directors may take into consideration that you are not using top-of-the-line equipment in your college journalism courses, but don't count on it. You will be competing with students who do have access to professional equipment, and if your video is poorly shot and out of focus you

Broadcasting students at Southern Illinois University
COURTESY OF MARILYN LINGLE/SOUTHERN ILLINOIS UNIVERSITY

will be at a great disadvantage, even if your story is a good one. The same applies to sound. If it is distorted, it will turn off news directors, so make sure the quality of your video and sound is good.

Should you use gimmicks on your videotape? Some news directors say they do not mind, provided they are done well. If you have a strong on-camera presence, a stand-up open on your tape may be effective. A montage of such stand-ups, if kept to five or 10 seconds each, might also impress news directors. But if you do not have a strong personality, you are better off opening your tape with strong video and sound. The vast majority of news directors will be evaluating your ability to package or wrap a story in a professional manner. If they are looking for a combination reporter-weekend anchor, they will be looking for samples of anchoring as well.

Professor Jill Olmsted of American University suggests putting about three stories on your tape, including a breaking story, a feature-enterprise story and a live shot if possible. She says, "Always put in stand-ups. News directors want to know how you look and handle yourself in front of the camera. For radio, they want to know you can create, write and deliver stories."

Professor Olmsted recommends slating your tapes at the beginning with your name, address and telephone number, but she admits that some news directors do not like this; they would rather see what you can do first. But, she points out, "at least you know that they can't lose your address."

Here are a few other suggestions from Professor Olmsted:

1. Your videotape should be ¾-inch format, not VHS or BETA unless specifically requested, because ¾-inch machines are in most news directors' offices. For radio, use an audiocassette.

2. Leave off the color bars. News directors get irritated at having to waste time sitting through the high-pitched tone.

3. Forget the on-air bios. News directors do not want to hear you telling them how much you want to work for them. The bios come across as staged, impersonal and phony.

4. Make sure that both the tape and its box list your name, address and phone number.

Also remember that most news managers will not return your tapes unless you include an envelope with postage. Sometimes it's possible to find short tapes that are being discarded by advertising agencies and TV stations to use for your audition tapes. Otherwise, the cost of buying tapes can be high, so you may wish to send along envelopes and postage in the hope that you will get your tapes back.

THE RÉSUMÉ

Although the audition tape is the most important job-search material you send to radio and TV stations, you also should include a printed *résumé*. Make it brief. If you are applying for your first job, news directors will know that you do

```
                        KAREN DRAKE
                        110 E. Main St.
                        Baton Rouge, LA 70810
                        (504) 555-1234
```

WORK EXPERIENCE

Summer 1991 Summer intern as assistant at assignment
desk, WBRZ-TV, Baton Rouge, LA. Monitored and logged satellite feeds, prepared read stories for anchors and
helped sports anchor select game footage for broadcast.
Accompanied reporters on shoots and worked teleprompter.

1991-92 Reporter and producer, "Impact," the Southern
University weekly TV news and features program on Channel
22 in Baton Rouge. Responsibilities included reporting
and producing a package each week, anchoring the program
twice a month, working the studio camera and shooting
ENG.

EDUCATION

1992 B.S., Mass Communications, Southern University
Major: Broadcast News sequence
Minor: Political Science
GPA: 3.4/4.0 On dean's list five of eight semesters

SPECIAL SKILLS

Proficient with Macwrite, Macintosh computer system.
Experience with Panasonic ENG cameras F-250 and AG460,
Panasonic 300CLE and WV-F300 studio cameras and Panaso-
nic AG-7750 and AG-7700 editing systems.

MEMBERSHIPS

National Association of Black Journalists

REFERENCES

John Spain, Station Manager
WBRZ-TV
Baton Rouge, LA 70832
(504) 555-5678

Professor Ted White
Chair, Department of Mass Communications
Southern University
Baton Rouge, LA 70821
(504) 555-9112

Professor Mike Kabel
Executive Producer, "Impact"
Southern University
Baton Rouge, LA 70821
(504) 555-3456

Figure 22–1.   A sample resume.

```
                                    110 E. Main Street
                                    Baton Rouge, LA 70810
                                    June 27, 1993

Mr. Frank Walsh
News Director
KTHU-TV
Centerville, CT 06880

Dear Mr. Walsh:

I would like to be considered for the opening you
listed in Broadcast magazine. I recently received
my degree in mass communications from Southern Uni-
versity, where I reported, produced and anchored
many stories for "Impact," the university's weekly
television program on Channel 22 in Baton Rouge,
Louisiana. The enclosed videotape displays some of
my "Impact" stories.

As the enclosed résumé describes in detail, last
summer I worked as an intern at WBRZ-TV in Baton
Rouge, where I performed various tasks at the as-
signment desk. I am sure that Station Manager John
Spain would tell you that I carried out my duties
with enthusiasm and diligence.

I believe that my experience with "Impact" and at
WBRZ-TV makes me an ideal candidate for the position
at WZZZ-TV.

I hope for a chance to meet with you after you view
my videotape. I can be reached at (504) 555-1234.

                                    Sincerely,

                                    Karen Drake
```

Figure 22–2. A sample cover letter.

not have much experience, so don't try to embellish your résumé. If your only experience is working with the university radio or TV station, list that first. If you have done an internship with a commercial station, that certainly should be listed first, with details about what you did. Do not start off the résumé, as so many students do, with your career goals. News directors want to know what you have done, not what you want to do.

List your education below your experience. If you have taken a minor in business, political science, economics or some other area that might make you more attractive to news directors, you should include that as well. Be sure to list any foreign languages that you speak fluently.

If you have won any awards from RTNDA, the Society of Professional Journalists (SPJ) or any other organization for your broadcast work, you should mention those citations. Also list any involvement that you might have with student chapters of RTNDA or SPJ, particularly if you headed up one of those chapters or served on any committees that might have taken part in regional or national conferences. Attendance at those conferences, by the way, is a valuable experience and a great way to make contacts with working broadcast journalists and news directors.

If you are proficient in computer skills, say so. Also list any cameras, editing systems, or other radio or TV control room equipment that you know how to use.

REFERENCES

If you have developed relationships with people in the field willing to give *references*, such as the general manager or news director of a radio or TV station where you did an internship, be sure to list them. Most news directors are not likely to call your journalism professor to ask about you unless they are really impressed with your résumé tape. But sometimes your professor can be helpful. He or she may be active in RTNDA or SPJ and may have served on panels with news directors at national or regional meetings. The news director you're contacting may even be a graduate of your university.

Unless your hobbies have some practical application, such as flying or photography, don't list them. News directors are not likely to be interested in your stamp or coin collections.

Put some effort into the way you lay out and design your résumé. If it shows creativity, the news director is likely to think that *you* are creative. Use a computer if one is available or consider services that prepare résumés.

Be sure to list your name, address and telephone number at the top of your résumé.

Figure 22–1 shows how a student who did an internship at a local TV station might organize her résumé.

COVER LETTERS

A brief *cover letter* addressed personally to each news director you contact should be included along with your résumé tape and printed résumé. Make sure you spell the news director's name correctly. Also be certain there are no misspellings or grammatical errors in the letter. If there are, the news director will never get to your résumé or your videotape. As this book has stressed throughout, accuracy is the most important aspect of journalism, and if you cannot be accurate in your job-search materials, you are not likely to find a job.

Your letter should be straightforward and honest. If you do not have much experience, say so, but stress the skills you do have. Make it plain that you are eager to learn and are prepared to work hard. Figure 22–2 is an example of a cover letter.

The cover letter accomplishes a number of things. It introduces you to the news director and lets him know where you heard about the job opening. It also tells the news director a little about you before he looks at the résumé, but it does not summarize the résumé. In this case, Karen Drake indicates what skills she would bring to the job and makes clear that she is enthusiastic and expects to work hard. The tone of her letter shows a modest confidence. The letter also mentions the name of her strongest reference, a TV station general manager with a national reputation. Note that the letter also expresses Drake's desire to hear from the news director. The letter is only four paragraphs, which is as much as any news director will probably read from someone applying for a job.

WRITING TESTS

Some news organizations, such as CNN in Atlanta, which encourages graduating students to apply for entry-level positions, require applicants to take *writing tests*. The best way to prepare for a writing test is to practice rewriting newspaper wire copy into broadcast style. Do several such rewrites before you take the test, and ask one of your professors or someone you are working with at a radio or TV station to review the copy.

THE JOB INTERVIEW

If you make an impression with your videotape, the news director may contact your references. If he or she gets a positive response, you will be asked to visit the station for a personal interview. The materials you sent got you an interview; the interview will decide whether you get the job.

As soon as you hear about the interview, talk to your professors about the station that has invited you. They may know someone at the station or something about the station's reputation for news. Another important way to prepare for the interview is to learn as much as possible about the city or town in which the station is located. Find out the name of the major newspaper in the city, and if you have time, have a Sunday edition sent to you. If there isn't enough time to do that, try to arrive in the city as early as possible before the interview and read through the papers. The chamber of commerce is also a good source of information.

If you can, arrive a day early. If you are after a radio job, listen to the station in your motel room. If you are after a job with a TV station, watch as many of the station's newscasts as possible. Appearing knowledgeable about the station and the city during the interview will let the news director know that you are interested enough in the job to have done your homework. For example, tell the news director that you arrived in town the night before and that you were impressed with the station's coverage of a breaking story. But be honest. If the story really was good, then the news director will be impressed that you knew it. But if the story was not that well done, you will lose points by saying that you thought it was. The news director will know better.

Once the interview centers on you and what you can do for the station, the pressure will build. This is when you must be at your best. Professor Jill Olmsted of American University warns against being overly concerned with pay, benefits, work shifts and vacations during the interview. She also says it would be a mistake to complain about your previous employer or college. And she advises, "This is your opportunity to show the strength of your personality and mind—so be energetic, but not hyper. Avoid vague, mumbling, rambling responses."

Professor Olmsted also says you should not be afraid to *ask* questions as well as answer them. "To a certain extent," she says, "you also are conducting an interview to determine if you would like to work for this person and organization."

MINORITY OPPORTUNITIES

During a recent national survey, the majority of news directors who responded indicated they are interested in getting applications from minorities, particularly African-Americans, who have strong writing, reporting and anchoring skills.

However, the number of minorities working in broadcast news has not increased appreciably over the last five years. There has been a lot of speculation and some research on why this is true, but none of it appears to be conclusive.

KRIV-TV News Director and Vice President Will Wright (left) talks to anchors Linda Cheek and Mikle Barajas.

COURTESY OF WILL WRIGHT/KRIV-TV, HOUSTON

Will Wright, an African-American news director and vice president of KRIV-TV in Houston, says African-Americans are at a disadvantage because they do not do enough internships that lead to many jobs in broadcast news.

Wright, one of only three black TV news directors in the nation, recalls that he broke into broadcast news as a desk assistant for CBS News in New York 20 years ago. Wright notes that he paid his dues at CBS, going for coffee, running copy and stripping wires. He believes African-Americans must be prepared to do the same through internships and entry-level jobs.

Wright adds, however, that those "who are determined to win in a business that is set up to discourage them have to be quick learners. Don't let anyone have to tell you twice what to do," he advises, "do it right the first time and you will succeed."

CBS News Correspondent Ed Bradley agrees that "menial tasks come with the territory . . . and when I got into broadcasting, I was a gofer." But he says that's the way entry-level positions work "whether you are black, white, yellow, brown or red." Bradley says he knows young African-American men and women "who are eager to take entry-level positions to get their foot in the door."

When asked if being African-American has had any effect on his career he said, "I think it has helped and hurt. It helped because I came along at a time when there was an effort to find more minorities who could do a job and I always showed that I could do a job no matter what they put me into." He added that being African-American may have hurt in some instances because there were people who wondered whether they should take a chance on hiring an African-American person for a given job because they had never done it before.

Asked how he thinks African-Americans are treated in broadcast journalism, Bradley said, "Better than we used to be, but not as well as I'd like to see. He adds, "I'd like to see more opportunity [for blacks] on the air and off the air."

THE OUTLOOK FOR WOMEN

African-American women have fared better than their male counterparts in broadcast positions at both local stations and the networks, but they also have been unable to make significant progress, particularly in management. Sheila Stainback, vice president for broadcast of the National Association of Black Journalists (NABJ), says she is unaware of any African-American women who are TV news directors. Stainback, an anchor for WPIX-TV in New York City, says three black women who were news directors a few years ago are now assistants in larger markets. The Asian American Journalists Association is aware of only two female Asian-American news directors.

But the reasons for the small number of women, black and white, in broadcast management are not entirely based on sex or race. "The demands of the job are harder for women," says Penny Parrish, news director at KMSP in Minneapolis. "It's hard to run a newsroom without that being the top priority in your life. Going into television didn't help my marriage and probably led to my divorce," she notes.

Susan Stamberg, a correspondent for National Public Radio and the first woman to host a national news program, says that women have done well at NPR but "it was not easy. A handful of us worked hard and we were good," says Stamberg. "We punched a hole through the wall and allowed a lot of other women to walk through."

Many women hold jobs with NPR as producers, editors, reporters and in other positions. But Stamberg also notes, "Women are paid less at NPR than they are at commercial stations."

As for why there still are no female anchors on major news programs on CBS, NBC and ABC, Stamberg calls it "ridiculous." She says, "TV is still living in the dark ages. Basic decisions are still being made by men. Women are OK as anchors in the morning but not in the evening."

Despite all this, Lou Prato, director of broadcasting for the Medill News Service in Washington, D.C., says, "More women are running and staffing newsrooms than ever before, and there are wider management opportunities in local TV news for white women." But he agrees that "it's another matter for black and Asian women, who only recently have been encouraged to pursue management careers."

Prato also notes that despite the growing opportunities for women, they "still have to deal with sexism, especially when it comes to pay." Female news directors, on average, make about 30 percent less than their male counterparts, but Prato says this differential may not be due to sexism alone. He says many women are unwilling to argue for more money because "subconsciously or not, women do not want to be perceived as overly aggressive."

Nan Siemer of WTOP-Radio agrees with Prato. She says most women feel that "they are lucky to have a job in broadcasting and aren't supposed to negotiate for wages." Because of this attitude, Siemer began a consulting service called Breakers, which, she says, teaches women how to get past the "glass ceiling."

Siemer says that one of the things she had to do in her own career was "follow the negotiating examples set by men because women were not giving me any examples to draw from." She says she is trying to teach women that "negotiation is not an evil word, that they can talk about money without being uncomfortable."

Vernon Stone, who heads research for the Radio and Television News Directors Association, says there are more women coming out of journalism schools and going into TV news than men, but he also notes that there is a much greater turnover in the business among women than among men.

The competition for jobs is going to be greater for women coming out of college than for men, particularly because many of the available jobs are in sports and those positions continue to be dominated by men. If you are a woman, there are still many jobs for you in broadcast news, but you are going to have to have good writing and reporting skills and may have to work harder to compete in what unfortunately is still "a man's world of broadcasting."

SOME FINAL WORDS

As many people quoted in this book have stated, broadcast news is exciting. It is a fascinating business, one that pays you to read newspapers and magazines; to interview politicians, celebrities and other exciting people; and to know what's going on in every part of the world before most other people. Unfortunately, because the work appeals to many people, the pay is not very good unless you have outstanding abilities that permit you to work in a large market. But for many journalists, money is not the most important consideration; the attraction is the challenges that await reporters every day.

You'll tell yourself how nice it is to be in a business that excites you so much you don't look at the clock except when a deadline is involved. Although you may be exhausted at the end of the day, you often will look for colleagues to join you for coffee so that you can recreate what transpired that day; to analyze what you and the news team accomplished and, of course, to commiserate about some of the things that went wrong. If you have trouble sleeping, it probably will not be because you're not tired but because you have trouble relaxing your mind.

You can join this exciting field, but remember: you'll need a dedication to develop your skills and a determination to pursue a career that is going to demand responsibility, accuracy and fairness in whatever you do.

Acknowledgments (continued from copyright page)

Parker, Nancy, story on prison visit. Used with permission of WAFB-TV, Baton Rouge.

Roberts, Cokie, feature story on Congressman Morris Udall. © Copyright National Public Radio ® 1992. Excerpts from National Public Radio's "Morning Edition" news were originally broadcast on National Public Radio on April 19, 1991, and are reproduced with permission from National Public Radio. Any unauthorized duplication is prohibited.

Rutz, Dan, chronic fatigue syndrome story. © 1992 by Cable News Network, Inc. All rights reserved.

Sevareid, Eric, "CBS Evening News" excerpts. Used with permission of CBS News.

Stamberg, Susan, interview with Alfred Eisenstadt. © Copyright National Public Radio ® 1992. Excerpts from National Public Radio's "Morning Edition" news were originally broadcast on March 13, 1991, and are reproduced with permission from National Public Radio. Any unauthorized duplication is prohibited.

Threlkeld, Richard, "Obituary for Dr. Seuss." Used with permission of CBS News.

Wall, Don, environmental report on possible dangers of electromagnetic fields, WFAA-TV, Dallas. Used with permission.

Welsch, Roger, "A Postcard from Nebraska," from "Sunday Morning." Used with permission of CBS News.

WISC-TV, Madison, Wisconsin, "Butter River Fire story," used with permission of Tom Bier, News Director.

INDEX